THE
GARDEN
DESIGN BOOK

THE
GARDEN
DESIGN BOOK

ANTHONY PAUL·YVONNE REES

Salem House Publishers
Topsfield, Massachusetts

For H & H

All photographs (unless
listed otherwise) by
Ron Sutherland

Designed by
Steven Wooster

Text editing by
Jonathan Hilton

Conceived and designed by
Anthony Paul and Steven Wooster
Duane Paul Design Team,
Unit 30, Ransome's Dock, 35 Parkgate Road
London SW11 4NP. Tel: 01 585 0277

First published in the United States by
Salem House Publishers, 1988
462 Boston Street, Topsfield, MA 01983

**Library of Congress Cataloging-in-Publication
Data**
Paul, Anthony, 1945–
   The garden design book.

   Includes index.
   1. Gardens – Design. 2. Landscape gardening.
3. Landscape architecture. I. Title.
SB473.P35 1988   712'.6   87 20811
ISBN 0 88162 273 7

Photoset by Rowland Phototypesetting Ltd
Colour origination by Bright Arts (HK) Ltd
Printed and bound by Tien Wah Press, Singapore

Plant naming
Some plants have had recent name changes. We have
used in most cases the old name. This will assist the
reader in referring to plants in many plant books and
some catalogs. Such examples are *Ligularia clivorum*
('Gregynog Gold' or 'Desdemona') which is now
L. Dentata. *Stachys lanata* is now *S. olympica*, *Euphorbia
epithymoides* is now *E. polychroma*. *Helleborus corsicus* is
now *H. argutifolius*. Where possible we have listed the
alternative names in the index.

FOREWORD

DESIGNING A GARDEN can be great fun and is a job that still gives me pleasure and rich rewards after 15 years planning gardens of all shapes and sizes around the world. There is no secret formula, no rigid blueprint to be superimposed on to the site. Armed with the right information and some idea of the final look you wish to achieve, there's no reason why your own patch shouldn't rival any of the gardens we have found to feature in this book.

If you look at the introductory pictures on the following pages, you will notice that they show gardens looking from the inside out: increasingly, our gardens are becoming extensions of our living space and to get the best out of them, you have to give them the same consideration you would your house interior. There is not just the color, texture and shape of features to be planned for, but furniture, ornaments, lighting and all the other elements that help it to function smoothly as well as look good.

A relaxing, easy to maintain environment seems to be what we are all looking for in today's ideal garden. It was that need, and the new enthusiasm apparent among owners of yards and gardens everywhere that prompted us to put this book together.

We found that most garden design books bombarded the reader with garden plans and technical details which only succeeded in confusing the issue or which tried to bully them into following some designer's ideas to the letter. This book, we hope, can offer better than that. We have tried to provide you with a wealth of pictorial ideas from which you can choose a style and look that fits your garden and your lifestyle. To feature the best possible range of ideas we photographed 15 professional garden makers around the world, in Europe, America and Australia. It was important that each gardener presented a style that you could easily relate to, incorporating good practical design ideas which could be easily executed using local materials and within realistic budgets. We also included a few more extravagant ideas where we felt they were particularly innovative or exciting. After all, that is what clever budgeting is all about: being able to afford the occasional indulgence. We then broke down those design ideas into elements that you could tailor into your own personal garden plan and drew up a rough set of guidelines to show how to put them into practice. The intention was first to inspire, then to inform.

About the Book We begin by presenting the garden designers, their philosophies and their styles, selecting from each his or her best ideas, which we felt could be adapted and used for your own garden. You may, of course, want to employ the help of a garden designer yourself, and this book will also show how you might work together successfully.

So that you might see exactly how these ideas can be translated onto the site, *Applying the Principles* shows how to go about designing and drawing up a plan for your own garden. We have kept the number of plans to a minimum as most people find them difficult to follow.

Designs & Themes has been planned to give you as many ideas as possible for your particular type of garden, whether it is dry, shady or stony, or in the city or country. We hope this chapter will stimulate your imagination and that you will find many useful suggestions.

The following chapters begin to build up the total picture of a good-looking, hard-working garden from the basic framework of boundaries, paths and patios to advice on how to choose those special features, such as fountains, pergolas and garden ornaments. Nor have we forgotten that you will be wanting to spend a lot of your leisure time in the garden. *Living in Style* looks at swimming pools, spas and summerhouses, as well as at suitable garden furniture.

The most exciting design material at your fingertips is the plants themselves, so as well as detailing some of the best ideas for using stone, brick and lumber in the *Design Guide*, we have compiled a comprehensive guide to designing with trees, shrubs, perennials, grasses and bulbs. Here you will find how to blend plant shapes and colors to achieve a progression of stunning effects throughout the year. For quick reference, the plant lists and information section at the back of the book have been carefully devised so that you can select plants to suit most climates.

We had a lot of fun producing the book despite the hard work involved. We made many good friends among the garden designers we met all over the world and took the opportunity to compare notes and swap ideas.

The list of people to thank for making the book possible is too long to publish, but at the back you will find full acknowledgement to the garden designers, photographers and other people who gave useful advice, generous help and valuable time and assistance in producing the book.

A New Generation of Gardeners

The best of today's garden designers are creating lush, leafy environments, outdoor leisure areas and a living link between architecture and the landscape. Their easy-care gardens are the perfect antidote for the stresses of modern life, presenting not a mind-numbing dazzle of different, highly bred, hybrid colors, but a subtler, more relaxing blend of foliage shapes and forms, soft drifts of pastel shades and natural materials such as stone and lumber.

This shifting of emphasis does not mean that their designs are lacking in drama: striking plant forms, giant architectural foliage, shimmering stretches of water and thought-provoking sculptures all have their place within the new design of things, where every element is carefully selected and integrated to produce a harmonious unity.

Nor have our garden designers turned their backs on tradition. Classical features such as topiary and container planting have been enthusiastically adopted and adapted into more informal applications and settings and there is a noticeable oriental influence in the use of rock, lumber, water and architectural plant forms.

Central to their work is a feeling for nature and an understanding of how plants can be encouraged to perform well; but the most practical priority is that the garden be easy to maintain yet retain interest all through the year.

ANTHONY PAUL

ANTHONY PAUL has an affectionate understanding of the natural landscape and his particular affinity for water in all its forms is one of the basic motivating forces behind his design philosophy. Early memories of a large, natural water garden as a child in New Zealand, and the influences of working in the water-dominated landscape of Holland, where the ecological nature of gardening was pioneered, have given him an enthusiasm for the ever-changing, reflective qualities of lakes and ponds. Natural structural features and dramatic, architectural plant groupings are evident in every project he undertakes, whether it is a small, contained area such as a roof garden for a private client, a large urban development for a public authority or, indeed, his own garden

▷ Anthony's own house is perfectly framed in shades of green by a background of mixed pines and in the foreground, dramatic planting of giant Peltiphyllum peltatum and spiky Sparganium erectum. Fringing one of the ponds, they create an ideal setting for a sculpted figure.

▷ A lumber deck extends from the house to overlap the water of the main pond. Softened by the lush foliage of water-edge plants like Ligularia clivorum 'Gregynog Gold' and tubs of spiky Phormium tenax on the surface of the deck itself, it makes the perfect place to relax.

▷ A strong blue geometric structure and terra-cotta pots of grass-like Cyperus alternifolius and C. papyrus, the feathery ferns Microlepia strigosa and trailing Hibertia scandens frame an uninterrupted view of the garden beyond this lovely poolhouse complex. At ground level (below), extensive use of lumber decking around the main pool and whirlpool softens and mellows the area and provides a practical surface underfoot.

▷ Green plants, water and a simple pergola structure have been used to enclose a formally paved seating area which is reached via a neat lumber bridge. This small but very secluded atmosphere is heightened further by the use of vigorous climbers and lush water-edge plants along the side of the pool, including bright yellow Trollius, Iris laevigata and Ligularia clivorum 'Gregynog Gold'.

in England – a semiwilderness of native flowers, woodland and water in the form of ponds, bog gardens, streams and waterfalls.

Underlying approach

Anthony places great emphasis on the easy-to-establish, low-maintenance aspects of his garden designs, and he has no doubt that this approach has led to their success as gardens of the eighties, whatever their size or location worldwide. Create a garden that is close to its natural habitat, he believes, and you avoid the overwhelming feeling that you are constantly struggling against the elements just to keep it under control. A more natural garden leaves you more time to observe and enjoy its features at your leisure.

Large, informal areas of water and indigenous planting satisfy important criteria for Anthony, for not only are they interesting and easy on the eye, they are also less trouble and more economical to establish, usually requiring only a modest financial outlay. These are important considerations for a generation of gardeners looking for relaxation and diversion rather than constant hard work.

The final result of this approach to garden design, happy to flourish in its own native habitat, requires none of the tedious and time-consuming maintenance chores common to the artificial, formal garden – weeding, planting and pruning. Instead, there is only the simple and occasional lifting, dividing and cutting back of more rampant established species and the introduction of new features to the basic framework of the garden.

New design ideas

Anthony reviews his own garden on an annual basis. It lies in a sprawling English country setting not far from London and while the main theme of ponds and natural planting with a lumber-decked leisure area close to the house remains basically unchanged, he focuses on and targets particular areas each year to give them a special lift and to create pockets of the garden that are always new and different. He believes that every garden, no matter how beautiful or thoughtfully designed, requires this type of treatment if interest is to be maintained over a period of many years.

The types of changes Anthony makes may take the form of a new bridge or a new design for a series of stepping stones, a shallow bog garden or an intimate and secluded Japanese-style area inspired by a magnificent maple tree and reinforced by the introduction of pebbles, boulders and oriental pots of bamboo.

Anthony's own garden represents an excellent example of his landscaping principles. He

◁ *Note how the warmth of an old brick wall has been picked-ed up in the purple red foliage of* Vitis vinifera *'Purpurea' and the purple-leaved* Malus *'Lemoinei', trained to provide both vertical and horizontal interest. In contrast, spaces between the plain gray paving slabs at ground level have been planted with large-leaved* Bergenia cordifolia.

⊲ A group of old farm buildings makes the perfect sheltered setting for an outdoor swimming pool and conceals it from the rest of the garden. Appropriately, the pool surrounding is a mix of old brick and lumber laid on two levels with large terra-cotta pots of Phormium tenax 'Purpureum' and Cordyline australis providing architectural plant interest. Forming part of the pool design is a grouping of Arundinaria murielae and Fatsia japonica contained by large boulders and round, smooth pebbles.

▷ An excellent example of lush but controlled planting: a wide variety of interesting foliage plants is given shape and form by paths of pebble, stone and decking. Anthony has cleverly combined and contrasted the tall, spiky grass Miscanthus sacchariflorus and golden pokers of Ligularia stenocephala 'The Rocket' with broader-leaved plants such as Hosta lancifolia and Ligularia clivorum 'Desdemona'. Lumber and stone are softened by bright, low-growing ground cover like Alchemilla mollis and Pachysandra terminalis.

inherited the framework of a much older garden consisting of several large but overgrown ponds, surrounded by a mass of jungle-like undergrowth and a quite exceptionally beautiful collection of mature trees. The ponds have been cleared after years of neglect and are now fringed with dramatic, lush plants such as *Gunnera manicata* and *Rheum palmatum* and the waters reflect the soft colors of hostas, *Rodgersia* and rushes.

Grass, gravel and bark paths provide endless, meandering routes around the garden, where drifts of wild flowers have been encouraged to grow among the trees: bluebells, violets, primroses and tiny wild orchids.

The area around the house is a blend of home and garden. There is an extensive lumber deck running directly from the house to overlap lawn and water and softened with tubs of bamboo, ferns and sweet-smelling herbs. The deck surrounds the house on two sides and Anthony has used lumber pergolas and bamboo screens to divide it into more intimate 'garden rooms': one provides a raised and sheltered dining and barbecue area, and another is fitted with a wooden hot tub.

⊲ Plants of special interest can be grown in containers and positioned where they will provide most impact. Here, the lovely autumn tints of an Acer japonicum 'Aconitifolium' make an eye-catching display among a grouping of large stones – a delightful focal point where the lumber deck changes direction.

Anthony has found these principles adapt well to any size or style of garden, and commissions in Europe, Africa and the Far East have only served to stimulate his imagination and consider new variations on his central theme. Like many of our designers, his architectural appreciation of plant shape and size and system of informal planting balanced by paving or decks, softened with tubs and containers, applies itself equally well to a small yard patio, stylish poolhouse or a large, sprawling country garden □

RICHARD HAIGH & ANNIE WILKES

RICHARD HAIGH and Annie Wilkes are the inspiration behind *The Parterre Garden*, a shop and landscaping service that specializes in creating a complete, tailor-made outdoor environment. Their approach is more like that of a team of interior designers than landscape architects – perhaps appropriate since they view their projects as outdoor rooms or living areas to be designed, equipped and furnished to suit the owner's lifestyle. Their own preference is semiformal but simple: boundaries hidden by climbers such as *Wisteria*, honeysuckle and ivy, walls and hedges creating smaller, more intimate garden areas with trees and shrubs to provide shade. An important design criterion is that it should not be possible to see all the garden at once, with the overall atmosphere being mysterious and inviting yet, at the same time, bold and stimulating.

Although they work mainly in Sydney, Australia, the look is typically English – cool, secret and slightly classical, with lots of shrubs, terra-cotta and paved surfaces to create a decorative but harmonious garden. Most of *Parterre's* customers lead busy lives and there-

fore seek a place to relax, not labor in, so it is a look that needs to be carefully controlled to survive the hot, dry climate in summer without a huge amount of work.

Instant maturity

The general design is devised by Annie, who begins with an analysis of the raw materials she has to work with: climate, soil, local plants, surrounding view and the client's preferences. She always takes note of existing trees and shrubs and uses these wherever possible to add instant maturity. Next, she will fill in the framework of existing or newly planted trees with strong hedging elements, which she finds ideal as a background for flower and foliage color. These she amasses into large areas of a single plant type for a bolder, simpler effect.

Green is a predominant color in a *Parterre* garden, with leaf shape and texture and sometimes a touch of silver or gray foliage adding interest and variety. Where color highlights are used, Annie prefers the softer hues and applies them in single drifts.

Annie likes to incorporate several seating areas within the garden, providing perhaps

◁ A row of sheared box (Buxus sempervirens) and Agapanthus *is visually contained by a terra-cotta edging. The deep green and earthy red make a pleasing natural combination.*

▷ A small courtyard is enclosed by a wonderful formal arrangement of green and silver foliage. Soft floppy Lambs Ears (Stachys lanata) and lavender edge the sheared box and Convolvulus cneorum. *Vertical interest is provided by sheared standard trees and twisty bark* Ficus benjamina 'Exotica'.

summer and winter eating places or a small breakfast patio. This approach not only maximizes the garden's potential, it also saves moving furniture around to follow the sun.

Materials are selected to blend naturally with the overall theme, using soft, rustic surfaces such as lumber, stone and terra-cotta: Parterre very seldom use white, which they find too glaring in hot sunshine. Often, paved areas will be continued into the house using a matching flooring of, for example, sawn sandstone and coordinating pots of indoor plants.

Another feature of a *Parterre* design is topiary, which is where Richard's expertise comes into play. Bay, *Buxus*, *Ficus* and *Thuja* are pruned at sapling stage to create balls, spirals, tiers and cones and used as focal points – the elegant final touches to a garden or patio design. They may be placed symmetrically in pots and other containers close to the house or within the garden where they can complement the architecture or add more of a classical note to an informal, rambling style of garden.

Further ornamentation in the form of sculpture, containers and garden furniture is considered with great care, and these pieces are often designed by *Parterre* themselves and positioned where they will blend with and add impact to surrounding plants and features. They often like to soften such features with plants to encourage a more natural feel and they make extensive use of Japanese Mondo grass, which remains green year-round, and white Alyssum to spill over the edges of a pot, around a pool edge or between paving stones □

◁ Parterre *are expert at combining sheared foliage shapes with interesting containers and amusing garden ornaments. Terra-cotta tubs and urns and animal sculptures (above) feature largely in their garden designs.*

△ *Herbs, sweet smelling plants and interesting variegated foliage add interest to patio and courtyard areas. Here, free-flowering white and mauve lavenders have been chosen to accompany the green-splashed-with-white foliage of* Lamium, Ficus benjamina *'Exotica' grown as standards, and terra-cotta baskets of* Soleirolia.

◁ *Climbing plants can be easily trained around wire frames to create unusual and interesting shapes. This technique works best with container-grown plants and here a garden ornament has also been incorporated into the design.*

GILLES CLEMENT

GILLES CLEMENT is a passionate and active supporter of what he calls the French *mouvement* toward wilder, more natural gardens. Gilles first became fascinated by the concept of a cultivated wilderness nearly a decade ago when he started to look seriously at the way plants grew in the wild. He loved their facility for regenerating themselves without the need for intensive care and, tired of the traditionally formal style of garden popular since the 14th century, he began to move toward a landscape where plants are grown in more unruly groups.

Taming a wilderness

Gilles realized that in order to maintain the richness of nature at its best, it was going to be necessary to interfere in some way to keep such a garden looking good year-round. He was convinced that it must be possible to control such an environment without destroying it, and it is this concept that is at the heart of his *mouvement* – where changes come slowly and more naturally with the turning of the seasons and where design and maintenance are disguised beneath the semblance of a completely natural combination of plants.

▷ The pure gold of the Californian poppy, *Eschscholzia californica*, shines out in a predominantly green design. The garden is a solid blend of foliage shapes, from the trees behind that frame the house to a massed planting design including gray *Senecio greyii* and blue *Ceanothus*.

▽ A light gravel path has been softened by a mixed edging of border perennials of gray- and green-leaved plants such as *Cerastium*, *Stachys lanata* and *Primula pulverulenta*. *Behind*, is the hogweed, *Heracleum mantegazzianum*.

△ *Light foliage, green and gray plants make a charming and relaxing surrounding for a seating and lounging area. The stronger forms of a sheared box and bright red* Rosa *make a stimulating focal point.*

◁ *Strong blues and greens and dramatic foliage plants have created a dense, rich design. Architectural* Rheum palmatum, *the white spikes of the Foxtail Lily,* Eremurus, *brilliant blue* Aquilegia *and the lightest pink Peony create the contrasts.*

The immediate impression you get when you enter one of Gilles' gardens is of the rich profusion of green foliage with the occasional splash of color. This may take the form of a bright flower or eye-catching leaf shade and it will be just enough to draw your attention or to lift an otherwise unremarkable corner. Indeed, it does look as if the garden grew spontaneously and is somehow merely a fortuitous accident of nature.

Look more closely, however, and you start to see how carefully the underlying framework has been planned. There is a subtle balance of shapes and colors relying on a strong collection of evergreens against a background of shrubs and trees. The overall effect is one of completeness cleverly built up from ground level, where large leaves may touch the ground or the soil be smothered in ground-covering plants, and then up through a blend of foliage shapes and softly colored blooms to the dramatic backdrop of shrubs and trees behind. There are no gaps for weeds to flourish in or for individual plants to get out of hand.

Surprisingly perhaps, Gilles has found his natural style of planting particularly suited to new gardens, where a raw plot can be given an almost instant maturity, and that it blends extremely well with modern architecture. For example, in a large garden he designed in Normandy, where the soil is clay and the climate temperate and humid, his aim was to restore the harmony between the architecture of the house and its surroundings.

The house is new, designed in traditional Normandy style, and is already covered in fast-growing *Clematis montana* 'Rubens'. Laurellike *Phillyrea angustifolia*, sheared into formal dome shapes, completely hides the pillar supports to the roof and serves as a green, leafy link between the house and the main garden. In a very shady part of the same garden, Gilles has designed an area of delightful shade-tolerant plants that produce beautiful scents and colors: splashes of bright orange in the foliage of *Pieris* 'Forest Flame' and the scented blooms of azaleas, such as *Rhododendron luteum* and *R. mollis* □

ROBERTO BURLE MARX

ROBERTO BURLE MARX is generally considered not so much a garden designer or landscape architect, as one of Brazil's leading and most exuberant artists. He has a rare talent for capturing and transforming the elements of his local tropical landscape and architecture into an exciting, seemingly wild union, and is indeed an artist of many talents: trained in both painting and botany, but capable of turning his hand to lithography, design and decoration.

Creating eyecatching and memorable landscapes does seem to be where the bulk of his energy lies and some of his designs are reminiscent of futuristic scenes from science fiction magazines, dominated by unusual shaggy trees, exotic, giant shapes and hot, glistening colors. Burle Marx has the knack of emphasizing the strangeness of the materials he uses, with skeletal rock formations or geometric architectural shapes that demand a reappraisal of familiar forms. Elsewhere, plants or beds of pebbles will be laid out in great swirls of color, contrasting brilliant red against deepest green or perhaps using more subtle shades of color as if he were painting the design with a brush from a palette.

Interpretations of nature

Many of his design concepts for undulating lines and great snaking curves of plants, paths or water are inspired by his many excursions up the Amazon looking for new plants to enhance his gardens. Other trips to inaccessible regions all over the world have produced further fascinating species to be discovered, brought back and acclimatized in Brazil. This mixture of native and exotic varieties is one of his distinguishing trademarks, for while he has a great feeling for and an obvious love of nature, he tends to interpret it in his own way.

It has been said that Burle Marx likes to take nature to pieces and then put it back together again in association with other, less natural forms. This aspect of his work can be seen in his use of blocks of stone and plants to imitate distant mountains and his reputation for complementing the architecture of surrounding buildings with his designs.

Nature may certainly be his inspiration, but it is also true that he is not afraid to use natural forms to suit his own needs. Long study of a particularly interesting twisted tree, for example, resulted in a convincing plastic reproduction for use in one of his gardens.

Strength and size

His general philosophy when designing one of his hot, lavish tropical gardens is that it should arouse wonder and a sense of euphoria. This he accomplishes with combinations of strong color, curious shapes and the sheer, astonishing size of many of his chosen specimens. He constantly tries to maintain variety by distributing different groups of plants with imagination and a good sense of asymmetry, although he never overdoes it by using too strong a color or too many dramatic effects.

The result is a far cry from the formal, regimented gardens once so loved by designers, but Roberto Burle Marx finds that his technique combines well with the strong geometric form of modern architecture.

Tropical brilliance

There are certain elements that Burle Marx particularly enjoys and he will often incorporate them into a new design. He loves water, for example, which he winds away out of sight or confines within a more formal, but not regularly shaped, pool. The water is usually smothered in water lilies and its edges hidden

Tropical plants with their vivid colors and strange forms need careful handling to show them at their best. The superb pink *Aechmea* needs only its own deep green spiky foliage for an ideal setting.

△ With an artist's appreciation of shape and color, light and shade, Burle Marx frames a dense background of sultry greenery from a cool terrace. A close group of terra-cotta urns and vases adds foreground interest and a contrast of textures. Their variety of shapes and sizes makes a pleasing combination, unified by the fact that they are made of the same material: you could achieve the same effect with any group of related containers, ornaments or even large pebbles in shades of gray or pastel colors.

beneath lush water-edge plants. He also has a fondness for smooth pebbles and, of course, for his plants, which provide such a splendid display of tropical shape and color, from the cacti and large palms to one of his special favorites, *Heliconia*, a relative of the banana, with its leaves opening to an elegant fan shape.

It takes considerable skill to balance and harmonize such plants and Burle Marx makes good use of green foliage plants, the tropical landscape offering plenty of opportunity to select large, bold leaf shapes and more subtle ground-cover material. This he uses among brick, stone and tiles of surrounding edges, paths and buildings, creating a softening, lush effect of greens, ranging from lime to almost blue, and many different shapes, from sharp spikes and fleshy, water-retaining plants to the great fronds of the palmate species.

The overall effect of one of his gardens serves several purposes. In the crowded city garden, it creates a welcome feeling of green countryside, a place to relax among the noise and dust; in the large country garden, such a backdrop of planting is the perfect setting for many of the richly colored tropical flowers that require a strong but not competitive foil.

In either setting, the effect is often breathtakingly beautiful when framed from the window or veranda of a nearby building. Cleverly arranged groups of plants can thus be appreciated for the shapes and patterns they create en masse, not simply for the charm of their leaf shapes when seen close to, and are indicative of the dual nature of his designs.

Roberto Burle Marx is always careful to ensure that his gardens will appeal from every angle. Borrowing from nature means that every design sits comfortably in its setting yet still retains the unique stamp of its creator □

△ A formal pool planted with water lilies (Nymphaea) *creates a calm focal point for close-cropped grass, cool gray pebbles and spiky leaved Bromeliads and Sansevieria. Strong architectural forms provide further contrasts against a backdrop of dense, jungle-like foliage.*

▷ *The silver pathways and lush but carefully balanced tropical vegetation which provide such an excellent foil for modern architecture are recognizable trade marks of a Burle Marx design. Here, an interesting variety of foliage shapes and blended shades of green are made up from Heliconia,* Vriesea *and* Beaucarnea. Ophiopogon japonicum *has been used as a dense grassy ground cover to the right of the path.*

▽ *Burle Marx displays his great talent for blending architecture into a seemingly natural setting. The long low lines of this two-level tiled roof are perfectly balanced between towering tropical trees and a reflective stretch of water. Groups of* Neoregelia compacta *dominate the scene and another bromeliad,* Vriesea schwackiana, *is in the foreground.*

JACQUES WIRTZ

JACQUES WIRTZ maintains a policy of creating 'green spaces' whatever the size, style or location of the garden he is designing. It makes his designs particularly appreciated in inner-city areas where his gardens represent oases of calm and tranquility. Jacques has created gardens and parks all over Europe and in Japan, but his roots are in Belgium, a country where a commitment to modern architecture requires strong garden concepts to soften and balance the dominating structural forms.

Dramatic foliage forms

A Wirtz garden is instantly recognizable by its greenness. Jacques enjoys blending and contrasting shapes and textures of leaf forms rather than mixing multicolored blooms, and relies mainly on clever arrangements and juxtapositions of foliage to create his rich effects.

Despite the apparent formality of his gardens, Jacques likes to combine dramatic or natural plant types, such as lush, fast-growing water plants, smothering ivies and wild rhododendrons, and he is not afraid to use these wilder, shaggier forms with more formal features, such as sheared box hedges or clumps of hedgerow to edge and delineate paths. He is also fond of topiary, pruning *Buxus* and *Taxus* into apparently spontaneous shapes and surrounding them with dense ground cover to produce a continuous flow of sculptural greenery reminiscent of rolling hills and an echo of the Japanese style.

Jacques Wirtz may prefer an orderly, controlled type of garden, but he is careful to keep maintenance to a minimum. He knows that the majority of his clients have little time to spend actually working on their gardens, and that they would prefer a restful, trouble-free environment to be enjoyed during their leisure hours. Thus, every aspect of his designs must work hard. He uses mainly herbaceous plants and is particularly fond of iris – he has been known to design whole gardens based around different varieties of this one species.

Similarly satisfying his need for dramatic, low-maintenance features, Jacques has a passion for planting trees within all his gardens. He feels that too many people do not give trees sufficient thought and appreciation; they tend to use them simply as a convenient backdrop, whereas he likes to make them into a special feature, using their shape, color and habit to create special effects, as in the example of *Catalpa bignonioides* 'Aurea', which he grows for its beautiful yellow color. He appreciates strong forms in shrubs, too, and will make extensive use of good architectural forms such as *Viburnum* and *Cornus*.

Creating calm from chaos

Jacques' own garden has been created from an old, neglected kitchen garden, which was once a regular arrangement of vegetable beds and fruit trees. On to the skeleton of this very formal layout he has grafted a leafy landscape.

Faced with a long, shady pathway bordered by ancient apple, plum and mulberry trees and edged with box (*Buxus sempervirens*) that had not been cut for 20 years, Jacques resisted the strong temptation to rip it all out. Instead, he pruned them at random to about 2 m (6½ ft) high in a variety of shapes, which created the sinuous effect of foliage snaking either side of the 150 m (490 ft) path. The rest of the garden picks up the theme, with arrangements of sheared *Buxus*, *Ilex* and *Taxus*.

Small garden tactics

The techniques employed in his own garden apply themselves equally well to smaller gar-

△ A neat low hedge of box Buxus sempervirens encloses and shelters this swimming pool area, yet allows views of the garden behind. More dramatic topiary forms in the shape of domes and cones continue the line of the hedge to make an architectural setting and a shady bower for a piece of sculpture. Well-weathered brick and lumber have been blended to make a safe and practical, but very natural, surface around the pool and on the patio. With a simple lumber bench softened by topiary, it is not only a pleasant place to sit, but it also disguises the end of the pool.

◁ In Jacques Wirtz's own garden, a wide, pleasant path shaded by fruit trees and edged with an unruly, undulating hedge of box has been tamed into a vivid green, leafy walk. The surrounding landscape is one of different shades of green and interesting sheared hedges.

dens. In one example, Jacques tackled a small, walled city garden by flanking the traditional path with something unexpected – dense plantings of horizontal-growing shrubs such as *Hydrangea paniculata* 'Praecox', *Viburnum plicatum* 'Mariesii', *Fothergilla* and *Cornus florida*, and a rectangular sheet of water between the wall and garden for clumps of *Iris sibirica*. A low fringe of *Buxus sempervirens*

◁ For a new house on the edge of the woods, Jacques has planned a group of oaks, Quercus palustris, *close to the house and a screen of pink-bloomed rhododendrons. Bonsai forms on lumber plinths and sculpture provide interest on a patio paved with Belgian blocks.*

▽ A narrow city garden contains elements of surprise when the classic straight path is edged with hedges of sheared box on the one side and a narrow pool of water with Nymphaea *and spiky* Juncus *on the other.*

borders the beds and softens the edge of the pathway. Among the unrelieved dense green foliage *Catalpa bignonioides* 'Aurea' provides a highlight of color and interest.

In another of his gardens, also surrounding a modern house but this time one built of red cedar in the middle of a pine wood, Jacques planted a dense thicket of bamboos, particularly *Arundinaria murielae*, clumps of *Rhododendron ponticum* and a glade of *Quercus palustris* to provide shade for a simple terrace.

Jacques Wirtz's talent for combining strong planting features with modern architectural forms naturally comes into its own when he is asked to design a pool or patio area. Topiary forms and hedges are often used to link the area to the house and to the greenery of the garden beyond. In this way Jacques can combine his plants with natural materials, such as lumber and stone, for an overall impression of comfortable formality □

IVAN RUPERTI

IVAN RUPERTI admits that he is not a plants-man, keen to fill his garden with many and rare species. He prefers to use readily available, and thus economical and easy to grow, varieties to create relaxing and low-maintenance landscapes. Based in Switzer-land, Ivan works closely with architects throughout Europe and the Far East and enjoys a challenge to his planning and design-ing skills – replanting a windswept island on the Italian coast or designing a prealpine garden that looks beautiful in summer despite being under thick snow for the rest of the year.

He has never been attracted to Mediterra-nean flora, but is drawn instead to cooler, softer-colored plants – magnolias, camellias and azaleas are particular favorites. In keeping with his low-maintenance philosophy, Ivan tends to select perennials, with each area of the garden designed to have two or three flowering periods a year. He is also fond of decorative features and will incorporate a stone wall rather than planting a hedge, or use a simple bench or eye-catching sculpture to enhance surrounding features rather than merge with them.

Water and rock

Visits to Japan have inspired Ivan Ruperti, awakening a new appreciation of rock, sand and water and the age-old concept of the garden as a universe in miniature. Thus, water has become central to all Ivan's designs, creat-ing what he describes as a 'living mirror' as the dominant feature. He loves the design poten-tial of water, not just because it is aesthetically pleasing and easy to maintain, but because it fits into the surrounding landscape so well.

His own current garden was designed and landscaped before the house was barely finished, with major features laid out and the pond dug at an early stage. The plot is sloping and triangular in shape, mostly given over to water, and he has used excavated material from the basement of the house to build a dam to contain the water.

The pond is edged with a pebble and boul-der beach that leads up to the house via a series of natural pebble and lumber steps and the wide, calm expanse of water is crossed by heavy railroad ties and a series of large stepping stones arranged in a zigzag pattern. Ivan was anxious to create a smooth transition between house and garden and, at the top of the steps, the house fronts the garden by way of a full-length conservatory, which provides useful protec-tion for his half-hardy plants in winter. Pink and white pelargoniums will flower in the conservatory all winter before being taken outdoors for the next summer; more winter blooms are supplied by *Datura suaveolens*, *Bougainvillea* and camellias.

The use of natural materials such as wood and stone and massed background planting of azaleas, camellias and rhododendrons help the garden blend with the surrounding land-scape, just as the design of the house harmo-nizes with the nearby village church and church tower □

▷ *Ivan Ruperti designed his garden to blend naturally into the view of roof tops and mountains beyond its boundaries. A large informal expanse of water reflects light and its surroundings with planting kept to a minimum and the pool edged or crossed with stone and lumber. The rocks and stones planted with pink and gray alpine plants lead up toward the house where pink Pelar-goniums are overwintered in pots to be brought out in summer and coordinated into the general plan. The overall style is simple and relaxing, lead-ing the eye naturally away toward the distant mountains which dominate the surrounding land-scape.*

MICHAEL BALSTON

MICHAEL BALSTON is a perfectionist. He has a thorough, scientific approach to garden design that leads him to check and then double-check every element of his plans to ensure that the final result is exactly right. Yet for all this, his gardens have a verdant, almost rampant informality. Only the fact that he achieves just the right balance of shape, height and color reveals the painstaking work that lies behind each impressive creation. Despite their almost mathematical planning, Michael Balston's gardens always have the ability to surprise and delight.

Garden analysis

Groundwork for Michael, who is based in the UK, begins with an analysis of the brief in relation to what the site has to offer – aspect, slope, drainage, soil chemistry and so on. When he is sure what he is up against he will begin to lay out a series of areas, assessing each in accordance to its purpose and in relation to its surroundings.

Michael is equally rigorous in his control of plant textures and colors to ensure the correct blend of contrasts and harmonies. He will plot foliage masses according to season or color groupings against season and annual growth. The same attention to detail is applied to the structural elements of his designs, such as pergolas, walls, paving and sculpture. These he uses not only to give an immediate enclosure for shelter and privacy in a new garden, but also as a contrast with plant textures and colors as part of the overall effect. As you would expect from a perfectionist, all these elements are plotted on to the main plan, then honed and refined until he is satisfied.

Viewed through his designer's eye, Michael finds the shapes, colors and patterns created by plants of special interest but he uses them sparingly – his designs are composed predominantly of gray, green and blue foliage with an occasional, strategically placed splash of white flower color or a sprinkling of white and pink flowers. Some plants remain favorites because of their shape: *Phormium*, for example, and *Viburnum plicatum*. Others, such as clipped yew or holly, *Lonicera pileata*, *Viburnum davidii*, and *Asarum europaeum*, he likes to use for their texture.

Coping with problems

Michael's inventiveness comes to the fore when asked to tackle a real problem site. The tiny north-facing terrace city garden shown here was heavily shaded and had a fall of 3 m (10 ft) from front to back. Drainage was also poor. Michael decided to introduce broad steps to give a feeling of depth and created a small sitting area at the upper level. The steps are useful as seats and as platforms for displays of potted plants opposite the family room at ground level. High-level fences of tubular steel and wire support quick-growing climbing plants, which provide privacy from the rear, and tubular steel arches filter the view into and out of the upper-level sitting area. Another device is the use of large foreground masses of shrubs, which suggest greater space behind □

▷ *A profusion of contrasting foliage forms disguise the carefully planned framework beneath Michael Balston's design for a small city garden. The effect is achieved mostly through a blend of contrasting foliage shapes in shades of green, blue and gray, with the occasional spots of color from quick-growing annuals like* Impatiens. *Michael likes to mix container-grown plants with more permanent planting to add variety, and employs climbers and sprawlers like* Hedera, Jasminum officinale *and* Cotoneaster *on trellis, walls and screens for vertical interest.*

△ One of Michael Balston's particular skills is the way he blends and contrasts foliage shapes and colors. Here, a shaped pyramid of box is the corner linch pin for a varied plan of feathery Cimicifuga, soft broad-leaved Alchemilla and the spiky-flowered Acanthus spinosus.

◁ A dense background of green foliage and wilder natural plants is perfect for showing off an unusual or particularly fine plant specimen. These beautiful lilies are almost luminous against the fresh green, cut leaves of a Philadelphus and the unobtrusive yellow and green of that excellent ground-cover plant Alchemilla mollis.

◁ *Formal elements contrasted with more unruly plant forms can create exciting areas within the garden. These ornamental, white-painted tubs have been planted with twisty-stemmed bay trees* (Laurus) *and a covering blanket of trailing* Hedera *for strong visual impact. Easy-to-maintain raised beds between contain quick-flowering plants like Anti-rrhinums* Cosmea, *Foxgloves* (Digitalis) *and fluffy white Astilbes. Black and white marble paving tiles and giant classical urns against a background of dark green have created an elegantly bright but intimate seating area where the shape and color of its plants can be appreciated from the comfort of a fine lumber seat.*

RICK ECKERSLEY & LISA STAFFORD

ICK ECKERSLEY and Lisa Stafford consider their client's lifestyle one of the most important determining factors when creating a garden. They like to assess both their functional and aesthetic requirements – how they will be using the garden, the style they prefer, favorite colors and materials – and work from these in conjunction with the site potential of soil, climate, light, shade and so on. Because they are based in southern Australia, a mild climate ensures that pools and barbecues come close to the top of many priority lists and they are careful to integrate these into the design. In a formal garden, for example, a swimming pool will often be symmetrical to relate to surrounding features such as a summerhouse or pergola; in a less formal setting, the pool may be simpler and more natural.

When their research is complete, planning tends to follow a set routine. First, Richard and Lisa will select a style appropriate to the type and character of the site and then develop this into a series of individual spaces geared to the owner's needs, incorporating areas for entertaining, sunbathing, cooking and play, as required. A lot of care is taken to make sure that these are well planned, balanced and suitably scaled to the size and shape of the garden.

Hard surfaces are an important element, often planned to complement surrounding building materials, with paving continued through to the house and around a pool or, where space permits, extended to make large patio or play areas. Care is also taken to ensure that plants are compatible and will grow together happily, encouraging a lush, mature feel yet minimizing maintenance □

△ Carefully chosen and well positioned, shrubs make excellent focal points, especially on the patio where they can be isolated by screens, paving and other structural forms.

◁ **Far left** Lumber and trellis have been cleverly used to create more intimate shady areas within the main garden, and softened by a climbing Kiwi Fruit (Actinidia chinensis) and hanging wire baskets of Brachycomes, Swan River Daisies, Impatiens, Cerastium and mixed silver-gray foliage.

◁ Simple slabs laid haphazardly make an attractive informal path along the side of the house. These types of area are often hard to design but by using a strong yet carefully balanced planting design, a would-be dull area has been totally transformed.

▽ Often it is the juxtaposition of unusual plants and materials that creates the most interesting effects. These lengths of pipe have been arranged in a group of differing heights and widths and then planted with dramatic subjects to make an exciting subtropical landscape.

HENK WEIJERS

ENK WEIJERS represents a generation of garden makers who have
learned to work with and appreciate
the everchanging nature of plants.
Strong, beautiful plant shapes and an organized but slightly unruly look typifies his
approach to garden design and, at first glance,
his gardens seem almost overwhelmed by
plants. Yet within this jungle of foliage, every
plant has its place and the seasonal show is
planned to provide year-round interest.

Henk has a natural understanding for the
use of water, and he has a talent for designing
both ornamental and swimming pools so that
they appear to be an integral part of the garden.
Dense groupings of water-edge plants around
the perimeter of ornamental pools are dramatic and help to hide the true limits of the plot.
Pools are encouraged to flourish with water-
loving plants, fish and wildlife to produce a
very natural, relaxing atmosphere that is full of
life and constant variety. Lumber-decked or
paved leisure areas within the main design are
often linked by paths and bridges across the
water to provide access and continuity.

Reacting against tradition

Henk's style is perfect for his native Holland
where garden space is precious and needs to be
made to look as expansive as possible. Thus,
boundaries are hidden by clumps of foliage
plants, such as *Miscanthus sacchariflorus*,

◁ Henk loves to use water in his designs, not just for its light-reflecting qualities, but for the wide variety of lush water-edge plants it can support. This large informal pool encompasses most of the garden, its limits hidden by the dramatic foliage of Iris sibirica and I. laevigata, Ligularia clivorum 'Desdemona' and other water-loving plants. A low lumber bridge provides an opportunity to observe fish and lilies at closer quarters.

◁ **Far left** Lumber decking around the pools provides walkways, bridges and seating areas, the exact boundaries of the water disguised by planting of Scirpus and clumps of the giant grass Miscanthus sacchariflorus. Dense planting and high walls have created an exciting, very private garden in an urban area.

39

Verbenas, Typhas and *Alchemilla mollis*, which all help to create his characteristic, slightly wild gardens.

Low maintenance is another important priority, and for that reason Henk never incorporates lawn areas into his designs, considering them a waste of space. He prefers to plan for plants with strong foliage shapes and colors that will be appreciated throughout the year, yet require little attention. He is also aware that gardens are for relaxing in, and within the basic framework of soft, blended colors and natural forms, he includes decks and patios screened by trees and larger-leaved plants to create sheltered, private areas. The occasional bright splash of plant color is included to add a vitally important element of contrast and interest.

The shape and form of Henk Weijer's gardens tend to flow with the apparent natural growth of the plants; they have no underlying logical pattern or geometric framework. Instead, they engulf the whole area, flowing around seating, softening the edges of decks or spreading across the surface of water to encourage the impression of a single garden entity. Only the relaxation areas are more clearly defined. It is a style that is very much in strong contrast to the more usual, very ordered type of Dutch gardening tradition, and one that relates directly to today's lifestyle seeking a

△ A double row of standard Catalpa makes a delightful feature in a garden with little vertical interest and provides useful shade for a seating area. The fresh green and yellow of Alchemilla mollis smothers their base and makes an unusual informal hedge around the area.

▷ Henk has an unerring eye for contrasting shapes and colors. On the one side of this narrow path is a rockery arrangement of spotted Pulmonaria, snowy white Chrysanthemum parthenium and dark green Prunus laurocerasus; on the other are the fluttering leaves of Arundinaria japonica and Lysimachia punctata.

no-fuss, relaxing environment within cities and other urban centers.

This natural, easy-care theme is also borne out by Henk's use of simple designs and natural materials, such as stone and lumber for seating, decks, bridges and other constructional features, which, softened by exuberant foliage and mirrored in the still surface of a gleaming pool, quickly become an integral part of the overall design.

Henk's gardens are for all the family to appreciate and enjoy. They are fun for children of all ages with their walkways, secret areas, junglelike profusion of plants and pools, and for adults, too, looking for a quiet retreat where they can soak up the sunshine or entertain friends within the privacy of a fascinating screen of plants □

OEHME, VAN SWEDEN

WOLFGANG OEHME and James van Sweden are an American-based design team fully conscious of the need for easy-care, highly enjoyable gardens for towns and cities. Both their amenity and private garden designs are distinctive in that they provide year-round interest for the minimum of maintenance, creating an effect that is at once easy and sophisticated, yet controlled and very natural looking. They aim to achieve a stylized but never over-formal landscape of flowing plants used en masse, choosing only the sturdiest and most reliable types and positioning them where they will have maximum impact. De-

nse ground cover takes care of weeds, while grassed areas are kept to a minimum or substituted with self-limiting plants, about 60 per cent of which are herbaceous.

Much of their work is based on a close observance of the life cycle of such plants, seeing how the garden subtly changes in color, size and density with the seasons as their sequence of growing, flowering, seeding and then withering completes itself with the minimum of human intervention.

Theory into practice

When commissioned to landscape a public park, Oehme, van Sweden were faced with the

▷ *Plants with white or yellow flowers can be used to highlight dark, shady corners. Here,* Ligularia clivorum *beneath a tree has the advantage of dramatic foliage, too, and has been allowed to make a large clump of golden daisylike flowers and huge circular leaves.*

▽ *Careful massed planting produces sweeping blocks of contrasting colors and textures, balancing spiky grasses such as* Pennisetum *and* Miscanthus *with the gold of lilies and* Achillea *in the foreground and the purple pokers of Purple loostrife behind. It is the use of such a limited palette of colors and their strict segregation that gives this design its impact.*

task of scaling down a vast open space to a more human scale. This they accomplished by breaking the area into a series of gardens with sheltered seating around a central expanse of lawn. Planting had to maintain year-round interest yet be sturdy enough to survive a certain amount of neglect. Their solution was to use large, ornamental grasses to give height above an immense container of intersecting expanses of *Epimedium*, *Bergenia* and *Liriope*, underplanted with hundreds of daffodils, hyacinths and tulips.

Elsewhere in the park, a dense row of *Sophora japonica* is underplanted with a succession of bulbs to be followed by sweeps of *Rudbeckia fulgida* edged with *Ceratostigma*.

By way of contrast, the owners of a small walled garden in a busy city center requested a low-maintenance area with outdoor seating that would form an attractive backdrop to a glassed-in room at the back of the house. The garden was heavily shaded and sloped toward the house.

They divided the garden into two levels with steps leading up from a small seating area close to the house. To create a feeling of extra space, large, dramatic plants were used not only to mask the real boundaries but also to suggest a more generous perspective.

Because the garden serves as a constantly visible backdrop to the house, plants were chosen to provide a succession of varied shapes and colors throughout the year. After the first burst of early bulbs come the tulips, followed by a long season of herbaceous plants and, in winter, showy ground-cover plants □

▽ *These large clumps of different grasses provide a splendid contrast of form, texture and color, the feathery forms of the seedheads rising attractively from the massed mounds of the leaves, set off to particular advantage against the dark foliage behind. Easy to maintain and good to look at for year-round interest, this design scheme exemplifies the success of Oehme, van Sweden's philosophy of blending art with nature.*

BETH CHATTO

Bᴇᴛʜ ᴄʜᴀᴛᴛᴏ is a plantswoman, a dedicated English gardener in the great tradition of Gertrude Jekyll. Her love and understanding of plants, and why they look and grow as they do, have led to the development of a beautiful, informal garden and one of the most fascinating plant nurseries in Europe.

Beth's own garden testifies to her unflagging hard work and enthusiasm and to her un-doubted skill in choosing and blending plant shapes and colors to maintain year-round interest. Her achievements are all the more impressive when you realize the nearly im-possible task she set herself almost 30 years ago: to carve a garden landscape out of a three- to four-acre acid wasteland.

The land featured a shallow depression of low-lying, mostly water-logged soil with a spring-fed ditch running through it. Compris-ing mainly bramble, willow and blackthorn, the only things to commend it were a boundary of fine, ancient oaks and the water-logged depression itself, which, to Beth, suggested visions of lush, water-loving plants and calm, reflective pools.

Natural selection

Working virtually single handed for the first ten years, Beth relied on her own love and knowledge of plants and on the inspiration of her husband's extensive understanding of the natural environment of plants and how this influences the way they grow. Her aim, in common with many talented modern garden designers, was to create an informal garden that could be enjoyed in every season. Low maintenance was a priority, too, and this she achieved by keeping the ground covered with foliage for as long as possible, thus suppressing weed growth. Beth has also devised a method of mulching any bare areas with straw and bark, which means she rarely, if ever, has to water in summer.

Each area of the site was gradually cleared and the soil fed and improved; planting was to follow Beth Chatto's philosophy of choosing plants as close as possible to their natural environment, taking into account shape, size and color. Tall, larger-leaved foliage plants would be employed to create bold effects; shrubs and other plants positioned close together to make dense groupings.

A dry, southwest-facing area was tackled first, enclosed by walls to make a sun trap. Drought-loving plants were introduced into raised beds that could be more easily main-tained and enjoyed closer to eye level, creating a real Mediterranean atmosphere; hot, dry and scented with plants such as santolinas, diffe-rent-colored sages, *Yucca* and fleshy house-leeks. Below, in the depression, the ditch was dammed to create a five-pond water garden enclosed by leafy, water-loving plants. Steps link this area to the drier, arid garden above, and you can feel the change of temperature as you step down.

The shady, northeast-facing part of the garden has been designed as a delightful wood-land, planted with spotted *Pulmonaria*, hos-tas, ferns, primroses and spring bulbs □

▷ *The large, informal pools in Beth's damp garden are framed by a dramatic backdrop of water-edge plants, including Iris laevigata, giant Gunnera chilensis and the glossy ribbed leaves and creamy flowers of the Great Water Dock, Rumex hydrolapathum. She likes to balance this dense, lush green effect with drifts of more colorful perennials such as Veronica, Alchemilla or Mimulus luteus.*

△ Wide grassy paths provide pleasant poolside and woodland walks through Beth's own garden, brushing water-edge or shady plants on either side and crossing a narrow neck of water by means of a simple wooden bridge.

◁ Beth is renowned for her exciting and unusual combinations of plant shapes and colors. Here she shows her skill in blending shrubs and perennials beside a pool. Large clumps of Phormium tenax 'Variegatum' have been contrasted with gray-leaved Salix repens 'Argentea', Salix lanata and the tiny smothering foliage of Vinca minor 'Bowles Blue'. The plant forms create perspective and architectural interest with a pleasing texture of varied leaf shapes.

TAKASHI SAWANO

AKASHI SAWANO in not only one of Britain's leading Japanese garden designers, he is also a master of both modern and classical styles of *Ikebana*, the Japanese art of arranging flowers. Such a thorough training in the identification and appreciation of plant form and shape has, not surprisingly, manifested itself in meticulous landscape designs where, with a keen sense of detail and a light hand in blending shapes and colors, he creates exquisite miniature landscapes in the classic Japanese tradition.

The essential elements

Takashi is an expert at combining the traditional elements of Japanese gardens – groups of carefully chosen and manicured plants, areas of raked sand, the position of rocks and boulders and the introduction of water features – which are all intended to represent the more natural landscape of mountains and seas.

He also has a special talent for introducing bamboo and stone ornaments or arrangements

of pebbles to his designs so that they complement the overall effect: thus, a small stone lantern might stand half hidden by foliage, or water pour gently from a length of bamboo on to a careful arrangement of smooth stones.

When it comes to plants, Takashi has a preference for blending dense green, ground-cover varieties with wall-covering climbers and taller, architectural species to achieve a good continuous spread of foliage. You rarely see bright flower color in one of Takashi's gardens. Instead he uses subtle shades of green and yellow foliage to balance and give life to the more somber grays and buff colors of the stone and sand features. Overall, this type of color scheme is very easy on the eye, designed to encourage relaxation and an enjoyment of an undemanding garden environment.

Embracing the ancient Japanese principles of creating a landscape in miniature means that Takashi Sawano's gardens adapt themselves very well to small spaces, making them ideal for the usual restricted garden sites of our modern cities, such as a patio, yard, roof garden or terrace.

Another of Takashi's talents lies in linking indoor and outdoor areas by using Japanese elements, such as stone, bamboo and plants, both inside and out. Floor-to-ceiling glass doors create the impression of a single area and, from inside, turn the garden into a living, ever-changing framed picture that can be appreciated throughout the seasons. Depending on the weather, the doors can either be opened or closed □

◁ *The classic Japanese raked gravel patterns, rocks and formal planting fits well in a small walled garden, where a low green plant carpet is in strong contrast to the sheared and manicured shrubs. A carefully positioned Japanese lantern provides a focal point.*

△ Water is an essential element of the Japanese garden and can be as simple as this small bamboo water spout, trickling water into a large urn buried up to its neck in smooth wet pebbles and surrounded by rocks, ferns and the yellow-spotted foliage of an Aucuba.

◁ Viewed from the house, the garden is as perfectly framed as a picture. The plan is predominantly green and gray, the high wall smothered by Clematis montana which blends with a backdrop of trees beyond the garden. Interest is maintained primarily through the varied colors and shapes of the foliage like feathery ferns and yellow-splashed Aucuba japonica, so the garden looks as good in winter as it does in summer. For added excitement and to mark the changes of the seasons, Clematis montana produces a splendid display of small pale pink flowers in spring and brid-- f ---

MIEN RUYS

MIEN RUYS can boast a long gardening pedigree and an impressive background in experimenting with plants as an element of design. For 60 years she has been exploring the potential for using low-maintenance perennial plants within the formal framework of landscape gardening – and with no small measure of success. At her home in Holland, Mien has built up a complex of 25 different gardens within the boundaries of one large site where visitors can see a wide variety of ideas and settings.

Strong forms and shapes

Although plants play a significant role in all her garden designs, Mien believes in using them as only a part of the total landscape plan. She prefers to begin designing the architectural lines of the garden, then softens these with a profusion of herbs and wild plants, particularly those with strong architectural form and shape. These she groups together in bold and always interesting arrangements, blending

▷ *A shady walk beneath a dense canopy of Alnus incana 'Aurea' is a medley of greens and yellows. The winding path of bark chips is edged with daisylike Buphthalmum salicifolium and spires of yellow Verbascum nigrum.*

▽ *Mien is not afraid to blend formal with more unruly elements. Here sheared spirals of Buxus sempervirens stand sentinel either side of a jungle of giant sorrel and the bright yellow flowers of Tropaeolum canariense.*

△ *Massed planting in the borders provides blocks of solid color and interesting textural effects. The creamy heads of* Sedum telephium *are graduated toward the bright yellow of* Achillea *'Parker's Variety', orange* Helenium autumnale *'Moerheim Beauty' and the feathery whiteness of* Phlox paniculata.

◁ *Within the formal confines of a paved and lumbered patio, a rich profusion of plants is contained by raised beds and wooden plant containers. The large round leaves of* Petasites japonicus *make a dramatic contrast with feathery, pink-tipped* Tamarix parviflora *and sweet-scented flowering thymes, blue-flowered* Agapanthus *and mauve-blue* Lobelia. *Stout lumber pergolas and meshing smothered by an attractive orange flowered* Eccremocarpus scaber *provide vertical interest.*

and contrasting shape and size with the same care as color combinations are chosen, and here she has a distinct preference for greens and yellows, with perhaps just a touch of red and pink.

During the 60 years Mien Ruys has been developing her own gardens, she has experimented with and created a diverse collection of different designs. These range from an early wild garden planted in the shade (first created in 1925) to an herbaceous border where she demonstrates that you do not have to plant in lines or position plants with their backs against a hedge or fence. One garden shows how the color of leaves can be used as effectively as the color of flowers, with gray- and brown-leaved shrubs making the point; another is a sunken garden with an enclosed, intimate atmosphere; and there are several examples of roof gardens with ideas for using all types of containers.

As a true garden architect, it quickly becomes apparent that structures and paved surfaces also play an important role in all her gardens and she makes good use of features such as pergolas, decks, paving, pebbles and garden sculpture. Railroad ties are often used and in a variety of ways – as a rustic bench below a cherry tree, for example, as edging for pathways or to mark a change of level.

Mien believes that a garden should maintain interest all year round, so here again careful planting is important to create areas full of sun for the summer, wild areas of bulbs for spring, trees and shrubs for autumn color or good, strong shapes for maximum impact on winter days □

△ Where a meandering path around the garden parts ways, a millstone bubble fountain in a bed of pebbles makes a dramatic feature. The formality of the brick path is contrasted with a strong planting design with the giant leaves of Petasites hybridus *running along its length and a blend of bright green* Hosta fortunei 'Aurea', *tiny* Prunella webbiana 'Rosea', *and* Artemesia nutans 'Silver Queen' *in the foreground. Behind is blue gray* Macleaya cordata 'Yedoensis' *and a beautiful* Hydrangea aspera.

▷ Water-edge planting around an informal pool offers scope for some interesting flower combinations as well as dramatically contrasting foliage shapes. Providing plants are grown in massed groups and not a jumble of different colors, the result can be stunning. Here, against the foreground planting of various greens of Iris and Trollius, yellow Day lilies (Hemerocallis) are the companions of crimson Astilbe and the tall purple spires of self-seeding Lythrum salicaria. These beautiful plants glow with jewellike brilliance against the deep shade of surrounding trees.

ULRICH TIMM

ULRICH TIMM is very much a modern garden architect, intent on blending the garden with its surroundings and creating private garden 'rooms' with unexpected views of the house or of other aspects of the garden. He lives and works in Hamburg and draws a great deal of his inspiration from nearby architectural structures and buildings, always striving to make the house and garden appear as one by matching stone or brickwork in the garden to that used in the construction of the house.

Ulrich Timm also prefers to keep his use of materials as natural as possible and he employs both stone and lumber for edging walkways and for walls, again making sure that they blend with any neighboring buildings, and thereby continuing the theme of creating a

single entity. He not only likes to edge his pools with pebbles, for example, but will also use them to build walls or simply pile them up as decorative features.

As well as formally training as a landscape architect, which has given him a good understanding of the basics of design, Ulrich is also skilled at combining plants to create specific effects, thanks to six years' experience working in a plant nursery.

Designing with plants

In general he favors informal planting groups with blocks of single color set against a strong background of trees. This is immediately identifiable in his own garden, which combines more formal beds with a wild flower meadow area. Here he has also created several formal paved areas for sitting and enjoying the sun at different times of the day. One of these is close to the house with raised planting beds and a pebble-bordered water feature that continues into the main garden.

To combine effectively all the elements of his design, Ulrich also introduces a variety of levels, which not only help to break up the garden visually, but also serve to link different areas. This is all part of his philosophy of creating garden rooms so that you can spend your leisure time in various parts of the garden enjoying many different views of, say, the house or the landscape beyond its boundaries.

Within his garden, Ulrich is keen to use perennials and shrubs rather than plants that require a lot of tending, and he is particularly interested in using hedges as design features. While his designs rarely produce an instant garden, he has a talent for laying down a good, permanent framework that will grow and mature with the minimum of care. This is at the core of Ulrich's concept of gardening □

◁ This delightful seating area under the shade of trees uses the borrowed scenery of the landscape beyond the garden. Wild flowers in long grass encourage the feeling that it is set in the midst of a meadow.

▷ Over large areas, just one or two brilliant colors are often more effective than many. The mass planted borders of this semi-formal design have been planted with yellow and crimson Rhododendron against a background of greenery.

◁ The large informal garden always benefits from being divided into smaller, more intimate areas. Here, Ulrich Timm has continued the formal lumber deck out from a shady terrace to create a sunny patio and interesting walkways between raised beds. The decking has been used to border a semiformal pool complex beside the patio. A steep change of level and the use of stone and pebble create interest and contrasting textures against the rest of the garden, which is an informal background of grass, trees and shrubs, to produce a relaxing green landscape viewed from the house.

▽ Taller, more architectural plants can transform a garden design into an altogether more interesting landscape. This giant bamboo towers above a lagoon-style pool edged with large pebbles and boulders and surrounded by more formal grass areas. Apart from adding height to an otherwise level area, this attractive plant creates fine dappled shade.

HIROSHI MAKITA

Hiroshi Makita has been fully educated in the classic Zen tradition and expertly taught *Shimbumi*, the Japanese art of creating serenity and harmony in a garden. Hiroshi now lives and works in America where his style of garden design is still essentially Japanese and very much in demand among a suburban society looking for a peaceful, easy-care setting.

Not surprisingly, the traditional Japanese blend of natural materials, such as stone, water and timber, has struck the right chord with garden owners hungry for soothing yet dramatic landscapes. Hiroshi has found that the basic Japanese principles adapt easily both to different lifestyles and to Western architecture.

In one of his gardens, Hiroshi found that the Japanese device of incorporating trails or winding pathways worked very well for a client who was keen on keeping fit: he now enjoys jogging round a circuitous, meandering route between fine hostas and azaleas and has the chance to put his stamina to the test over a steeply arched bridge.

Creating an integrated whole

To Hiroshi Makita, every garden is a work of art and he puts much love and care into his designs. Great emphasis is placed on the use of stone and water and also on a bold background planting of fine trees and shrubs. Hiroshi likes plants with strong, well-defined lines, such as *Enkianthus*, azaleas, Japanese maples and rhododendrons, which lend themselves to being pruned.

A typical garden might include extensive planting of *Liriope* and rhododendrons with moss and azaleas pruned into softly domed pillow shapes in imitation of the natural contours of the land. As much as three-quarters of his planting may be evergreens. Hiroshi believes that this provides year-round interest and a natural background for other plants.

While Hiroshi's designs have a mostly natural bias, he puts great emphasis on structures and objects, such as bridges, lanterns and gazebos, which are designed and constructed to blend perfectly with their surroundings and provide extra points of interest. As well as being a talented designer he is also a skilled craftsman, expert at working in wood or stone, and he generally builds his own benches, platforms, waterspouts, bamboo screens and fences. His bridges have almost become his trademark, and these may range from a simple zig-zag of planks to an elegant, arch.

Perhaps his gardens work so well because Hiroshi has the patience to pick and sort every stone, rock and pebble that is used in them and because he so obviously loves every element that goes to create an intimate, tranquil and, at the same time, stimulating environment □

▷ *Hiroshi Makita is a master at blending unusual plant forms with natural materials like stone and lumber in the classic oriental style. He designs and makes many of his own ornamental and structural features, such as this beautifully designed, low lumber bridge which crosses an area of water and slab stone designed to look like a natural pool, edged by a spectacular Miscanthus sinensis 'Gracillimus' and more formal clipped plant shapes.*

△ *Makita's gardens look good in winter as well as summer. A heavy fall of snow has enhanced this small corner with its stone sculpture and dark evergreens.*

◁ *The jewel of the Japanese garden is the Japanese maple which produces such spectacular foliage colors in autumn. Even after the leaves have dropped, the maple continues its beautiful display.*

▷ Japanese maples are invaluable not just for
their delightful summer foliage and vivid
autumn tints, but also for some fascinating trunk
formations like these twisted dark forms that even
make an eye-catching feature through the starker
winter months.

▽ Using plants in a natural association with
other materials is an art form the Japanese
understand and practice in their designs. Here,
rough rock and lumber steps lead up a winding
path softened at the edges by ground plants in
autumn shades of gold and brown.

APPLYING THE PRINCIPLES

A good idea is worth nothing if it cannot be put into practice. If the pictures on the preceding pages and the suggestions that follow have inspired you or sparked off further ideas, you will no doubt be keen to know if they will work in your own garden. There is only one way to find out, and that is to employ the same methods used by the professionals – diligently draw up a set of plans and then plot them accurately onto your site.

In the following chapter you will find out exactly how it can be done and you are advised to take the information to heart if you are planning major work in your garden. Initial enthusiasm to see an idea take physical form often leads to shortcuts with disastrous and potentially expensive results.

Give yourself the chance to weigh up the pros and cons of every element, fine tune and adjust your plans so that every feature functions correctly, and you will be rewarded with a garden that not only looks good but also performs the way you want it to – at a price you can afford to pay. Remember: inspiration tempered by patient attention to detail is behind every successful garden design.

THE MASTER DESIGN

THIS BOOK IS intended as an inspiration and as a means of presenting some of the most exciting options available in garden design today. The selection of designers on pages 8 to 60 will have provided you with some insight into the superb effects that can be achieved and shown how many apparent problems are overcome, but the last thing you should attempt to do is slavishly reproduce an exact copy of somebody else's garden – even if that were possible. This chapter will help you to select the creative elements you need from the ideas and photographs presented, then show you how to draw your own plan – one exclusively tailored to your own garden and your life-style – for a completely individual and, for you, practical garden environment.

DRAWING THE PLAN

So how do you go about choosing the right features and how is the final effect achieved? Start by drawing a list of priorities of the types of features you would like to see in the garden, those that your family will need and any major items that must be incorporated into the plan, such as a greenhouse, swimming pool, covered garbage area or tanks for central heating fuel supplies.

Next, ask yourself who will be using the garden and for what purpose. If you have children or pets, you need to plan for play and exercise areas, while those who enjoy entertaining require barbecue and dining facilities. Perhaps the garden will simply be a retreat, a place where you can relax away from the noise and stress of your business life. You must also ask yourself what you want from the garden: is it to be vegetables and fruit, cut flowers for the house, a fine view or a series of outdoor leisure areas suitable for all the family and their varied interests?

Another point to take into consideration is the amount of time you are prepared to spend on maintenance once the garden is finished: does it need to be virtually maintenance free or is the occasional weeding and shearing all part of the relaxation process for you? For some people, the garden must be designed to look after itself for several months of the year while the house is unoccupied, yet be ready to spring

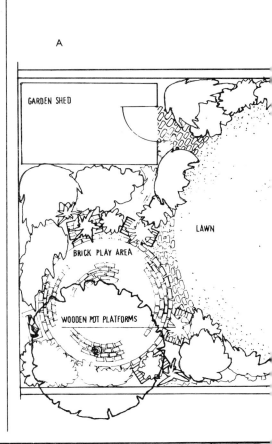

A

GARDEN SHED

BRICK PLAY AREA

WOODEN POT PLATFORMS

LAWN

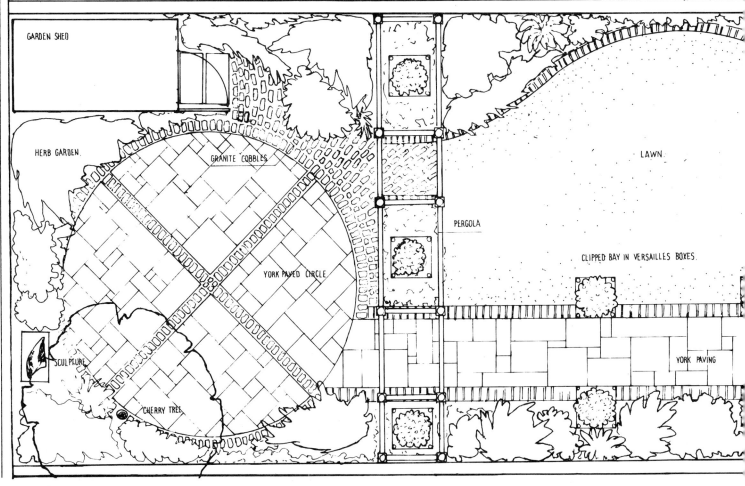

GARDEN SHED

HERB GARDEN

GRANITE COBBLES

YORK PAVED CIRCLE

SCULPTURE

CHERRY TREE

PERGOLA

LAWN

CLIPPED BAY IN VERSAILLES BOXES

YORK PAVING

This small city garden was developed by designers Anthony Paul and John Duane for clients with a young family. The clients were shown two concepts, plan **A** and **B**. Plan **B** was chosen for its more classical feel as it was thought to be more in keeping with the interior of the house. Both designs had allowed for a small space with play equipment for the children at the rear of the garden but plane **A** had water in the design and it was rejected as a possible hazard to the children.

Color scheme was developed around soft pastel shades in both flower and leaf forms. Herbaceous plants such as verbascums and potentillas were planted, as were variegated thymes and gray-leaved olearias and santolinas to give a silvery effect, making the plant material look light and feathery. A small herb garden was planted around the garden shed, including dill, sage, fennel, lovage, mint and thyme.

The garden is shown three months after planting (p.65) and blue and white annuals have been added to give some structure for the first season. The standard weeping roses, 'Swany', give a very pleasant scent at night, as do the white tobacco plants (Nicotiana) included especially for this effect.

The client wanted to be able to eat out in the garden at night so lighting was carefully designed to highlight the feature plants and planting boxes.

The walls were painted white to give an illusion of a greater space and to help reflect the night lighting. The hard materials used were traditional stone for paths, cobbles for the edges and gray-blue engineering bricks as a trim to the paving.

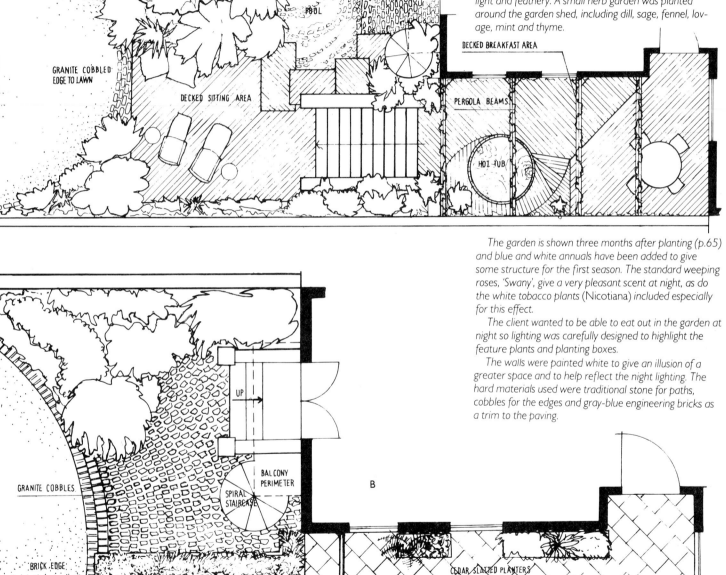

GRANITE COBBLED EDGE TO LAWN

BALL FOUNTAIN

POOL

DECKED BREAKFAST AREA

DECKED SITTING AREA

PERGOLA BEAMS

HOT TUB

GRANITE COBBLES

BRICK EDGE

UP

BALCONY PERIMETER

SPIRAL STAIRCASE

B

UP

CEDAR SLATTED PLANTERS ON EITHER SIDE OF STEPS

CEDAR SLATTED PLANTERS WITH TRELLIS ON WALL

FRONT OF CONSERVATORY

CEDAR SLATTED PLANTERS WITH TRELLIS ON WALL

back into life with the minimum of effort when the owners return.

Keeping costs under control

Finally, there is the question of budget. Planning your garden as a total project from the outset not only produces a more exciting, unified look, it also enables you to cost it and to modify where necessary. Nothing is worse than a half-finished plan, left in a state of limbo because money ran out; or a garden which so obviously started off on the right track, but which later strayed and standards allowed to drop as funds became low.

It is far better to replan along more modest, but no less exciting, lines from the beginning – and many of the ideas you see will be surprisingly budget conscious – or to create a basic framework that can be built on and developed over a period of years as money becomes more readily available.

Once you have your list of essentials and some idea of the time, effort and money these involve, you can begin to consider what style of garden you would like to enjoy. A larger garden may encompass several different styles; a smaller plot maybe only one. But the informality of the wild or country garden, more formal classical or high-tech features can be matched to the style of your home, its surroundings or simply your own whims.

Designs & Themes on pages 71 to 112 will show you the variety of features and effects it is possible to achieve. In many ways, the look – and cost – of your garden will be dictated by the materials you choose and, here again, it is worth paying close attention to your immediate environment: indigenous plants and local stones and woods will naturally look more in keeping and they can be adapted to a wide variety of garden styles. They will also be less expensive to bring in □

THE PLAN INTO ACTION

Once you have a clear idea of the type and style of features you are looking for in your garden, and have placed the major elements into priority order, you can start to see how they might fit into the actual site.

Step by step

Begin by measuring the garden and make a note of any permanent existing features, such as attractive trees and shrubs, outbuildings or drainage or septic tanks. Transfer your measurements on to graph paper to make a scale plan and mark in some indication of shade, aspect, permanent features and any changes of level.

Now you can begin to plot in your additional features, juggling with the information you have assembled until it looks right. No doubt you will have to make some compromises, but always opt for removing unsuitable elements rather than trying to squeeze them into a position where they will not look right. Work in pencil initially so that you can go back and change the position of features, or make correct-scale cut-outs and move these around on the plan until you are satisfied.

The next step involves transferring the paper plan to the garden proper, checking measurements carefully and marking the garden with a series of pins and strings to represent the shapes of the features you want to include. Sometimes it helps to position solid objects, such as boxes, cartons or old pieces of carpet, to indicate planting areas, raised pools, and other, similar features.

It is vitally important that you now spend time viewing the effect from every conceivable angle. Live with this arrangement for a few days and walk round the garden making sure that the sunny areas are indeed sunny, that the 'paths' do not have impractical twists and turns and that the overall design will work properly as well as look right. It often helps to view the effect from the house, especially an upstairs window, since this will throw it more strongly into relief. Anything you are not happy with should be amended at this stage.

If you are now satisfied with the type and position of the features, you can sit down and plan more specific details, such as the plants and materials to be employed. Here it is important not to go out and buy on impulse. Instead, make a list of exactly what you need. Calculations for materials must be checked and double-checked, taking into account their suitability as well as availability. Draw up a

△ As you transfer the basic framework of your design onto the garden, it will take recognizable shape once paths, paving areas and screens are installed. The addition of plants produces a fuller picture immediately, but it will not be until the plants mature over the seasons that your garden will achieve the full effect of the original plan. Depending on the type of plants you have chosen, you can sometimes produce a mature garden in a short space of time. This small suburban plot was transformed within a matter of months. The stage-by-stage photographs show how the design was built up.

detailed planting plan so that you can expertly balance plant shapes, colors and sizes, marking in expected heights and spreads. You should be aiming for year-round interest and plant suitability, not just foliage and flower variety. Trees will provide height as a focal point or backdrop; evergreen shrubs, climbers and ground-cover plants your basic framework, with herbaceous plants and smaller decorative plants to highlight specific areas. You will find additional information on designing with and choosing plants in *Designing with Plants* starting on p. 173.

Once pins and strings have been adjusted and you have established where and how you are going to acquire plants and construction materials, the actual work can commence. The first things to go in must be any essential services – drainage, if necessary, electricity and plumbing for lighting and water facilities. Now is the time to start doing any remedial work on your soil if it is necessary. You can follow this with any building work, such as

paths, patios, boundary walls and fences, pergolas, pools and changes of level – your garden framework in fact.

This completed, planting can begin and, finally, the design details – ornaments, pebbles, sculptures, pots, containers and furniture – positioned where they will have the greatest impact.

With everything in place and plants beginning to establish themselves, your ideas will at last have taken shape and by the end of the first year or two you should be able to see your plan maturing, particularly if you have opted for fast-growing plants or the slightly wilder effect preferred by many of the successful garden designers we have featured. It does take patience, but with the final look firmly in your mind, you will see it becoming a reality season by season. If you wish, and have the time and money, spaces can be temporarily filled with extra plants or fast-growing annuals while the main plants are growing to a more mature height and spread □

Splashes of color are added all over the garden with pots and boxes planted with bright flowering plants such as this Swan River Daisy (Brachycome iberidifolia).

Cedar planting boxes, oiled with teak oil, were built to fit over old step surrounds and a blue and white design of violas, geraniums, cornflowers and trailing lobelia has been used to adorn both sides of the steps.

Trellis entrances to the children's play circle divide the garden into two distinct areas. Fast-growing climbers such as passion flowers and jasmines will quickly climb up the trellis in the next year. The terra-cotta cheetahs were brought in from the clients' last garden.

LIMITATIONS OF SOIL & SITE

Your garden will naturally impose certain restrictions on what you can and cannot do. While many of these can be overcome artificially, it generally involves spending time and money when, in most cases, you would do better by choosing more indigenous, easy-care types of plants and features.

Climate

Climate is a vital factor, not only affecting your choice of plants but also the types of materials you use. Bear in mind that fierce sunshine can be just as damaging as strong wind and frost. Your local climate is easy to identify in very general terms: alpine, for example, and very cold during the winter months, temperate, subtropical or tropical. But every location experiences its own microclimate, particularly in a temperate area, where one garden can vary to the next; or on the coast, where salt wind makes it difficult to grow very much even when sunshine and rainfall seem perfect. Frost, wind and sun are the determining factors and you must learn which plants are best equipped to deal with the conditions on your particular site.

Choosing plants and materials that can cope is half the battle, but there are ways you can modify conditions slightly to allow a rather broader range and provide a more welcoming environment. Shelter from wind can be supplied by trees and shrubs or by erecting fences, walls and screens – these are also useful for casting shade. If you do not mind the extra maintenance work involved, glass, straw and burlap can be used to give some protection for tender plants from frosts in winter, while thick mulches and timer-controlled irrigation systems will help to relieve drought conditions in hot, dry weather.

Site

You need to take a long, hard look at the actual site of your garden before assigning specific features to your basic plan. You must consider its aspect, for example – that is, which areas are north or south facing – for it is this that will determine not only your choice of plants but the position of patio areas, too. It is not always sufficient to presume that south facing will be warmer; remember that areas facing east will warm up quicker, particularly earlier in the year when the hours of daylight are less. West-facing areas will receive the lingering warmth of summer sunsets – perfect for evening entertaining and dinner party patios.

△ Where temperatures and weather conditions are extreme, the right choice of plants is a key to success. While this walled patio protects the plants from the wind, it is also a real sun trap. Tall trees and the walls themselves help to provide shade, and the plants have been specially selected to withstand fierce sunshine during the summer months.

◁ Use of natural materials helps any structural features to blend with the rest of the garden. Local materials will naturally look more in keeping and are often cheaper. Here, a simple lumber bridge has been carefully chosen, its color and texture matching the surrounding rough stones and pebbles along a stream bed.

Any slope to your site will make a difference too, providing on the one hand interesting garden contours but, on the other, potentially expensive leveling and backfilling costs.

Poor drainage may well need to be rectified, which is another expense and one that has to be considered before any work is begun. A high water table may dictate a raised swimming pool rather than a sunken one. Few sites are perfect and the most common problems are that they are either too exposed, often the case in country locations or with roof or balcony gardens, or, more usually in cities, that they are heavily shaded by surrounding trees and buildings. Shelter will alleviate the former problem, but there is little you can do about the latter, other than to concentrate on shade-loving plants and to install visually-lightening features such as water and mirrors or use white paint on walls, fences, screens and so on.

Soil

Again, soil is very rarely perfect, but it is important that you find out exactly where its shortcomings lie so that you can adjust your choice of plants accordingly. Owners of new properties often find that the problem is that there is little, if any, topsoil and in this case you will have no option but to import it.

By closely observing the soil in both wet and dry conditions, and by rubbing it through your fingers, you will quickly discover whether it is too fine and sandy, thick with clay or, hopefully, a pleasant, crumbly tilth. Testing its pH levels, either by sending a sample for analysis by a soil testing center or by using an inexpensive home kit, will determine the exact alkali/acid level, which is an important consideration, since some plants can be sensitive to too much lime or peat in the soil.

It is possible to improve soil type by the addition of organic matter and chemicals, but you must realize that this is a continual process and will need to be kept up. It would be difficult to change your soil type permanently, although Beth Chatto (see p. 44) has made significant inroads into providing better drainage for a hopelessly waterlogged site.

Sandy soil, which is too freely draining, benefits greatly from the addition of plenty of organic matter, as does a clay-based soil. With clay, it is important to build in a better system of drainage, using material such as rubble, old bottles or purpose-made drainage pipes under a perforated plastic sheet, to keep the surface soil intact.

A peaty soil tends to be too acidic and an occasional dressing of lime will help to provide a more balanced pH, while a too alkaline soil is full of calcium and spells instant death to lime

△ Plant groups will flourish if they all enjoy the same type of soil and site conditions. These can be created artificially, as in the case of this verdant bog garden where an area of soil is kept permanently moist by means of a perforated plastic lining concealed by pebbles.

▷ Leisure areas require careful siting to make the best use of all the available sunshine. This may mean positioning patio areas away from the house, as in this small suburban garden where a seating and sunbathing area has been created at the far end of the plot. Lack of privacy and population can also be problems in city gardens. Here fences, screens and dense planting baffle traffic noise, block out fumes and ensure necessary privacy.

haters such as camellias and rhododendrons, and needs lots of manure or compost.

You can only improve your soil so far, and if conditions are totally wrong for the plants you want to grow, you will have to install them in tubs, pots and raised beds full of a suitably formulated soil. Otherwise, it is sensible to follow the line of least resistance and choose plants that have at least an inclination toward local conditions.

One important point to bear in mind when assessing and testing soil types is that results can vary from area to area within the same garden. So take care to make a series of tests and you may be able to plan your planting to produce an excellent variety of plants.

Size and shape

Short of buying more land and extending or moving elsewhere, there is not a lot you can do to change the physical size and shape of your garden. There are, however, a multitude of visual tricks you can employ that will create the impression of space or disguise your garden's shape and dimensions.

A small or uninteresting, long, narrow strip of a garden can be disguised by paths describing indirect or circuitous routes and the introduction of screens of foliage and flowers so that you are never really sure where the actual boundaries lie. With a small garden, it always helps if you cannot take it all in with a single glance. Other visual tricks employ reflective stretches of water or mirrors to magnify and add light. The positioning of focal points, the use of certain colors, the direction of paths and the style of hard surfaces will all influence the apparent size and shape of your site.

In a large garden it is more necessary to minimize its expansiveness in some way. This can be achieved by the creation of more intimate garden areas within the site, linked by paths or walkways. Where possible, it is useful to extend the garden visually into the landscape beyond the boundaries □

△ In a large garden, it is a good idea to create small garden 'rooms' for relaxing or for grouping special collections of plants. A partial screen, like these lengths of lumber and carefully selected plants, not only establishes a boundary but allows the eye to wander beyond, so still extends the garden visually.

▷ There are various features you can incorporate into your garden plan to create visual illusions. A stretch of water will always magnify the space and make a garden look larger than it really is. Screens, lush planting and bold architectural specimens are useful for distracting attention and disguising the true boundaries of the plot.

DESIGNS & THEMES

Like interior design, garden design is largely a matter of personal taste and practical limitations. Within the confines of shape, size, soil type and, of course, budget, the trick is to make the garden work for you. And that is what *Designs & Themes* is all about – designing a garden to suit your lifestyle.

Before you start planning, you should ask yourself the types of questions a landscape architect would ask a client. For example: what type of garden suits your needs and inclinations? Low maintenance is often an important consideration; a busy job may leave little time for working in the garden but a pressing need for an enjoyable environment in which to relax. The large garden, with time-consuming, manicured lawns and weed-hungry herbaceous borders, may need rethinking.

You should also spend time assessing what is important to you in a garden and deciding the types of features that appeal most. You may have a preference for hard or soft surfaces: lawns and decks, for example, rather than stone and brick.

This section is divided into styles, or themes, with ideas and suggestions for all sizes of garden. Some you may not have thought of before; others you may have liked but not realized they were possible. Use the ideas presented here as a means of establishing in your own mind exactly the type of garden you want and see how it can be adapted to your own circumstances. The *Design Guide* (p. 209) and *Designing with Plants* (p. 173) will provide additional advice.

THE CITY GARDEN

DUE TO INEVITABLE pressures on space, gardens in many urban centers may be small, sometimes no larger than a few paving slabs square. But no matter how small it might be, the city garden performs an important function: it provides valuable extra room for living and is, in a sense, an extension of the house, allowing space for sitting, eating and relaxing.

Modern urban architecture tends to emphasize the actual building and largely ignores the environment in which it is set, making it even more important for the individual to use the garden area to its maximum extent. This is not the difficult task it may initially seem. Every type of garden has advantages as well as disadvantages, and the city garden is not without its plus points.

Admittedly, some city gardens are fairly small and narrow, and the proximity of other buildings may make them shady. Unless some garden-loving owner has lavished love and plenty of humus on it over a period of years, the soil will also tend to be poor and thin. But perhaps the worst problem the city gardener can face is the type of garden found on new housing developments: extremely small, bordered by inefficient and unattractive fencing that offers little or no privacy and full of stones and rubble. In urban centers there can be the problem of pollution to contend with, too.

All these factors sound rather negative – but take heart! It takes only a little planning and imagination to turn a yard into a little piece of paradise and there is much to be said in favor of having only a small space to look after. A small garden is more controllable for one thing, keeping maintenance to a minimum, and,

▷ Maximize your assets by designing house and garden as one. Hard-wearing flooring continued across both areas provides indoor and outdoor living spaces and encourages a feeling of continuity, emphasized by plants grown in containers that can be positioned inside or out according to the weather. A Dracaena marginata, the handsome Phoenix robelinii and a glossy Ficus benjamina 'Exotica' are useful for creating strong architectural interest.

▽ The city garden often presents the designer with a difficult shape and situation. This site includes a steep change of level which has been resolved with lumber steps and walkways around an ornamental pool and deep beds filled with easy-to-maintain shrubs and trees like Acer palmatum 'Dissectum' and sheared box.

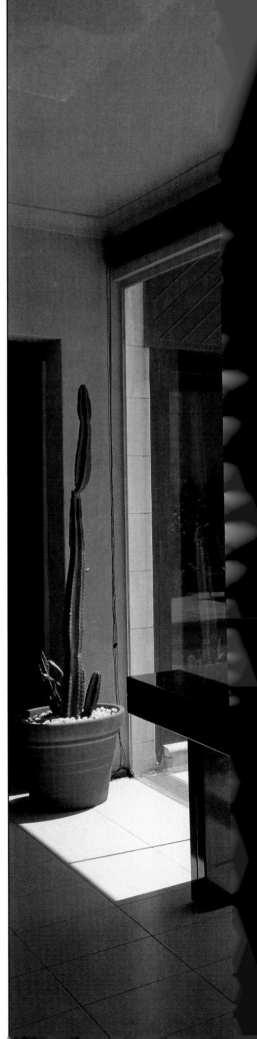

because it is sheltered, the seasons will be longer, thus allowing you to grow more unusual and tender plants. The reduced size also means growing fewer plants and using less building materials, making a full and interesting garden easier and less expensive to achieve.

The role of the city garden

The city garden represents more than just a plant-filled space: it is a buffer between your house and the pressures of city life. This is why the way you design and plant your garden is so important – low-maintenance features mean that it will not be regarded as a chore but rather as a relaxation, an enjoyable experience with the added benefits of the sight and sound of wildlife and the refreshing scent of the earth

and flowers. The garden should also afford you privacy, so that you do not feel observed, and space in which to relax and unwind.

Privacy and shelter do not necessarily mean high walls blotting out light and sunshine. Lacy screens around the patio, for example, or pergolas and quick-growing climbing plants good ways to avoid the neighbors and they have the advantage of being good to look at.

The concept of the mobile garden – large pots of plants, sculptures and movable decks that can be lifted and repositioned – is perfect for the small city garden because it can be modified and redesigned as the mood takes you or your requirements change.

Even small gardens benefit from being divided into different areas, paradoxically

▽ A tiny patio, crammed with interest, provides the perfect retreat of scent, shape and color. Bold planting provides areas of particular dramatic interest using giant Gunnera manicata, the tall thistle Onopordum and Hosta sieboldiana. Smaller foliage plants blend softly shaded leaves and flowers of gray, mauve, yellow and blue.

▷ *A lumber deck makes the perfect link between house and garden in this subtropical courtyard. Softer and more natural than paving, a deck can be constructed to follow the shape of your house and be continued into the garden in the form of bridges and walkways.*

▽ **Below right** *Remember that the areas close to the house will be viewed directly from indoors and should provide a pleasant screen of plants and interesting features. Trees and shrubs are important here on a practical level to provide a screen against noise, wind and pollution.*

△ *Ideally the patio should incorporate a strong design of permanent planting backed up by a selection of tubs and containers of mixed annuals to add color in summer. This bold pattern of fleshy Hostas, grassy Phalaris and a fine specimen of the Chinese Loquat tree makes a dramatic background for bright summer flowers and white-painted garden features.*

making the garden appear larger than it actually is by providing the observer with a variety of points of interest and changes of mood. Thus, pebble areas could be interspersed with grass or planting beds, areas raised or designed so that they curve away from the eye of the observer, and you could even allow a little patch to grow wild with long grass and meadow flowers. Try also to incorporate features such as stained lumber for deck or pergola supports, some unusual paving patterns or a thought-provoking piece of sculpture. Seating or relaxing areas could make use of contrasting plants with soft, downy foliage, such as sage (*Salvia*) or *Stachys olympica*, or the large-leaved *Hosta sieboldiana*. Consider, too, adding a fountain or other water feature for the soothing sound of moving water. Many water features can be constructed so that there is absolutely no

danger for young children or pets.

The patio

The patio is an essential ingredient of the city garden, linking the house to the garden proper, and providing a flat, dry area for outdoor furniture. There is no reason, however, why it should be limited to a meager area just outside the back door. Why not have two or three patios round the garden, positioned to catch the sun at different times of the day? This approach could well eliminate the need for a lawn. This semiobligatory patch of green, so small as to be virtually useless and representing a weekly mowing chore, can be a waste of precious space that could be better employed as an all-weather surface.

Do not always assume you must use paving when thinking about patios; there are many exciting surfaces that can be used (see *Design Guide*, p. 209). Perhaps the most versatile and inexpensive alternative surface is lumber decking (see p. 122), which is used extensively by many internationally recognized garden designers. With its warm, natural appearance suited to so many garden styles, it is the perfect material for the easy-care city garden, and one that can be continued through to the house or conservatory. It is also easy to lay and can be used to create patterns and designs, incorporating seating and raised areas or stained and colored for special effects. Wood has the additional advantage of being light and easy to handle where access to the garden is difficult, such as in a house with no side entrance.

Other, less usual, patio ideas for the city garden include breaking up the main area with pebble beds, planting areas or, perhaps, even a small formal pool. These, as well as built-in features such as seating, sandboxes for children, and barbecues, are invaluable for making the most of a small space.

Using water

Whereas interior designers use mirrors in small houses to create the illusion of space and light, landscape architects use water for the same effects in the garden. The sound of moving water is undeniably soothing and relaxing, but the changing patterns of the sky in a still-water pond is of equal, visual, benefit, as is the chance to observe the antics of fish, frogs and insects – inevitable wildlife visitors even to an urban water feature.

The secret of success with water features is to be ambitious with your plans. Just because the size of plot is limited, do not necessarily scale the feature down. A stretch of water spanning the width of a small garden, for example, can be crossed by stepping stones or a bridge, to add adventure and a certain sense of mystery to the area beyond.

Small features can be exciting, too, when imaginatively designed and properly integrated. A small, formal pond could be edged and shaped to match its surroundings: or a pond set within a deck can be given a raised lumber frame. Alternatively, set it with colored pebbles in a paved patio area.

Moving water features need to be chosen with equal care. If your garden is simply not large enough for a stream, waterfall or large fountain, then consider instead a small bubble fountain spilling over an old millstone or urn, or a small water spout in a patio wall. Here you should avoid the ubiquitous lion's head or other clichés, and install, if the setting is right, an original sculpture (see p. 148), an old brass faucet or a simple Plexiglas lip curtaining

◁ *Where doors and windows can be folded back to allow direct access to the garden, lush arrangements of foliage plants on both sides will encourage a feeling of continuity between house and garden, and an attractive leafy environment for dining or lounging. Here a large trough has been planted with ferns and Chlorophytum, to create the impression that the garden has spilled indoors.*

▽ *Unusual paving ideas can create exciting areas within the main garden. These terra-cotta sections serve a variety of purposes: according to size they create paving and plant containers, as well as a circular edging for a small pool.*

water into a small pool or well below.

The wild city garden

A wild garden may seem at first a curious option for the city dweller. Yet, with the right plants and features, it is surprising how quickly the local wildlife population moves in, creating an environment that is forever full of variety and interest.

Wild is a good theme for a town or city setting. A natural, wild garden full of native plants requires minimal maintenance, surviving for the most part on its own resources – results, though, will tend to be somewhat unpredictable, since you can never be quite in control. A wild garden is tremendously relaxing, too, a real retreat of softer colors and subtler scents – qualities that can often be absent in over-cultivated gardens.

Patience is required with a wild garden in order to give it time to establish itself, and some control needs to be exercised over unwelcome or particularly invasive weeds. But part of the pleasure of this type of garden is watching your plant collection grow over the years, adding new species and finding that some mysteriously appear of their own accord.

The plantsman's city garden

A small garden also gives you the opportunity to specialize. This might take the form of a one-color garden, where you restrict yourself to flowers and foliage of a single hue. It also offers you the chance to develop and display your talents for garden planning by maintaining interest through shape, texture and size within the restrictions of a single color. Or perhaps you would prefer indulging in a scented garden or an evergreen foliage garden of shrubs and trees. Your options are vast.

The real plant lover will not hesitate to start a collection of rare and unusual plants, and the garden will be small enough for you to give them the special attention they require. Again, the restriction of size makes your task easier, since you will be able to fill the area available without it costing a fortune. Plants can be acquired from friends and fellow enthusiasts or from specialist nurseries supplying exotic and little seen forms of heaths, shrubs or alpines.

Unlike most small city plots, the plantsman's garden is not designed to be maintenance free or quick to establish. It represents more a labor of love, and the relaxation and pleasure come from tending the plants and seeing them grow and flourish over a period of perhaps many years □

△ An attractive patio garden can be created in the smallest area, even on the roof. Lumber decking makes a lightweight surface underfoot for loungers and containers of colorful plants, with interesting foliage plants like Aucuba japonica providing year-round interest and brighter flowering annuals a special summer display. Painting the back wall white has helped to bounce extra light into this particular design.

ROOF GARDENS

Establishing a roof garden is an excellent way to reestablish a corner of nature among the acres of concrete and glass in the urban landscape. You must ensure, however, that the structure itself is of the right type and sufficiently strong to support the weight of damp soil, trees, containers and furniture. You should obtain the advice of a qualified surveyor and plan accordingly.

Apart from this, the main problem you will face is the garden's exposure to weather: high winds, lashing rain and, in summer, uninterrupted sun. Wind can be largely combated by using light screens or plastic netting designed specifically for the job. You will also need proper drainage to cope with rainwater run-off, which can be channeled into a waterbarrel for use in dry weather. Wherever possible, use lightweight soilless soil mixes and sturdy, yet light, wooden screens to add variety and visual relief.

▷ *If you are lucky enough to own a level roof area surrounded by taller buildings you will find they afford the protection and shelter to grow a variety of plants. This lumbered area makes a fine rooftop patio, shaded by sheared Ligustrum in terra-cotta pots of trailing Lobelia. Passiflora caerulea has been trained on overhead wires for additional shelter and interest.*

◁ *You can make excellent use of all available space in a small, enclosed roof garden by planting vertically as well as horizontally. In this one, shrubs such as Lilac (Syringa) and rhododendrons have been planted in containers to provide colorful, scented shelter, with smaller ground-cover and flowering plants in raised containers on ledges at several levels.*

THE COUNTRY GARDEN

THE COUNTRY GARDEN is often large and sometimes rambling, making it hard to cultivate and expensive to maintain. Also, because it will often be bordered by fields and simple stock fences, exposure to wind and frost may be a problem. Privacy can often be a fallacy, too, since country houses tend to cluster together in village communities.

The first priority, then, may be a screen, both for privacy and shelter. It is unlikely you will be able to afford the miles of high walls that once surrounded English estates; nor is extensive fencing desirable, from either the cost or aesthetic points of view. The answer is to plant trees and shrubs that not only create a wind break and effective screen, but also blend well with both the garden and the surrounding countryside.

A large garden offers the ideal opportunity for more ambitious features, such as tennis courts and swimming pools, and these, too, will need screening from the main garden and protection from prevailing winds. You will probably want some form of vegetable garden, perhaps herbs or fruit trees, also seating and lounging areas. Once you have established the types of elements you would like to include, you can start to slot them together into the available space, like a jigsaw puzzle. In fact, dividing the garden up into different areas is the best treatment for a large site; it makes it

more manageable for one thing, which is an important consideration in an age when most of us cannot afford an army of gardeners, and, for another, it is also a more interesting and varied use of the site, offering changes of mood and of angle, allowing it to be more fully utilized.

Based on traditional elements it may be, but the new-age country garden embraces the current passion for things natural, with softer, wilder plants and flowers and a basic framework of low-maintenance trees and shrubs. With this in mind, consider the bigger plants, such as the enormous *Gunnera manicata* with a spread of leaves up to 4 m (13 ft) across. For fast-growing ground-cover to suppress weeds, the large-leaved *Petasites japonicus* is ideal (although it can become very invasive), as is the distinctive spotted lungwort (*Pulmonaria*). Green and gray foliage is restful on the eye and the perfect background for drifts of soft, natural-colored plants, such as the perennial *Ligularia clivorum* 'Desdemona', which produces wedges of tall, orange, daisy-like flowers, purple foxgloves (*Digitalis purpurea*) or the lovely lilac of *Bergenia cordifolia*, with its clusters of bell-shaped flowers above giant, round, green leaves.

These structural and exciting plant forms all need to be planted in large groups to gain impact and to give form to the garden's overall shape. Restrict annuals to tubs and containers around the house where they can be easily cared for, and grass can be allowed to grow long with paths simply mown through a few times a season to create wonderfully informal trails leading to special features or points of particular interest.

Among this soft semiwilderness are more formal areas, paved for seating or with regular beds for herbs, vegetables or special collections

◁ No country garden is complete without a clump of nodding hollyhocks and, with their large, tall flower spires, they make a good screen or wall cover. Usually they need staking, but here they are contained by a metal fence, making them easy to maintain.

▷ This large country estate makes full use of the surrounding landscape. The semi-formal pool has been planted to create a very natural effect and is highlighted with clumps of beautiful lilies: in the foreground, the waxy Arum lily (Zantedeschia aethiopica), and, in beds contained along the sides, the more informal yellow Day lily, Hemerocallis.

△ The country garden may appear as a haphazard but happy blend of different plants, but needs to be carefully planned for success. Shape, size and color have been expertly blended to provide a series of contrasts: tall feathery clumps of Arundinaria murielae, low growing, deeply marked Hosta 'Thomas Hogg', delicate Day lilies (Hemerocallis) and spiky yellow Ligularia stenocephala 'The Rocket'.

◁ Massed planting of shade-tolerant plants beneath trees can make a delightful wood-land walk. This interesting variety of foliage plants is clustered around the unusual twisted trunk of a fruit tree making a colorful mass of greens, whites and yellows: Hosta sieboldiana and white Phlox provide important highlights.

of plants. These are 'secret' places that you come across by surprise, offering new vistas and changes of atmosphere.

The cottage-type country garden

Traditionally, cottage-type gardens have a bit of everything – vegetables, flowers, herbs, fruit and trees. The modern cottage-type gardener creates clearly defined areas around the main garden that can be more easily controlled and planned, or incorporates edible delicacies into more ornamental features. Many vegetables are attractive enough to grace the flower beds: feathery carrot tops, globe artichokes or frilly pink and green cabbages.

Medicinal and culinary herbs can also be attractive plants in their own right. Consider the design possibilities of the tall, bronze fennel (*Foeniculum vulgare*), growing to a height of 1.5 m (5 ft) with splayed umbellate heads of deep brown-gold; or sturdy tansy (*Tanacetum vulgare*), with its dark feathery foliage and deep yellow button flowers. Allow the herbs to form banks of scented foliage and flower color and so provide a fine visual feast.

Fruit trees and bushes can be used flexibly, too. New hybrid berry varieties produce more compact growth studded with crossbreeds, such as tayberry and tummelberry, and they are as good looking as any ornamental shrub.

▽ *Large gardens in country locations can often be overexposed and will need careful screening and sheltering. Note how informal tree planting and sheared hedges create more intimate patio and planting areas. Another problem with such gardens is that they may front directly on to a street and so may require a tall fence or wall for privacy.*

VEGETABLES & HERBS

Herbs, fruits and vegetables are traditionally essential elements of the country or cottage-style garden, a separate area set aside and protected by walls or screens; or parsley and thyme, strawberries and cabbages, grown amongst the flowerbeds in a small plot. Don't reject the idea of edible plants within your master plan because you think they are too much trouble or you do not have room to hide them away. Often they look as good as they taste, and they can be as valuable to the garden designer as any other plant.

▷ **Top** *Traditionally the country* potager *was designed as a decorative as well as a productive garden with formal beds of herbs and vegetables divided by small paths and paved areas for sitting and relaxing. This formal vegetable garden captures the true spirit of the* potager *with decorative features, such as a sundial and an ornamental bird bath, among the plants. One of these might form the center piece of the* potager *or, as here, be positioned to create an additional focal point.*

▷ *The formal herb garden can be time consuming to maintain and small blocks of plants may not produce sufficient for your needs. In many ways, a larger informal herb garden is more practical and produces an attractive display of flowers and foliage into the bargain. In this plan, herbs have been combined with flowers and salad vegetables behind a screen of pole beans and large-headed sunflowers.*

△ *Vegetables can often be as attractive as any flower. These Savoy cabbages produce spectacular curly heads and have been planted with bright flowering* Tagetes *– a good companion because it will help to keep away white fly.*

Apple, pear and cherry trees, with their superb spring blossom and fine branch patterns, are too good to banish to a crowded orchard, especially if hung with climbing roses or wisteria.

The woodland country garden

Large or small, a garden given over to trees and shrubs with grassy walks between and studded with wild bulbs and flowers is simply magical. Planning and planting trees requires foresight. Unless you are lucky enough to have a few mature specimens already, it will be years before the full impact of your design can be appreciated.

The secret is not to choose too wide a variety. Try instead for a subtle blending of local species in groups or coppices, with the occasional special, strategically placed, specimen tree. You will need spring interest with the showy blossom of a wild cherry (*Prunus avium*) or a Japanese rowan (*Sorbus commixta*) and a mixture of evergreens and trees with striking autumn colors. Oak, beech and maples can usually be relied on for brilliant autumnal colors, made all the more vivid if balanced with patches of deep green evergreen pines and spruces.

The woodland garden is a shady place and you need to choose plants with care if they are to survive. You cannot go far wrong with those that have adapted themselves naturally to the rich, damp soil and dappled sunlight of the woodland – ferns, ivies, bluebells, primroses, lily of the valley, violets and orchids.

The wild country garden

The woodland garden is wild in its way, but if you would like the chance to appreciate the more sun-loving plants, it is just as easy to create a natural meadow, grassy bank or stream and bog garden. Meadow areas can be seeded with wild grass and flower seeds. For other plants, however, you need to observe their natural habitats in order to create a realistic effect in cultivation.

Water is one of the most exciting wild features, offering the chance to cultivate entirely different plants and the opportunity to observe a wide range of wildlife in the form of

birds, insects, frogs and fish. If you have a source of natural water, check that it is free from pollution at all points before it reaches your garden.

A bog garden is worth the little effort it takes to install. You can use any badly drained patch of land or create one in any other position using punctured pool lining material topped with rich soil. Once established, plant specimens such as the exotic lily *Cardiocrinum gigantum*, which produces large trumpet-shaped flowers, marsh marigolds (*Caltha palustris*) and the stately water iris (*Iris laevigata*) create a fine display. These moisture-loving waterside plants tend to be rampant growers, so it is best to plant just a few choice plants rather than many different species.

The country garden in a city

There is nothing to stop you taking the essential elements of the country garden and transferring them into a smaller space in a city. The country patio, for example, with massed herbs and wild or cottage-type flowers in containers, works well. Or you could leave a small corner of your plot to grow wild, with perhaps a small pond.

Rather like bottled spring water, you can capture the essence of the countryside in your city yard. But take care: try to cram too much in and you risk ruining the total effect □

◁ *A profusion of flowers is often more effective when you stick to a limited range of colors. Pink and mauve combine well together and in this case have been used at every level, the deep purple climbing* Clematis *and* Thalictrum dipterocarpum *making an elegant display. Large clumps of lilac-flowered* Nepeta *have been used for ground cover.* Sedum spectabile *provides creamy highlights, while* Monarda didyma *produces hot pink blooms.*

△ *The area under trees is all too often left barren and unattractive because few plants will tolerate the deep shade. Yet there is a surprising number that will flourish in more shady conditions like this selection of woodland plants, including the Male fern,* Dryopteris filix-mas, *and a wide variety of* Primulas.

△ **Top** *A large garden will often provide the opportunity to create a semiwild natural area with a small pond surrounded by native grasses and wild flowers. Sheltered by trees or large shrubs, it makes a delightful secret garden away from the house.*

THE WATER GARDEN

DRAMATICALLY FORMAL or wild and sprawling, there is a style of water feature to suit every situation and all types of garden. Water is without doubt one of the most stimulating, adaptable and exciting raw materials the landscape designer has to work with. When you consider how versatile it is, adapting itself to any shape or size, creating still, tranquil pools or fizzing fountains and gurgling waterfalls, as well as supporting a fantastic range of animal and plant life, it is not surprising that it features so prominently in the best of modern landscape architecture.

Water as a feature of garden design is not a new concept; the Egyptians were building lily pools as long ago as 2000 BC. But because of the low-maintenance aspects and the wonderfully relaxing qualities associated with any type of water feature, it also strikes a particular chord with today's gardeners.

Design potential

It may be that you need to work a little visual magic in order to make a garden appear longer or wider than it really is. Here, a mirrorlike stretch of water reflecting the sky and surrounding trees and plants can effect such an illusion for very little expense. Perhaps the background noise of traffic is intrusive. If so, then the soothing sound of a moving water display, such as a waterfall, spout or fountain, will create its own aural diversion.

Water can be used for many such 'tricks' if it is employed boldly and with imagination – no tiny molded-plastic pools in standard shapes barely large enough for a single water lily. If you have just a few square feet of space, go for something with some style – an old trough or a high-tech cascade in the corner of the patio. Thinking big even in a small garden will be well rewarded, not just with less grass to mow or beds to weed, but with a new concept of the garden being a place of constant change and movement.

Suitable plants

It is not just the design potential and low-maintenance aspects of water that makes it so attractive to the landscape architect and gardener alike. Water plants are among some of the loveliest grown, offering tremendous variety of shape, size and color. Yet few are difficult to grow – in fact, many are vigorous and need keeping in check in order to maintain a good balance of different species.

For still pools there are the beautiful water lilies, with their classic, large, padlike leaves and superbly petaled blooms turning their faces up toward the sunshine. For most people these plants are a must. Also to be seen on the surface, although less spectacular than the water lily, is the pretty water violet, a good oxygenator with pale mauve flowers and bright green leaves. On the pool margins, water-loving plants will flourish to produce large, dramatic foliage and strangely shaped, if not brightly colored, blooms.

Water plants tend to have soft, subtle colors, which further endear them to the modern designer. Even the bright, sovereign gold of the marsh marigold (*Caltha palustris*) has a warm, buttery hue. Blues and mauves are almost luminously soft and pinks tend toward raspberry rather than cerise. Bearing in mind that their shapes and colors will be blurred and magnified in the water's surface, flowering plants are best positioned in solid clumps of a single species to create banks and drifts of one color. Too many different plants look muddled and confused and it is difficult to stop them swamping one another.

It is among the water-edge plants that the garden designer can really display a talent for grouping and combining different plant shapes. It is not just the flowers that are attractive with water plants; the leaves, too, are often dramatic and boldly shaped in spikes, swirls and delightful giant saucers. Some, like *Peltiphyllum peltatum*, have enormous, parasollike leaves, while *Rodgersia pinnata* has deeply cut, star-shaped leaves. The incomparable *Gunnera manicata* has foliage large enough for a person to shelter under like giant parasols. Other plants have leaves with fascinating markings or color ranges. One of the best groups is the hostas, with deeply veined, almost three-dimensional, leaves and a variety of shades through many types of green to soft gray verging on blue.

Contrasting with these softly rounded or fleshy-leaved varieties are the reeds and rushes, the iris and the sagittarias, with their sharp spikes and arrowheads rising from the water's edge like some mythical Excalibur. *Typha* produces the classic, tall, brown pokers that give it its common name of false bulrush, while the flowering rush (*Butomus umbellatus*) displays a spreading flower head like an upside-down umbrella. What could offer more contrast than two other rushes, the corkscrew rush (*Juncus effusus* 'Spiralis') and

▷ You needn't restrict yourself to one pool when planning a water garden. Here, a complex of pools is linked by lumber walkways and shaded by a pergola covered with plants. The climbers make interesting reflections in the water's surface and the spaces between lumber and pools have been planted with purple-flowered varieties such as Lythrum salicaria.

◁ A clever way to integrate a swimming pool into the garden is to link it with a formal ornamental pool by means of paved areas and raised beds of plants. Shrubs and plants in pots and containers around the swimming pool disguise its function yet keep the plants away from the water. This ornamental pool is also slightly raised to give it particular emphasis.

▽ This central pool needs only minimal planting to show off its strong architectural lines. The geometric brick edging has been incorporated into a slate and brick patio design and a few lush plants in pots are all the planting necessary. The starkness of its shape leads the eye away toward the rest of the garden setting.

△ A water garden can be adapted to suit any
shape or size of plot. This informal pool
shows how two changes of level have been used to
advantage. Simple lumber steps make all parts of
the garden accessible and provide viewing platforms from both above and close to the water's
surface.

▷ A large rectangular raised pool makes the
perfect centerpiece for a formal garden.
The strong architectural shapes of water-loving
plants are the perfect foil for the formality of
sheared hedges and patio areas, the raised brick
coping softened by large clumps of Ligularia stenocephala 'The Rocket' and the water's surface
enlivened by water lilies (Nymphaea), mixed
Typhas and Juncus.

the Zebra rush (*Scirpus tabernaemontani*
'zebrinus'), respectively spiraled like a corkscrew and striped in cream and green, for a
wonderfully decorative effect? It is the sagittarias that have strongly shaped leaves in the form
of arrows, as well as the bonus of lovely flowers
in summer.

But the water garden is not content to stop
there. Moist, damp conditions are perfect for
many types of plant, which often give few if any
flowers but have spectacular foliage – the
grasses and ferns. Umbrella Grass (*Cyperus
alternifolius*) describes itself, producing thick
clumps of 'umbrellas' on slender stems, and
Canary Grass (*Phalaris arundinacea* 'Picta') is
very strikingly striped in green and white.
There are several species of variegated grass in
addition to dark green and blue/gray forms.
There is even one with bright yellow foliage,
Carex stricta 'Bowles Golden', which really
lights up a dull, uninteresting corner of the
garden or creates a dazzling display when
planted in large, informal groups along the
water's edge.

△ No pool is complete without a few ornamental fish which will help keep the water clean and can often become tame enough to swim to the side of the pool for feeding. A water garden attracts a surprising variety of wildlife too, not just frogs and toads but also interesting insects and birds.

△ A stretch of water is a valuable design asset and always lends an air of tranquility to a design. To emphasize its calmness, you should try to restrict planting to the edges of the pool and keep the center free, producing a shining mirror image of sky and surrounding features. This technique is also useful for producing areas of light in a small garden, as here where a large pool in a small plot has been planted with colorful water-edge plants to achieve maximum effect in the minimum of space: strong purple Lythrum salicaria and sunny yellow Lysimachia punctata dominate the planting plan.

▷ The semiformal pool easily conjures up an oriental atmosphere when edged in stone and lumber and with plants carefully chosen for their dramatic effects. In this small yard, large boulders, collections of pebbles and sculptural plant forms have created a definite Japanese atmosphere. The pool is linked to the house by means of a lumber deck so that it can be enjoyed all the way round and gives the impression that the water is larger and deeper than it really is. Features and focal points have been chosen to encourage the feeling of a natural landscape, using a large interesting rock among the water lilies in the center of the pool and slabs of slate and simple containers around the garden.

Pools and ponds

Blending and balancing plants is one thing; choosing the right style of water feature is quite another. You can opt for the classic formal pool with paved or lumber edging to suit a formal garden, or you could go for a complete contrast and install a wild area including pond and meandering stream. The same principle applies to large, rambling gardens, where a small formal area with pool and fountain, a few fish and seats make a welcome change of pace and a place of order among the less-controllable features.

With the formal pool it is the frame that is important – its edging should blend harmoniously with its immediate surroundings, be they stone, lumber or sod. Informal ponds and pools need the opposite treatment – complete disguise and softening of the banks and edges using plants, grasses and, if large enough, jetties. Moving water features, such as streams, water courses, waterfalls, cascades and fountains, can be treated in much the same way. The basic rules are design them simply and keep them in style and you should not go far wrong.

Formal pools tend to be small, or at least moderately sized, for reasons of cost and because of the desire to avoid large, unsightly areas of exposed edging. Today's garden designers now look more for soft edges and mingled, natural features, even when they are trying to capture a more classical atmosphere in their garden plans.

A formal pool can be as small as an old stone trough, sink or water barrel, large enough to supply a gleam of interest in the garden and to support a few water plants. If more space is available, then you can have a square, circle or rectangle or, for the adventurous, fake moats, canals and pools bordered with stone, lumber or sods. The formal water feature is ideal as a visual link with the architecture of your house, creating the illusion that it is surrounded by water, and providing spectacular water views.

The informal pool or pond can also be successful when space is limited, but it is at its best over large areas where a good variety of moisture-loving plants can grow to form a subtle, multicolored background to the water's surface. This type of pool really does look after itself, establishing its own biological balance and requiring very little maintenance, bar the removal of dead foliage and the thinning of rampant species. A smaller pool is best fitted with an electric filter to keep the water clear.

Streams and waterfalls

Moving water features are an effective device for drawing attention away from the real shape and proportions of your site. A small stream crossed by simple bridges or stepping stones, can lead you round a garden in such a way that you never really realize its true length or width.

Waterfalls are another attention grabber, adding height and excitement. You could incorporate a traditional rocky fall or a more hi-tech interpretation, with water spilling from gaps in an ornamental wall.

Fountains and waterspouts

It is not just the sound and motion that makes a fountain a popular feature in the large pool, it also helps keep the water fresh and oxygenated. Steer well clear of mass-produced fountain ornaments and go for something simpler and more tasteful: plain water jets creating geometric shapes, frothing plumes or a slight bubbling motion that will enhance your planting.

Fountains can also create a focal point with a fine fountain sculpture. If this proves too expensive and space is tight, an inexpensive bubble fountain frothing water over an old millstone or decorated urn will fit neatly into the smallest patio. Waterspouts are even more compact: a trickle or stream of water into a stone bowl, trough or basin □

THE ORIENTAL GARDEN

IT MAY SEEM extraordinary that a form of garden design developed over a thousand years ago should have a particular relevance today. Yet many Western landscape designers are adopting and adapting oriental design principles. The traditional oriental garden is based on the natural landscape, albeit translated into an unfamiliar form (to Western eyes), which is a concept close to the hearts of today's designers. There is also the undoubted attraction of the low-maintenance aspects of this type of garden, of course.

Traditions and adaptations

Ancient China was the home of the Zen garden we know today, where features were carved into real landscapes incorporating hills, trees, plants and, most importantly, water. As gardens became smaller, the scale reduced and became more representational – a landscape in miniature with rocks instead of mountains, ponds instead of seas and trees and shrubs shrunk in order to maintain balance and proportion.

The philosophy behind the oriental garden involves an enjoyment of beauty and relaxation of the spirit. This is particularly true of the smaller Japanese-style garden, where vistas of imaginary mountains, seas and plains in the yard transport the appreciative observer to grander, more natural, landscapes. The important factor with this type of garden is its minimalism, so do not be tempted to overdo things by adding too much.

Practical considerations

Careful planning is central to success. It is important to make a scaled drawing of the proposed design on graph paper and plot your features to gain some idea of how they might work (see p. 62). If you find it difficult to visualize how this will appear on site, transfer your plan into the garden using stakes and string to delineate contours, paths, streams and any other features.

▽ *In the oriental garden, trees are of prime importance as a design feature, carefully positioned and brought to the correct point of maturity to achieve special, but always very natural, effects. They may be selected for their interesting foliage, their striking form or their spectacular autumn color, then blended and grouped into dramatic landscapes. This Japanese temple ornament is surrounded by a glorious Acer, in full autumn color, against a complementary background of deep green coniferous trees.*

◁ The more extensive oriental landscape often sets large informal pools and natural planting against a strong backdrop of trees. Paths and walks around such a garden are an important element of the design, leading through woodland and across the water to various resting points, where the view may be enjoyed or a cocktail drunk. This classic ornamental bridge leads to an oriental summerhouse.

▽ Garden ornaments add to the charm and authenticity of an oriental design, but they need to be chosen and positioned with care. Created from a natural material like well-weathered stone or slate, and surrounded by green foliage plants, they will form an integral part of the landscape.

▽ *A delightful oriental corner makes an interesting change of tempo in a small suburban garden. Enclosed by bamboo and brushwood, the Japanese stone garden ornament has been used to create a focal point, half hidden by foliage and reached by a simple gravel path. Such an area might be incorporated into a patio or garden to provide a quiet spot for eating or meditation.*

▷ *An oriental-style garden can be adapted to any size or type of site. By using simple Japanese features and a minimal amount of planting, you can capture just the right atmosphere even in a small, walled garden.*

▷ *This clever oriental design shows how well the style adapts itself to small spaces. A tiny inner courtyard glistens with wet stone and lush green plants around an informal pool. The dramatic foliage plants* Aspidistra elatior *and* Rhapis excelsa *are perfectly balanced with bamboo, rocks, paving, pebbles and a couple of carved stone lanterns. The garden provides a delightful view from the narrow bamboo terraces or the windows of the house, while a random pattern of stepping stones allows the area to be crossed and enjoyed from all angles.*

In the oriental garden, the empty spaces are as important as other, more solid, features and you should be aiming for a good visual balance. Also, try to maintain a subtle combination of colors – mainly pale shades of greens and blues, with natural autumn colors provided by trees and shrubs. Bright flowers are rarely used en masse, but they may be employed in small areas as a contrast to green foliage. The affinity with nature means that oriental gardens eschew rigid geometric shapes, such as circles and squares, and favor instead asymmetry and the creation of many points of interest as opposed to a single focal point within the garden.

Plants and other features

As an integral, rather than a dominant, part of the overall design, plants need to be chosen for their architectural qualities as much as for their coloring. Trees tend to be shaped and pruned to resemble older, well-weathered specimens – an art seen at its most extreme in the Bonsai, or miniature tree. There are many species of tree that will help to create the impression of a mature, natural habitat: oriental favorites include the Japanese maples, the Japanese cedar (*Cryptomeria japonica*), mountain laurel (*Kalmia latifolia*), Chinese sweet osmanthus (*Osmanthus fragrans* 'Au-

rantiacus'), pines, cedars and cypresses. You may also feel inclined to include a bamboo or two, either grown as a fluttering grove or in elegant containers. *Arundinaria japonica* is one of the best, growing easily to a height of 3 m (10 ft). It is hardy with glossy, dark green leaves and strong canes. The yellow grooved bamboo (*Phyllostachys aureosulcata*), with its distinctive yellow-striped stems, is used extensively in Japanese and Chinese gardens as a contrast plant (see p. 184).

Where every element of the garden has equal weight, special care is needed in the choice of other features, too. Rocks and boulders are best selected locally to look as natural as possible. Surrounding areas also need to be in keeping: bamboo screening and fencing are excellent both for protection against wind and as a design feature. Lumber structures, such as pergolas, decks and walkways, are equally suitable and, if left natural or stained with rustic reds, blues or grays, can capture exactly the right atmosphere. Finishing touches can include traditional stone lanterns and bowls, but bridges and pagodas require just the right touch to be successful. The oriental garden is all about balance and contrast; it needs a gentle hand to achieve the correct subtlety □

THE STONE & ROCK GARDEN

I N SOME GARDENS there may be only a few inches of poor soil on top of the bedrock and, in these circumstances, major excavation or the addition of tons of topsoil and humus is expensive and often impracticable. A better solution is to exploit the site's natural features and create a stone and rock garden using plants adapted to a free-draining soil.

Similar problems are faced by an owner of a garden that has been concreted over at some stage: to dig it up, dispose of the rubble and reclaim the land is frequently more trouble than it is worth. Here, the answer is a complete container or raised-bed garden (see p. 110). Sometimes, of course, you may want to create an artificial rocky area in order to add texture and height to a dull design. In this case, rocks and boulders need to be chosen with care and arranged to look as natural as possible.

Design ideas

Although a stone garden does not rely heavily on living greenery, it can be as stunning and every bit as relaxing as a more conventional garden. The secret is not to go for too many surfaces and colors. Concentrate instead on achieving a variety of textures and shapes, from large slabs of rough, speckled granite to masses of small, smooth pebbles. Contrast pebble or gravel beds with smooth slab steps or use stepping stones to create bridges and paths, and larger boulders to add height and mass.

Suitable plants

A rocky terrain, whether natural or not, is an ideal environment in which to grow alpines. These plants thrive in poor soil but they do, mostly, like plenty of sun. There are some, however, such as the *Acaena*, which has lovely silvery to bronze foliage, and the tender, but much prettier, mother of thousands (*Saxifraga stolonifera*), which produces a mass of trailing white flowers, that will tolerate shade. Also tolerant of partial shade are primulas, small cyclamen and the white anemone (*Anemone nemorosa*).

Another idea is to install plants that resemble stones in your stone garden. There is a surprising number to choose from, including the pebble plant (*Lithops*), which needs very little water and thrives in warm climates. The tiny *Titanopsis*, which is covered in what appear to be warts, is also suitable, but it prefers an alkaline soil. In the warm stone garden, you could grow *Conophytum*, sometimes called living stones, or mesems (*Argyroderma*), a strange looking plant shaped like split pebbles and producing flowers in summer □

ۆ

△ A rocky informal garden may recreate a mountain woodland area with a dry stream winding its way through shrubs and boulders to run under a rustic wooden bridge. This illusion cleverly suggests the coolness of water, using light gray chippings for the suggested stream among the richer brown bark chips that mulch the thin soil between shrubs.

◁ A natural or contrived rocky outcrop is perfect for designing an informal waterfall where the water is allowed to spill over a series of rocks and boulders into a small stony pool below. The rocks are best arranged to look as natural as possible, softened with plants, like this bright lime-green Euphorbia epithymoides, hot pink Rhododendron × hybridum and a small red maple, Acer palmatum 'Rubrum'. This effect relies on selecting a water pump that is capable of handling such a large volume of water.

◁ **Far left** Small rocky areas or stone gardens are useful for creating a change of texture and interest within a very different environment. This may take the form of a rock and pebble planting bed to display Arundinaria murielae, Fatsia japonica and Euphorbia wulfenii beside a swimming pool where they will be protected from chlorinated water, or a small pebble area (inset) planted with the curious rosettes of Echeveria within a patio design.

THE SHADY GARDEN

MOST PLANTS, and particularly those that produce showy flowers, will flourish only where there is plenty of light and sunshine. Shady areas of the garden, therefore, require particularly careful planning in order to avoid straggly looking plants and bare patches of earth under trees and close to walls.

Shade is a frequent problem in a narrow city garden, where high walls and nearby trees and buildings can overshadow the entire plot. In woodlands, too, the shady, damp ground beneath close-growing trees is suitable only for specially adapted plants. You may also wish to create a shady area from choice in order to provide shelter in a bright, sunny garden, using trees, large plants or a pergola, so that a comfortable seating or dining area can be enjoyed when the weather is hot.

Lightening shady areas

There are several garden design tricks you can use to add a little more light to an unavoidably dark area. Mirrors, used sparingly, will reflect any available light as well as give the impression that the garden is larger than it actually is. Water will also pick up the faintest gleam and create a patch of light (see p. 140). High walls

and fences can be painted white or cream in order to reflect light and also to provide a good background color for climbing plants.

Using plants

Plants themselves can be of help in this situation: those with white flowers or yellow leaves are extremely useful brighteners, and there are quite a few species that prefer shade.

If you choose carefully, it should be possible to stock the shady garden with an interesting variety of shape and color – all the more so since a surprisingly large number of shade lovers produce sweetly scented flowers. If deep, unrelieved shade is your problem, then suitable flowering plants are few: the trilliums perhaps, making a good show of pink, white or red flowers, or the lovely blue mass of *Omphalodes cappadocica*. The only alternative is to grow plants in tubs and move them periodically to sunnier areas to pep them up.

Ferns and ivies are well known shade-loving foliage plants, but less obvious ones include the tiny green *Soleirolia*, the large, shiny leaved *Fatsia japonica*, the deeply ribbed hostas and the spotted lungwort. Another good plant for shady gardens is the bamboo, which is a tall, elegant and vigorous plant □

△ A shady area may be created by enclosing it with walls or screens and building a pergola above, and then smothering the area with shade-tolerant plants. This cool courtyard has been planted with a variety of foliage plants to create the impression of the forest floor: spiky Agapanthus campanulatus, sheared green Buxus, Polystichum ferns and Rodgersia podophylla. Splashes of color are provided by pots of Pelargonium × hortorum, Hydrangea macrophylla and golden Rudbeckia fulgida.

◁ A shady path to the back door has been intelligently planted, making a delightful leafy entrance. The walls on either side are completely smothered with a curtain of shade-tolerant greenery: Hedera, ferns and a glossy Camellia, with baskets of colorful annuals.

▷ **Center left** *Shade-lovers often have interesting or dramatic foliage which can be combined and contrasted to devise some spectacular leafy effects. This narrow path is almost enveloped by a dense border of the fern Poly-stichum setiferum with the deeply veined leaves of Hosta sieboldiana 'Glauca' and Fagus sylvatica.*

▷ *Pink- and white-flowered plants are useful for bringing dark areas to life. Fast-growing Impatiens will quickly and easily grow to smother and highlight such a spot.*

THE HOT, DRY GARDEN

I N A HOT, DRY GARDEN there is the constant chore of trying to keep your plants well watered – a particular problem in mid to late summer when there may be water restrictions. Even if plants do not die, they will almost certainly be stunted, leaving you with bare patches of soil, which only speed up the loss of moisture from plant roots. The end result is likely to be a soil poor in humus, thin and free draining. The solution, as always, is not to fight the natural inclinations of your site but to make a virtue of them.

Line of least resistance

In a Mediterranean-style garden you can concentrate on plants accustomed to exposed, sunbaked conditions. These tend to be large, extravagantly shaped plants with brilliant flowers to soak up the sunshine. Most also have some sort of built-in moisture-retaining device and often grow from a central rosette close to the ground or adopt a mat-forming habit to ensure that maximum soil surface is shielded.

Beth Chatto had an inspired idea (see p. 44) with her impossibly dry area near the house. She created a patio with raised stone beds densely planted with Mediterranean foliage shapes and masses of flower color in summer.

Drought-tolerant plants

A familiar Mediterranean plant is the *Nerium oleander*, which produces pink, white or red flowers among narrow, dark green leaves, as is the beautiful rock rose (*Cistus*). On limey soils, trailing *Campanula isophylla* is suitable and has masses of pale blue, starry flowers, while you will have to look hard to beat the intense flower colors of the cyclamen.

For foliage, consider the dragon tree (*Dra-çaena draco*), which has blue/gray leathery

▷ *A surprising variety of plants will tolerate dry, exposed conditions and can be used to highlight a poor stony area in full sun. This carefully chosen variety of flower and foliage colors makes a successful patchwork, only a few feet high: the green-gray of* Phyla nodiflora, *gray wooly* Stachys lanata *and* Nepeta × faassenii *are highlighted by the bright yellow flowers of* Anthemis sancti-johannis.

▽ *A dry, sunny garden may exploit the soft grays and greens and the heady scents of those plants which flourish in dry conditions. This light gravel path winds through an interesting arrangement of shapes and textures: great clumps of scented* Lavandula spica, *the gray* Santolina chamaecyparissus *and the pretty striped grass,* Phalaris arundinacea *'picta'. Further contrasts are provided by lusher plants such as* Hostas, Iris *and the dramatic creamy plumes of a* Yucca recurvifolia.

leaves, and a few of the ferns that will tolerate dry conditions: the deer's foot fern (*Davallia canariensis*) and the Hart's tongue fern (*Phyllitis scolopendrium*). Other drought-tolerant plants worth considering are the yarrow (*Achillea*), particularly A. *taygetea*, which has silver-colored leaves, *Corydalis lutea* and the gray-leaved *Zauschneria californica*.

In this type of garden, the cacti and succulents are also your allies. Good examples to grow are *Sempervivum*, with tight, fleshy, green rosettes tinged with pink or purple; *Rhipsalis* making bristly, branched twigs with pink or white flowers and, later, white berries; and *Echeveria gibbiflora*, which produces a head of bluish, fleshy leaves and bright orange and red flowers on long stems.

There are numerous forms of cacti to choose from, many in shapes that can almost be described as grotesque. For a real oddity, look at the spiny *Ferocactus*, which resembles a ball of pink wool; also strangely shaped but better known are the prickly pear and the peanut cactus (*Chamaecereus*), which looks like a mass of spiny pickling cucumbers with red and yellow flowers. Many of these, however, are frost tender □

▽ *Dry-loving plants can be usefully grown in pots to be brought out and grouped in a sunny position. These fleshy succulents make good contrasting shapes and textures to move around the garden where needed.*

◁ *Arid, sunbaked situations provide the perfect opportunity to grow a fascinating collection of cacti and succulents. Their unusual, diverse forms offer plenty of scope for contrasting shapes. These giant Mexican organ pipe cacti,* Stenocereus marginatus, *tower above the prickly pumpkins of* Echinocactus grusonii. *Flanking the doorway are troughs of* Aeonium arboreum *'Zwartkop' with their dramatic, purple black rosettes.*

103

THE TROPICAL GARDEN

WHERE THE CLIMATE is favorable, a tropical garden is a magnificent collection of exotic shapes and vivid colors: ferns and palms, bright foliage, hot-colored flowers and giant leaves. These are the types of plant to grow if you have extremely hot, humid weather in your part of the world. Do not waste your time with bedding annuals, such as dianthus, clarkia and nemesia, which are better suited to more temperate climates: in the tropics they will either flower too early before making much growth or simply not flourish at all. Better instead to enjoy the beauty of such tropical trees and plants as the jacaranda tree with its blue spikes or the Frangipanni blooms, both with a heavenly perfume.

It is possible to enjoy these spectacular, tropical displays even if your climate is not exactly right. Where the summers are long, humid and hot but the winters cold, a temporary tropical garden of palms and exotic, flowering plants can be created in pots and containers, to be taken outdoors at the first sign of the really hot weather of summer and stored under heated cover in winter. While those people with a totally unsuitable climate, and the resources, may wish to retreat to the pool house or conservatory and enjoy a heated indoor tropical garden – the perfect surroundings for swimming, relaxing or entertaining.

Basic plant requirements

The tropical garden is extravagant in appearance. It needs, therefore, lots of plants with large or unusual leaves grown close together in order to create a junglelike effect. But to avoid a claustrophobic feeling, and to provide balance and contrast, you should also incorporate clearer spaces.

The exclusive use of strong, green architectural plants is very restful, but for a more ornamental, stimulating appearance, include some of the more colorful shrubs and trees and flowering plants. This is a design that needs a good sense of color blending and a certain restraint: even the foliage can be brilliantly colored and it is easy to overdo the effect. The showy, fast-growing *Cassia*, for example, can reach 5.5 m (18 ft) in only seven

△ Luxuriant ferns (Polypodium scandens) make exotic and necessary ground cover beneath the tall striped canes of a golden cane palm thicket (Chrysalidocarpus lutescens) and encourages a junglelike atmosphere. It is important to balance the dense canopy of leaves above with underplanting such as this.

◁ The brilliant colors and exotic shapes of tropical plants need careful planning if you are to achieve the correct balance. These reds, greens and oranges fully complement one another with a variety of lush, spiky and feathery forms. Dark purple Bromeliads (Neoregelia 'Dr Oeser' hybrid) edge an informal small pool which is highlighted by bright orange Epidendrum 'Boundii' and red E. cinnabarinum. In the water, Cyperus alternifolius has been planted while Cyathea medullaris, the Black Tree Fern, sets off the whole tropical scene.

▷ A tropical blend of sultry shapes can work well when isolated and confined within an island bed. Keep the plants close together and cover any bare soil with pebbles to help retain vital moisture and create a more lush effect. This tree, Barringtonia asiatica, has been underplanted with Alpinia, Canna and Cycas, with purple Hemigraphis used as ground cover.

years, smothering itself in pink or gold, pea-like flowers after several years.

Shrubs can be equally stunning: the fabulous, white starbursts of *Pavetta natalensis* among dark green leaves, the incredible, yellow, folded trumpets of *Thevetia peruviana* or the hot, red powder puffs of *Calliandra*.

Perennials compete bravely in terms of color and form. *Agapanthus africanus* has blue/mauve-striped flower heads on long stalks and the desert pea (*Clianthus formosus*), which creeps along the surface of the soil, has hooded red flowers with black swellings.

For moist areas and semishade, the ginger lily (*Hedychium gardneranum*) displays bottle brush blooms of yellow and orange. For coastal areas, *Osteospermum ecklonis*, a good ground-cover plant producing a profusion of flowers, is ideal because it will withstand salt wind and sandy soil.

It seems that there is every shape and shade for every situation among the tropical plants, but even by these standards there are some fascinating forms. The grass *Cortaderia selloana*, for example, produces giant, creamy plumes on long, reedlike stalks and *Licuala muelleri* has ribbed, fanlike leaves. Then there are the red-leaved cordylines, red-, gold- and green-spotted crotons and silver-bladed *Poa caesia*.

There are also many fruiting plants that can be integrated into a tropical garden design: the Passion fruit (*Passiflora edulis*) is a good climber and produces sweet, purple, seedy fruits; and mango, paw-paw and avocado are all attractive, fruit-bearing trees. You could also include some vegetables: okra, aubergines (egg plant) and chili peppers.

Creating a mood

An important aspect of the tropical garden is the need to create cool, restful areas, not just as a contrast to the heat and color of the sun and plants, but to provide somewhere to sit in comfort and to enjoy the shady pleasure of the plants and trees. Large plants can be combined with lightweight bamboo or grass screens and awnings or you can hang pergolas with climbing *Bougainvillea* or *Clerodendrum* for overhead shade.

A water feature is ideal for creating a feeling of coolness and a complete change of atmosphere. Pools must be partly shaded, however, and moving water features, such as waterfalls and fountains, should be only of modest size – trickling or bubbling types are best – because of the huge water loss through evaporation. A still, cool pool is the perfect opportunity to grow some of the more unusual water lilies or water poppies (see p. 188) □

◁ *Tropical plants can be controlled to make more formal effects. This beautiful shaded walk was created by growing a stunning canopy of the climber* Pyrostegia venusta *on tall pergola structures underplanted with feathery foliaged trees of* Thevetia peruviana. *The brilliant orange is balanced by thick ground cover: on the one side, grass-like leaves of* Ophiopogon japonicum *and on the other, purple* Hemigraphis alternata.

1 Vriesea hieroglyphica produces eye-catching rosettes of strong dark green- and lime-striped leaves which are perfect for lighting up dark undergrowth among ferns and other tropical plants.

2 A warmer climate provides the chance to grow some of the lovely, more tender tropical water lilies. Many of their flowers rise up above the water and some have the added bonus of fragrance.

3 Heliconias offer spectacular foliage and flowers. The leaves of this species are a deep green, against which the white and orange flowers stand out like candle flames.

4 Cordyline terminalis 'Atom' is useful for its brilliant cerise foliage which is at its best when caught by sunshine and contrasted against darker green-leaved plants.

THE INDOOR GARDEN

A GARDEN ROOM, conservatory or any other covered, plant-filled structure will make the ideal link between house and garden. It need not be large; even a glass lean-to a few feet wide serves a practical purpose as well as a valuable visual one. For not only does it prevent dirt and debris being trodden into the house, it has wonderful insulation benefits.

Important features

For plants, light is the vital factor, and so the indoor garden should incorporate as much glass as possible. Even so, in winter you may have to increase light levels with grow lamps if plants start to look a little sickly.

Heating is important, too, unless you intend to grow only hardy specimens and not use the room for sitting or eating in. If you cannot extend the household central heating, then it is best to use the dry heat of electric radiators.

Plants to choose

You should be looking for a blend of plant shapes and colors, positioning those that prefer sunshine nearest the windows and shade lovers further back. If you have space, encourage a few floor-standing plants, such as palms, to grow toward the ceiling, thus providing a visual link with larger, outdoor plants.

The best type of plants to grow are those that normally do well in the greenhouse – geraniums (*Pelargonium*), dwarf conifers (avoiding variegated cultivars if the light is poor), miniature roses, acacias and eucalyptus. Cacti and succulents would be a welcome, too.

Integrating the indoor garden

The indoor garden should relate closely to both the house and the garden in its fittings and design. Any furniture, fabrics or other soft furnishings should reflect the general style of the house and, wherever possible, try to install the same flooring right through from patio to house for a sense of continuity.

An indoor garden need not be attached to the house, of course. Any garden building would make an attractive setting, provided it had a glazed roof and received sufficient light to support plant life □

▽ *The pool house is the perfect place to indulge in an indoor tropical garden providing you can ensure plant material doesn't get into the water. These tiled raised beds contain exotic palms* (Howea fosterana), *and the superb white blooms of* Spathiphyllum *'Mauna Loa' are integrated into the total design.*

▷ *In a small conservatory or lean-to, plants are best grown in tubs and containers so that they can be moved around or replaced as required. A broad-leaved banana plant,* Musa paradisica *'Cavendish', spiky* Yucca elephantipes *and the palm* Howea fostereana *provide the height, with hanging baskets of purple* Setcreasea purpurea *'Purple Head' and green* Nephrolepis exaltata. *In the foreground is a glossy green castor oil plant* Ricinus communis *and, to smother the steps, a* Kalanchoe.

△ *It is important in an indoor garden to produce foliage at all levels, particularly close to the roof where it will provide a visual link with larger plant forms outside. This may be achieved using taller-growing species in pots on the floor or by hanging trailing plants from the ceiling. Here* Ficus benjamina *and* Philodendron *'Royal Queen' provide tall but strong foliage with a Boston Fern,* Nephrolepis exaltata, *suspended from the ceiling above.*

THE CONTAINER GARDEN

NY TYPE OF PLANT can be container grown – not just obvious spring bulbs, quick-flowering annuals and herbs, but also vegetables, trees and shrubs. On a paved patio, lumber deck or roof garden, you usually have no choice but to use plants in pots to soften hard, angular spaces and to add color and form. But there is much to be gained by creating a container garden at ground level or by choosing to include a container garden within a wilder, less formal area. Apart from the change of level and the new materials it might introduce, it offers you the chance to grow plants that cannot tolerate the chemistry of your garden soil. And, providing you are conscientious about feeding and watering, they can be easily maintained with the minimum of effort.

Choosing containers

Containers are visually as important as the plants in them and, therefore, need to be selected with care. Antique or oriental urns might suit a formal setting, while terra-cotta would be more appropriate for a country style of garden. Overall, though, try to achieve a balance of different textures and colors, with the roughness of terra-cotta or seasoned lumber, for example, contrasting with smooth stone or glazed ceramics.

A good arrangement uses containers of different heights and sizes too, balancing a

▽ Close groupings of flowering plants in tubs, with a single color theme, make a superb island display in the center of a starkly simple patio. Contained in these simple barrels are, among others, Verbena peruviana, tall heads of Cleome spinosa 'Pink Queen' and Eupatorium atrorubens.

◁ Plant containers should be chosen to suit their surroundings. This white-painted geometric tub is the perfect companion for white and pastel blue painted latticework over which a Wisteria sinensis has been trained. Its container companions are a spiky Iris germanica, gray creeping Cerastium tomentosum and summer-flowering Begonia and Dianthus.

△ Containers built as an integral part of their surroundings can be particularly effective – an ideal treatment for a lumber-decked area where tubs for plants can be constructed in matching wood. The simple, severe lines of the pergola are set off by a yellow and white planting theme against a background of foliage. White Impatiens sultanii and Chrysanthemum frutescens soften the edges of containers and are combined with Nicotiana alata and white Cleome spinosa.

▷ Use containers to make immediate and dramatic impact in otherwise uninteresting parts of the garden. The giant green leaves and beautiful hanging blooms of Nicotiana sylvestris rise from a foaming sea of Impatiens sultanii. Single color themes for containers are often the most effective.

shorter, wider pot full of bright colors with a tall chimney of, perhaps, cascading ivies or starry campanula.

Planting suggestions

Planting in pots follows the same design principles as the rest of the garden. You should aim for a strong background planting of taller evergreens, with a variety of foliage shapes and colors, embellished by a careful selection of flowering plants. Try to get away from the obvious combinations of plants. Interesting foliage plants, such as hostas, feathery gray *Senecio maritima* or the silver eucalyptus, could form the perfect backdrop for a dramatic Japanese maple, miniature rhododendron or the hardy and attractive Chinese fan palm (*Trachycarpus fortunei*).

Trailing plants are perfect for softening the edges of containers and for linking arrangements with their loose, creeping habit: ivies, campanula and creeping Jenny are just a few suggestions. Contrast these with something tall and elegant, such as a bamboo, and add a splash of color with a few annuals, choosing new favorites each year.

Scented plants are ideal in containers, positioned where they can be brushed against to release their fragrance. Big, bushy tubs of lavender or pots of herbs can be arranged near the back door for easy cropping. Fruits and vegetables can also make attractive pot plants, with stacked towers of strawberries or miniature cherry-type tomatoes bending under the weight of their fruit. Even dwarf beans, zucchini and sweet peppers make eye-catching, and tasty, container arrangements □

△ *Red and green make an exciting, contrasting color scheme which has an even more dramatic effect when several containers are pushed together to provide a large splash of color. These combine* Lobelia fulgens *'Queen Victoria' and red forms of* Nicotiana affinis, Pelargonium peltatum *and* Salvia coccinea. *The vibrant arrangement looks particularly good against the sheared formality of the hedge.*

△ *Fast-growing, small-leaved plants which produce an abundance of flowers make excellent container plants, especially when they spill over the sides of the pots. 'Hot' colors – orange* Tagetes patula *'Pascal' and bright yellow* Sanvitalia procumbens – *have been used here very successfully.*

◁ *Look out for more unusual containers and interesting planting ideas. A wide-topped dish or terra-cotta strawberry pot can be planted with stones and alpines to create a miniature rock garden in the corner of the patio. Pots of flowering* Pelargonium *provide bright colors when required.*

CREATING THE FRAMEWORK

Patios, paths, lawns, steps and boundary walls and hedges added as an afterthought will nearly always have a tacked-on appearance, never really merging into the main design or blending well with plant material. The secret is to plan your framework first and add the other features to it.

Defining and enclosing your boundaries will immediately give you a feeling for the shape and character of your garden, where necessary providing privacy or concentrating attention on a particular aspect. Entrances and exits to the garden are equally important, either hiding what is within or offering an invitation to step through.

Level, paved or decked areas for entertaining, leisure or play can be positioned where they will receive maximum sunshine or just the right amount of shade and then linked with paths, walkways or stepping stones across grass, water or planting beds to provide interesting rambles and safe, dry access. Walls, hedges and screens can be used to enclose smaller areas within the main garden, creating garden 'rooms' and making shady areas. All of this must be established before you can begin to soften their outlines with climbing and creeping plants.

GATES & ENTRANCES

WHETHER INTENDED as an exit or an entrance, a gate, door or archway within the garden creates a definite atmosphere and a certain anticipation of what lies beyond: its design and position can alter the whole ambience of the garden. An entrance is inviting and suggests a little mystery, while an exit may reveal further treats or blot out unwelcome surroundings.

True or false gates

An entrance or an exit need not be real at all, but a *trompe-l'oeil*. A false gate, for example, gives the impression that the garden leads somewhere, an illusion that can be accentuated by the installation of mirrors to reflect an existing path or vista. This trick works well with archways, too – an elegant arch set in a high wall that leads nowhere but reflects a delightful image of your garden.

The real thing, however, needs equally careful thought. A gate may dictate a change of pace, perhaps from a busy street to a quiet retreat, or signify a change of mood from one part of the garden to another – from a woodland area, say, to a formal lawn, flower plot or vegetable lot. In the country, a gate or stile frequently separates the garden from the wild beyond.

Using gates

In a small garden, a gate can be used as a frame: focusing attention through an opening naturally directs the eye to a certain point. But gates and doors can also serve a very practical purpose and may, therefore, need to be strong and secure in their construction.

Security and privacy could be important considerations, and a stout, lockable door within a high wall will act as a deterrent to unwelcome visitors or prying eyes. Simpler gates can be used to contain pets or children, preventing them straying into a busy road or into parts of the garden that are for adult or supervised use only. This can be particularly important when there is a swimming pool or large ornamental water feature in the garden.

▽ For a formal paved entrance you do best with plants in containers. The plants can be changed according to the seasons to maintain variety and interest: a fine display of bulbs in spring, bright flowering annuals in summer and an arrangement of evergreen foliage through the winter. A pair of palms (Phoenix roebelinii), positioned either side of the door, can be overwintered indoors. This symmetrical arrangement relies on the plants being the same size and on their being well looked after to keep them in peak condition.

△ Steps and verandas provide the perfect support for interesting creepers and climbers. One of the prettiest climbing plants for a house exterior is Wisteria sinensis, which produces scented pendulous racemes of white or lilac flowers. Wisteria flowers in full sun but likes its roots to be kept cool: here they are shaded by silver-leaved Atriplex lentiformis that has spread over the front steps.

Purpose and setting will determine the size, height and stoutness of a gate, but its style and the materials used should blend with other garden features. Wood, for example, generally looks good and suits both formal and wilder gardens. Yet ornate metal gates can look exactly right in the proper setting. For a decorative appearance in a more formal garden, create elaborate frames and surrounds with mesh screens, trellis, bamboo or reeds.

If security or privacy is not a priority, an opening may look better without a gate or door at all. This way you create tantalizing glimpses of what lies beyond a high wall or fence. Any opening looks better when softened with plants – climbers tumbling over the tops of walls, low ground-cover plants encroaching on doorsteps or a tangle of creepers and sweet-smelling flowers to push through on entering □

▷ A plain exterior has been brought to life with flowering plants, a promise of the garden delights within. Bright white Petunia × hybrida spills over the raised beds on either side of the gate; wall-mounted pots on the tall, formal gate posts have been planted with lovely golden Tagetes patula.

▷ An ornamental gateway is an excellent device for framing a view of the garden and drawing attention to a particular feature. This fine arched 'rainbow' bridge has been perfectly positioned so that it is seen against a background of tall trees through a rustic tiled and lumbered gateway.

▷ The classic narrow entrance to a large town house with its tall walls and ornamental railings seems to offer little opportunity for planting. Yet this can often be overcome by using plants in containers or, as here, creating a raised bed for plants along one side only of the steep steps. A mixture of spiky Cordyline stricta and the golden-variegated Aucuba japonica aureo-maculata makes an attractive display without obstructing access.

PATHS & PAVING

PATHS ARE MAINLY a convenient way of getting around the garden without the nuisance of wet or muddy feet, while larger areas of paving are ideal for lounging and entertaining. Both types of surface, however, need careful thought if they are to work well and look good within your overall design. In the Japanese tea garden, for example, paths are specifically designed to take the visitor on a leisurely route: the curves and detours will dictate the pace and resting points.

In your own garden, a circuitous route round a small garden may mask its limited boundaries. In a large garden, paths should never take a direct route but should intrigue and divert, leading in several directions and linking areas partly concealed from view.

Practical considerations

Your practical aim is to provide a clean, dry surface, so drainage is important. On some sites, you may need to provide retaining walls, drainage pipes and gullies. If you keep a careful watch during heavy rain you can note the natural drainage patterns of the site before starting. Note also the lie of the land: a large paved area on a sloping site will entail costly backfilling. If drainage is extremely poor or the gradient exceptionally steep, you may need to seek advice from an architect or land-drainage expert.

Other factors that may influence your choice of materials will depend on the weather. Severe frosts or prolonged, intense sunshine, for example, will soon reduce certain types of brick, tile and concrete to rubble.

Wealth of materials

Choice of materials for paths and paving is vast and will ultimately be determined by cost, availability and personal preference. In some cases, a patio, terrace or path will adjoin an

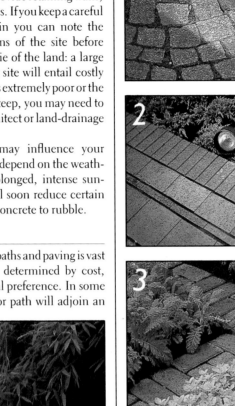

◁ *Brick lends itself to a variety of interesting patterns and designs. These broken samples have been cleverly used to create a circular patio by graduating the bricks so that the largest are used for the outer rings. The circle has been deliberately left incomplete to incorporate an informal pool planted with Iris, Hosta sieboldiana 'Elegans' and a tall Arundinaria japonica — far more natural and pleasing than if the circle had been completely defined.*

1 Rough-finished gray blocks have been laid to create a circular patio design. This versatile material also lends itself to infinite herringbone and weave effects.

2 A more formal arrangement uses new brick laid in different ways to create patterns. Placing the bricks on edge produces narrow stripes and borders.

3 Paving materials are useful for dividing planting areas as in this formal herb garden, where usually rampant Melissa, Thyme, Tansy and Fennel have been confined by narrow, mellow brick paths.

4 More unusual paving shapes are available for special effects. These interlocking sections have been designed around a central circular bed and neatly edged in a matching rectangular brick.

▷ Paving can represent a major element within your basic plan, used to design paths, walls, seating, patio areas and surroundings for a completely integrated effect. This awkwardly shaped garden has been divided into a series of garden 'rooms' and shows how versatile a single material can be. Small bricks have been laid in a variety of designs to enclose raised beds, seats, a barbecue area and a formal pool. The effect is echoed by a series of formal planting features such as sheared hedges and sculptured shapes (inset).

△ A random arrangement of dark bricks gives this wide path an immediate mellow appearance, its decorative border softened by lush foliage such as Ligularia stenocephala 'The Rocket' and L. clivorum 'Desdemona', Rodgersias and the fern Polystichum setiferum.

▷ Paving material can often be successfully mixed to produce certain effects. This irregular arrangement of weathered stone blocks has been contrasted with light stone chippings.

indoor or semiindoor area, such as a conservatory, summerhouse or pool house, and you will want to use the same paving materials throughout.

Within the limitations imposed by the materials themselves, there is scope for creating patterns and shapes. Individual paving units can be arranged in intricate designs – bonds, weaves or herringbones. Different sizes and shapes can be blended or contrasted or even built up into a variety of levels for additional interest (see *Design Guide*, p. 209).

Secondhand paving material such as flags, because of their natural mellowness and irregular shape, are ideal for patios or stepping stones, and these are best interplanted with low-growing or creeping plants, especially in cool climates where these types of plant have a better success rate. They do not, however, mix particularly well with other materials, since their rough, irregular appearance can look muddled. Also useful for covering relatively large areas, providing it is sensitively handled, is concrete. Exposed aggregate incorporated in the cement adds an interesting texture and ensures that the surface will not become slippery when wet – important for a pool area and steps. Concrete patio blocks and interlocking paving bricks are also available and these can be laid attractively in patterns.

If you prefer materials with a smaller surface area, then bricks and quarry or ceramic tiles may suit. Bricks, of course, are ideal for laying in geometric patterns, and are available in a range of colors and textured finishes. With tiles, it is vital that you choose the nonslip variety, especially if you are continuing the paving outdoors from an indoor conservatory-type area. Cobbles are another possibility, but they are uncomfortable and slippery to walk on and are most suitable when laid around large plants, shrubs or trees to create a change of texture within a larger, paved area.

Soft or loose materials, such as gravel, sand and lumber or bark chippings are becoming increasingly popular for creating a softer yet reasonably hard-wearing surface for pathways and walks. They tend to look particularly fine when combined with lumber structures, such as decks, pergolas and areas of trellis work. Be wary of bark chippings, however, where termites are a problem.

Mixing materials within a garden design can be most effective for breaking up large areas, creating further patterns or for making contrasts between hard and soft surfaces. It is important, however, not to mix too many types. More than two or three shapes and colors, even of the same type of material, tend to look messy and a little confusing □

A wide formal walk between tall hedging focuses attention on a fine sundial at the end of the avenue. The uniformity of the stark, sheared hedging is echoed in a path constructed from soft bark chips.

Paving needn't come to an abrupt end where it meets grass. These bricks have been fanned out into the lawn area, creating attractive patterns. The buff gray of the paving is highlighted in the darker colors of the planting bed, where the purple-leaved foliage contrasts with the dramatic green backdrop of Arundinaria japonica and Macleaya cordata.

STEPPING STONES

Stepping stones across any surface – wet or dry – seem to offer an irresistible invitation to cross. It may be a zigzag across a shallow stream, over grass, a pebble bed or bark chippings, but there is always the unmistakable impression of being led somewhere exciting.

Safety insists that the 'stones' should be large enough to stand on and spaced comfortably for stepping on to. They should also be level, stable and nonslip. Stones, of course, are only one of numerous types of material you can choose from: paving slabs or bricks and even wooden boards are all suitable. You will need to experiment to get the layout just right and remember that a straight line rarely looks as good as a staggered or winding design.

◁ *Breaking up the larger, more severe paving forms creates a less formal effect. Plain paving slabs have been set amongst pebbles to make a winding path between lumbered raised beds of dense planting, which combines a bold range of foliage shapes –* Hosta sieboldiana, Pinus aristata, Agapanthus campanulatus *and* Eccremocarpus scaber.

▽ *Simple log slices make excellent stepping stones across grass or water, if given a regular treatment of nontoxic preservative and periodically scraped free from moss or algae to prevent them getting slippery.*

◁ *Irregular rocks can be used as informal stepping stones providing they are flat-topped. They are a popular device in oriental-style gardens where they may lead across sand, grass or gravel to a bridge, summerhouse or pond, for instance.*

▽ *Linked colors and textures enhance these rough stepping stones, a more formally paved path and the smaller pebbles edging the water. The hard surfaces contrast well with the natural planting of ground-covering plants such as* Alchemilla mollis *and dwarf* Rhododendron.

LUMBER DECKS

As well as being a natural material that is warm and attractive to look at, lumber decking is an economical and versatile alternative to hard paving. Whether you have a large country garden or a small city yard, an oriental, formal or wild setting, lumber decking will adapt itself easily and unobtrusively. Stain it with colored varnishes, lay it in elaborate patterns or simply leave it rough-hewn and natural to create whichever effect blends best with the rest of your garden. No other material can cope so readily with being fitted round trees and other large features such as pools, or extended out from the house or over water in the form of an entertainment area or a jetty.

Materials to use

Decks are available in ready constructed and treated sections that sit just off the ground. You can lay these sections in a limited variety of patterns across a lawn or patio, and they are useful for lifting and rearranging wherever you need to make a portable and dry surface.

A more ambitious and flexible system is the type of deck you build yourself, using new or well-seasoned, secondhand lumber, to create paths, patios, bridges and jetties at whatever height you need to suit the terrain.

All deck lumber should be pressured treated. Durable timbers, such as redwood and red cedar, are excellent for deck construction since they do not rot or warp easily and will wear well with the minimum of maintenance. The less expensive softwoods, however, such as larch or spruce, are more commonly used and are suitable if given an annual treatment of preservative. Also, you will need to brush the surface of all wood once or twice a year with a stiff brush and a safe fungicide in order to keep it free from slime or algae growth. Apart from this, maintenance is simply a matter of testing any metal bolts and fastenings periodically for signs of stress or rusting.

Safety aspects

Platform-style decks can be very securely fastened to the side of the house by a system of supporting joists and steel or lumber ledger strips connected by bolts or nails. Free-standing decks are supported on joists and beams set into concrete footings. The size and number of supports depend on the extent of deck and whether the site is sloping: posts also need to be stronger if they are supporting any type of roof structure – open or solid.

All forms of elevated lumber deck require some building experience. It is also a good idea to check your local building rules and regulations before attempting anything too ambitious.

An integrated whole

Lumber decks will blend well with other wooden structures around the garden, providing a feeling of unity that can be softened if necessary with trailing and creeping plants. For privacy and shelter, trellis, screens and pergolas planted with quick-growing plants are an obvious choice. Wooden tubs, wooden furniture (built in and freestanding) and sunken spa baths also create a fine, harmonious effect. Any large expanse of deck will benefit from the addition of statuesque or sprawling foliage plants, shrubs and small trees, just like any paved surface □

◁ A change of level or a change of direction makes large areas of decking more interesting. Narrow planks can be laid at right angles or on the diagonal to create patterns, and here they provide a warm and practical surface around a swimming pool – very much in keeping with the half-lumbered buildings that surround the pool.

1 Free-standing, low sections of deck can be laid across grass, gravel or pebbles to make walkways, bridges and 'stepping stones'. Because they are completely portable, their position can be altered if required.

2 A deck extended across a pool just above the surface of the water makes a fine bridge and can be linked to lumbered patio areas. Here the effect has been softened by growing water-edge plants like Iris laevigata and Lysimachia punctata close to the edge.

3 Large areas of decking are made more interesting by allowing surrounding plants to spill over and blur the edges, and by placing tubs and containers in strategic positions. These terracotta tubs of sheared Buxus sempervirens have been arranged either side of wide lumber steps for a semiformal effect.

◁ On a sloping site, lumber decking is a far more practical alternative to paving, which involves considerable excavation and back-filling. This patio in Anthony Paul's own garden provides excellent views of the garden and has been designed to enclose a large tree which provides convenient dappled shade for seating areas. The deck was designed with spaces for planting and a handsome clump of Arundinaria japonica provides visual contrast as well as a practical windbreak.

STEPS

STEPS MUST TAKE you safely from one level to another without looking awkward or out of place; they should also form an integral part of the garden design and, therefore, need to be thought out carefully from functional as well as aesthetic points of view.

A change in level is always attractive and steps should invite you both to ascend and descend depending on the angle you approach them from. Even in a semiconcealed setting, steps have to be comfortable to use: the rise not too steep and the treads not too narrow. Pitching the treads slightly forward – approximately 0.3 cm per 30 cm (1/8 in per 12 in) – will ensure that water will not collect and so make them dangerous to walk on. Also, this will greatly extend the life of wooden steps.

Handrails are useful, particularly where the steps will be used by the elderly, disabled or the very young, or where the slope is steep. Make sure that rails are firmly fitted and made of materials that are sympathetic to those of the steps themselves: rope slung between stone supports, for example.

Scale and proportions

Visually, it is important that the steps fit the scale of your house, patio or surrounding landscape. A large, formal terrace leading down to a large lawn, for example, requires wide steps in suitably regal proportions; a small, low deck, on the other hand, would benefit from a short flight of much smaller steps, perhaps made of wood. Wherever steps join a path, they should always be of the same width, and long flights look better if they change direction once or twice, preferably with a platform or landing at these points.

Any nonslip paving material is well suitable for steps. Sensitively used, sensibly installed and softened with bordering plants, rustic lumber, concrete slabs, bricks edged with granite and even preformed concrete step units can be adapted and made to look attractive (see *Design Guide* p. 209) □

△ *Wide, shallow steps encourage a leisurely pace and lead easily from one level of the garden to another. Simple U-shaped slabs link more decorative paths on both levels and have been used to construct matching bench seating on either side.*

▷ *Steps need not be purely functional but can be used as a design feature, like this stone pyramid flanked by simple terra-cotta pots of summer-flowering Geraniums. Alternatively (see inset), they may lead to an interesting focal point such as a piece of sculpture, a pool or a specimen plant.*

△ *A flight of steep, short steps has been softened with massed foliage planting such as Hedera helix and Lonicera nitida 'Baggesen's Gold'. Using old, secondhand bricks immediately gives a feeling of maturity.*

▷ *Matching step materials to their surroundings and softening their edges with vigorous planting helps them integrate well into their surroundings. These brick steps are softened and decorated with tubs of flowering and foliage plants.*

LAWNS & SOFT SURFACES

GRASS IS NOT as popular in the garden as it once was; even small areas of lawn are time consuming to keep in good condition. Yet, used with discretion, grass can be a valuable design feature and an asset to the well-crafted garden. Grass areas should never be used simply to fill spaces between, say, trees and planting beds, but should be regarded as an important part of your total garden design with a full awareness of the shapes they make themselves.

There are many ways you can use grass in the garden without resorting to the predictable, suburban mown strip. You can combine it with other surfaces, such as lumber, brick or stone, to create paths and patterns (see page 116), or intersperse it with stone or lumber 'stepping stones' for interest and dry access. In a naturalized garden, grassy banks make attractive screening, especially when the top is planted with flowers or shrubs. For fun, construct a stone or lumber seat using living moss or grass as a cushion.

Maintenance and planning

With any grass area, you must be prepared to keep it in good condition – which means regular mowing, watering, feeding and occasional dethatching (removing compacted, dead material that builds up on the soil surface). For these reasons, it is worth ensuring that grassed areas are neither too narrow nor too difficult to mow by avoiding tight corners, narrow pathways and awkward curves, such as those around trees.

When patching an existing grass area, or starting one from new, seeding tends to make a stronger, more even lawn. Sods, however, achieve quicker, more predictable results. Whichever method you go for, it is essential

△ The flowery meadow makes a glorious natural display of colors in spring and early summer and is very easy to maintain, unlike more formal grassed areas. Here, a splendid carpet of buttercups, Ranunculus acris and R. repens, spreads out before a backdrop of purple Rhododendron ponticum and tall trees.

▷ Where large parts of the garden are shaded by trees, grass is often the most practical ground cover. A sculpture or other ornamental feature could be used to add points of interest. Here, such an area is separated from the main garden, reached via a small bridge and screened by a dense border of dramatic plants.

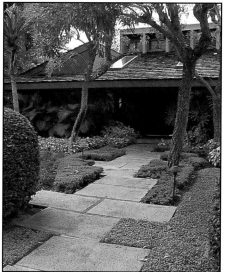

△ Grass is a good linking material between natural features and can be taken between borders or around pools to create relaxed walkways and informal paths. Larger areas can incorporate brick, stone or lumber paths or stepping stones for dry access to all parts of the garden.

that you choose the correct grass mixture for the type of use and climatic conditions the grass will be subjected to – a fine mixture if you want a velvety effect or a coarser mixture for general family use. There are also grasses recommended for extreme climates, such as Bermuda grass, for hot, southern districts.

Alternatives to grass

There are other types of plants you can use besides grass to create a lawn: some low-growing, creeping varieties will spread quickly over a given area provided that you weed between them in the first year or two.

Some of the sweet-scented herbs, such as thymes and chamomiles, actually enjoy being crushed or walked on once they are established, and they will emit a bewitching scent as well as creating a lovely, and weed-suppressing, carpet of subtle coloring.

Other surfaces

There are other soft surfaces useful for parts of the garden where you want to introduce a change of texture. Bark or wood chips are soft underfoot and reasonably hard wearing, although they do require edging with lumber planks to contain them. A thick layer should last about three years. Fir bark is another inexpensive alternative, as are wood shavings and nut shells, although none of these will last as long as chips. Another obvious material to consider is sand. Again, you will need to border a sandy area with stone, or similar edging, and it will need topping up periodically, depending on the amount of wear □

PLANTING BEDS

OR TODAY'S garden designers, planting beds do not necessarily mean long, straight herbaceous borders full of time-consuming perennials and annuals, or the artificial island beds so popular with England's early-nineteenth-century designer Humphry Repton. Beds are just as likely to be raised and contained by stone, brick or lumber in the tradition of Chinese raised vegetable gardens. They might consist of small planting spaces intended for a single shrub and set among decking or paving, or they may be larger planting areas following the natural contours of the landscape and planted with a subtle blend of shapes and shades to add form and variety to the garden throughout all the seasons of the year.

Raised and sunken beds

Raised beds are particularly useful when drainage is poor or when you want to grow plants that would not thrive in your general garden soil. The walls of the beds can be formal brick, rough dry stone or stout lumber, de-pending on the style of their surroundings. In the formal garden, semiraised beds owe their clearly defined edges to railroad ties, cope-stones or the modern terra-cotta equivalent to the traditional ornamental edgings.

Sunken beds are enjoying a new popularity for creating intimate sheltered areas: complete with steps and seating, they allow you to enjoy to the full the scents and colors of plants and flowers. You can use these sunken areas to create a theme garden by using only perfumed flowers, for example, or plants of a single color or those with distinctive and interesting form or foliage.

There is a new awareness of the balance of form and color in planting beds: eyecatching combinations of large, fleshy or short, spiky leaf shapes and simple color mixtures. Even country-style gardens are opting for drifts of one or two colors and softer, more natural plants instead of a profusion of bright shades, which can create a confused and muddled picture unless handled with care (see *Designing with Plants*, p. 173, for further ideas) □

▷ *Paved patios should incorporate planting spaces within the general design. This one has been edged with* Euonymus, Hosta *'Thomas Hogg' and other variegated plants for a low-maintenance foliage display. Brighter flowers have been restricted to* Petunia, Lobelia *and* Tropaeolum majus *in containers for quick summer color. The annuals stand out against a strong permanent background planting of a glossy green Chinese loquat and climbing ivies that disguise the boundary wall.*

▽ **Below right** *This predominantly gold and orange planting design is an informal version of the traditional herbaceous border. A careful blending of colors, forms and leaf textures includes* Tropaeolum majus *at the edge, while behind, the tall flat heads of* Achillea *'Coronation Gold' and orange daisies of* Helenium *'Moerheim Beauty' combine to make the required color blend.*

◁ *A neat brick edging and single color scheme make dramatic features of these island beds. The mauves and purples of* Petunia × hybrida, Salvia superba *and* Brachycome iberidifolia *are well contained within their circular planting spaces to make mowing the surrounding lawns easier.*

HEDGES

A HEDGE OF DENSE foliage – sometimes with the bonus of scent and flowers – makes an excellent windbreak, boundary or screen, and it is a more natural alternative to walls or fences. Although hedges are cheaper than fencing materials, you do require patience to grow them to a mature size. Also, varieties designed for shearing into formal shapes, such as privet (*Ligustrum*) or box (*Buxus*), need considerable maintenance.

There are, however, many shrubby varieties you can use that require minimal shearing and make most attractive hedges, including *Escallonia*, *Mahonia* and *Pyracantha*; or for a short, highly aromatic hedge you can plant rosemary or lavender. In the informal garden, a shaggy 'wild' hedge may be more in keeping: a mixture of hawthorn (*Crataegus*), beech (*Fagus*) and hazel (*Corylus*) interwoven with a variety of different climbing plants for added color.

Despite being slow to establish, hedges have many practical advantages as well as great design potential. Their softer, less aggressive outline is, nevertheless, an effective wind-

▽ *Hedges can create an air of mystery and surprise within a garden plan. Allowed to grow tall and sheared into strong, plain shapes they provide an excellent device for leading the eye toward a particular focal point or for dividing the garden into interesting compartments. Extra interest has been created in this garden by using different plants, and contrasting forms, to emphasize the simple geometry of the sheared forms.*

break, particularly in coastal areas where *Aucuba*, cotoneaster or hydrangea will shield more tender garden plants from the worst of biting, salty winds. As well, hedges also make effective noise and pollution filters.

Hedge sizes

A tall boundary hedge is an obvious device to screen the garden, but it can also be used to create special effects, to define the end of the garden or to break up the space and create different views. Plant them in dense shapes to make a bold statement or to hide an unattractive building.

Medium-height hedges are useful for defining and bordering garden features, such as drives, paths or walkways, without obscuring the overall view. This size hedge is also ideal for use as a sculptural form, sheared into amusing topiary shapes to make a focal point or special feature. Bear in mind that there are many fragrant and flowering varieties. *Choisya*, lavender and *Artemisia* are notable for their heady fragrance while, for massed flowers, choose a shrub such as broom (*Cytisus*) or barberry (*Berberis*).

Neat, low hedges, such as box, are generally grown purely as a decorative feature, creating miniature borders around specialist plant beds or elaborate knot gardens where different herbs are restrained within complicated patterns. These require almost daily shearing and care during the growing season, and so are only for the really dedicated gardener □

Hedging at its most ornamental: the sheared box design surrounds a central reflecting orb sculpture raised high above a neatly sheared wheel shape. Other sculptural hedge forms outside the design link it to the main garden and bright blooms have been avoided so as not to detract from its dramatic impact.

Deliberate gaps or spaces left within a run of hedging allow views of the garden or landscape behind. Alternatively, use them to frame a special feature like this ornamental stone sculpture.

WALLS & SCREENS

I N NEARLY ALL gardens, some form of wall, fence or screen is essential to give privacy and provide shelter for plants and leisure areas. Unfortunately though, it can often become too dominant or appear out of place in its garden setting. Yet there are many materials you can use to avoid this type of problem: stone, wood, brick, bamboo and reeds, for example, are all products which, if used carefully, can harmonize with any surrounding garden features and become attractive elements in their own right.

In the formal garden, weathered, rough materials tend to look most natural: old brick covered with ivy, for example, or simple dry stone walls in locations where stone is plentiful. As an alternative, many eye-catching effects are possible using shaped and rendered concrete blocks if you design and construct them well and then paint them to blend with their surroundings. For the high-tech or classic formal garden, painted metal-mesh grill trellis provides an airy type of screen.

Alternative materials

For a soft look, and one that is quick to achieve, a basic framework can be used to support bamboo or reed screens. This can look perfect

△ Small courtyards often need screening for shelter and privacy. Here, a focal point has been made of an ornate classical trellis in Greek style complete with urns and columns. The structure is covered in sweet-smelling Jasmine and the wall behind has been painted white to match its flowers.

◁ Peep holes and windows in screens or walls provide interesting views and add to their decorative effect. This ornamental lattice has been otherwise smothered with Solanum jasminoides.

▷ Rough wooden railroad ties make a strong and economical rustic fence in a garden shaded by a lumber pergola and featuring decks around and across a series of formal pools. The base of the fence has been softened by a planting design which links the two features.

1 Fast-growing climbers are useful for covering new walls or fences. This new brick wall is disappearing under an attractive blanket of Parthenocissus.

2 An unusual link design screen in steely gray is twined with Clematis, which produces a profusion of delicate leaves and flowers in contrast to its strong geometric form.

3 Well-weathered lumber is the perfect neutral background for a fine bamboo with its tall canes and light green leaves.

around an outdoor living area or in an oriental-style garden. In some locations, you may also be able to obtain wattle or brushwood screens.

Rather than install barriers of particularly ugly fencing panels, you can construct your own fences very simply out of logs laid horizontally or supported vertically: utility poles, railroad ties and even drainage pipes can all be used to good effect.

All forms of walls and screens greatly benefit from being softened by plants supported on trellis. Ugly walls can be disguised with climbing plants or an ornamental trellis painted white and hung with colorful pot plants. Screens and fences can be softened at ground level with containers of trailing foliage plants or, of course, you can cultivate a total screen of foliage using large and interesting specimens to create a jungle of form and color supported on a concealed framework □

▽ *Stout lumber poles, irregularly spaced and supporting mixed climbers including Lonicera and roses, make an unusual and informal screen.*

△ *Lumber planks can be arranged horizontally and spaced to produce a more interesting louvered effect. The base is disguised by tubs of green and gray foliage plants: include Eccremocarpus, Eucalyptus, Artemesia and Senecio.*

▽ *A close arrangement of vertical bamboo canes forms an attractive, natural screen for shelter and privacy. Here, the climbing Ficus pumila is being trained against it to provide additional plant interest.*

ADDING THE FEATURES

Like the icing on the proverbial cake, there are many nonessential but attractive and often useful features that can be added to your basic framework. Owners of smaller gardens will have to be more selective, but there is a style and a scale for every type of garden, whether you are choosing a piece of sculpture, a fountain or a plant container.

The primary purpose of these features is decorative and, simple or ornate, they need to be chosen to fit comfortably into their surroundings. The intention is that they complement, not stand out in contrast against, the rest of the garden. This can be achieved by selecting objects in a sympathetic material: lumber or stone, brick or terra-cotta to match surrounding architectural forms, or colors and styles to suit a general theme.

Here, more than anywhere in your garden design, you can afford to be original and imaginative and it pays to look out for the more unusual item or effect that may strike just the right note in your particular setting. These are also the features you may like to change and replace in future years to avoid monotony and to create a slightly different effect.

PERGOLAS

A PERGOLA is a three-dimensional structure that originally evolved as a means of displaying climbing plants, particularly in areas of the garden where there were no existing buildings or other supports. As such, it is a wonderful device for ornamental specimens such as vines, roses, fruiting plants and splendid climbers like clematis or wisteria, which produces an amazing canopy of scented, pendulous blooms.

Practical as well as beautiful

Plant-covered pergolas are now being used for new and more practical purposes. In a hot, dry climate, they create a welcome shaded area, ideal for lounging under. Also, in any type of climate, pergolas can be used to contain a private eating or living area, essential in a small city garden; or they can be used to define a cozy enclave in a larger space. As a green roof studded with sweet-smelling blooms or bright fruits, a pergola can link the house to other buildings or form a roof for a walkway.

Pergolas are usually of lumber, but they may also be made of metal, peeled larch poles (simply notched and fixed together), steel girders or rough-sawn lumber with natural or colored stains and varnishes. For a more sophisticated look, use brick or stone piers to support the lumber or metal poles; and for a

lightweight but oriental feel, you can even use bamboo poles.

Planning and planting

When planning, it is important to consider the height, width and orientation of the structure in relation to the rest of the garden. It is the plants that should be immediately obvious, not the structure itself, and what a wonderful selection there is, from the scented climbing roses and honeysuckles to fast-growing vines and even trees that can be trained to cling and entwine themselves.

With its scope for providing overhead interest as well as shade and screening, a pergola lends itself to many design possibilites. It works well with gates and entrances, for example, is ideal on a roof garden to give shelter and variation in height and it can be used to frame and accentuate a garden seating area. For total flexibility and excellent screening, combine climbing plants with materials such as rustic bamboo, lumber boards, louvers or delicate lattice fencing □

▷ *A pretty rustic pergola almost invisible under a mass of foliage (Parthenocissus) provides dappled shade for a small sunny terrace overlooking an informal pool. The leafy structure blends easily with the dense canopy of surrounding trees and its base is hidden in a hedge of sweet-scented Lavandula spica.*

△ *Exotic surroundings and dramatic architectural plants demand bold structural forms, such as this pergola, which echoes the arching and slatted shape of nearby palm trees in* its design. The base is literally swamped by a great enveloping hedge of Spathiphyllum 'McCoy' which provides both shade in hot weather as well as privacy.

AWNINGS & UMBRELLAS

SOME FORM OF overhead shelter will not only keep out the worst of the midday sun, chill breezes or summer rain during the day, it will also create a protected, secluded area at night, especially if combined with outdoor lighting. Whatever you design or build to protect you from the elements, it must, first of all, be practical and easy to use. A permanent structure must be capable of surviving all weathers, including high winds and the potential weight of any snow or rain that may fall. A temporary one must be simple to erect and take down and you will also need somewhere safe and dry to store it when it is not in use.

Your second major consideration must be the awning's appearance: you will certainly not want to add a feature that will spoil the look of the garden. A family patio, for example, may benefit from a bright, striped awning or umbrella, striking just the right note near a barbecue or at the poolside, while other parts of the garden may demand something less gaudy, perhaps constructed out of lumber, canvas or bamboo.

What to use

You can construct an awning in many ways using a variety of materials. For an effect that will blend perfectly with surrounding foliage, use bamboo or rush matting, lumber slats, stretched sailcloth or even some burlap, de-

△ *Stretched canvas over a metal frame provides excellent shade and shelter and here it has been supplied with circular windows admitting light and framing a fine palm.*

▷ A bright yellow awning extends over a well screened
patio to provide shade in hot weather and the impression of sunshine
on duller days. When not required,
it retracts into a neat casing fitted
to the wall of the house and can be
operated either electronically or by
hand.

▽ A wood and canvas free-
standing umbrella is a welcome addition to this sun-drenched
terrace beside the pool. Its clean
design and natural materials are
fitting within a stylish area of white-
painted walls and terra-cotta tiling.

△ In this small sun trap, light and shade are
well under control: a large canvas umbrella
provides a pleasant place for eating and entertaining while a dramatic black and white screen extends to make a sheltered terrace.

signed to roll or pull back on an overhead frame or pergola (see p. 136).

Alternatively, continental-style awnings are available and made to measure. These can be fixed to the side of the house to shade a patio or an upper-story balcony, and some come with matching side screens to cut out biting crosswinds. Good manufacturers carry a wide choice of fabrics that have been tested for their resistance to weathering and color fading. Many types can be operated electronically from inside the house.

Umbrellas

Not to be forgotten when considering shade in the garden are umbrellas and parasols. These excellent, versatile devices still have no equal when it comes to providing a wide spread of shade quickly on demand, yet fold away easily to be stored in the smallest of spaces. You can slot them into mounting holes in the middle of garden tables, decks or paved areas, or there are also freestanding models with weighted bases for lawns and pool areas. Again, designs vary from stripes and florals to plain calico □

WATER FEATURES

SMALL, ORNAMENTAL WATER features have their place in both the large and the small garden. Where space is very restricted, or if you are planning to construct just a tiny patio, a water feature, suitably scaled to match, can be used to provide a lively focal point. It will also become an eyecatching element of a more ambitiously sized water garden (see p. 90).

These small water features often take the shape of moving water, which can always be relied on to capture the attention of the eyes and ears. Or you may be looking for the right materials to enclose a formal pool, to be sparsely planted with a few architectural plants, and create an effect that relies on shape and the uncluttered gleam of water reflecting the sky and surrounding plants for its impact.

Choosing a style

Ornamental does not necessarily mean ornate and often the simplest ideas are best, using natural materials and basic shapes. Size and scale are also important if features are not to look diminutive and insignificant or too dominant in your garden setting.

Position will determine the shape and style of your water feature: if it is placed in the middle of a patio or large pool it will automatically become a focal point and can be more ostentatious. A less obvious feature, one that you want people to come across by surprise, is best designed as naturally as possible and tucked away into a corner or hidden from immediate view by clever landscaping or an arrangement of foliage.

As a design feature, the formal pool is characterized by having a clearly defined outline, based on a series of squares, circles or rectangles. It need not be symmetrical, though, and can be either sunken or raised as an integral part of a patio design, or can strike a clean note of order in the midst of a more informal garden setting.

Geometric shapes lend themselves naturally to a series of pools, perhaps interlinking or raised, made out of stone, brick, paving or lumber to match any surrounding surfaces. These materials are important as the formal pool cannot offer the same scope for dramatic water-edge and moisture-loving plants that a natural, informal pool can. But wide, raised

▷ *The raised pool is built to simulate an old well, designed in matching materials to the patio. The usual circular pool with a wide brick coping is the perfect feature for a rectangular garden bounded by a tall dark conifer hedge and smaller green sheared Buxus. In contrast to the lush planting of the rest of the garden, the pool provides only gleaming reflections and the decorative effect of a couple of pots of pink Pelargoniums on its perimeter. Moss has been encouraged to grow between the old bricks to produce a more mellow effect.*

▽ *On a small patio, an old faucet pouring water into a stone trough makes an excellent space-saving water feature. An ornamental gourd has been allowed to twine itself over the white-painted wall behind, providing additional interest with its finely shaped leaves and fascinating white fruits. A small submersible pump can be used to create any number of moving water effects like this.*

◁ *A trickle of water from a series of bamboo canes disturbs the surface of a tranquil pool in this very simple, oriental-style water garden, where features are kept to a minimum and stone and rock predominate. The sound and movement of this water feature make it an important but understated focal point.*

▽ *The simplest ideas often work the best with water. Allowed to trickle over a dark stone ball and circulating from a pump below, water makes an excellent surprise feature in an unexpected corner of the garden, or, as this is, in a leafy woodland setting.*

▷ *A small pebbled area contained within a decking design uses sunken and raised containers filled with water to make an amusing feature. One has been planted with tall Butomus umbellatus and the other with elegant slim reeds (Typha stenophylla).*

△ *Water may be used as a natural stop to define a boundary: a stone-parapeted moat lined with mosaic tiles is not only decorative, but it also separates the garden from a steep drop in levels.*

edging or copestones, if stable, make ideal platforms for standing plants in pots or for sitting on and enjoying the sight of plants and fish in the water.

A sunken formal pool fits very well into certain types of garden layout, too. It can be built into a lumber-decked patio or terrace, for example, edged in brick on a paved patio or even neatly integrated into an area of carefully manicured lawn. Sunken pools such as these should be stocked with just a few perfectly formed water lilies: miniature varieties can be used where space is limited. Also suitable here would be a single clump of erect reeds or an isolated group of stately iris.

In these circumstances, you need to keep planting to a carefully controlled minimum in case you lose the shape of your pool. Surrounding areas then have to be equally elegant. According to the imposed style of your garden or patio, you can use a collection of large, smooth pebbles, decorative pots of bamboo, raised beds of foliage plants, seating or a piece of sculpture.

Making the water move

Unless you are lucky enough to have a natural stream running through your garden, moving water features rely on the installation of an efficient pump to recycle the water. This means that a safe, external source of electricity must be close at hand if you are not to have the nuisance of running specially shielded cables all over your garden and then hiding them from view and accidental damage.

It is vitally important to select a pump that is capable of the job it has to do and that can cope with the volume of water it has to move over the proposed area. Pumps are of two types: they can be submersible (underwater) or sited above ground. Submersible pumps are more expensive but are stronger and tougher – above-

ground pumps will need some type of weather-proof housing and they cannot be left outside during hard winters.

Fountains and water spouts

Fountains provide a lot of pleasure and are relatively simple features to install, but consideration of their size in relation to their surroundings is crucial to their success. All too often they look out of proportion: if too large or ornate they tend to dominate or overspill the sides of the pool; too small and they are simply insignificant. Fountains can be as simple as a single jet of water, installed chiefly for the sound and sight of rising and falling droplets, or you can have several jets of varying power.

Depending on the type you choose, fountains begin as low as a domed or umbrella effect and can rise as high as 2.4 or 3.3 m (8 or 11 ft). At their most ornate, the fountain nozzle can be inserted into a decorative figure or sculpture to produce a range of special effects.

Another simple moving water effect, and one that is particularly suitable for patios, is the water spout – a steady trickle of water into a bowl, basin, small pool or collection of stones or pebbles which is pumped back up to the head by means of a submersible pump. Water can be made to spout straight out of a rough gap between stones or bricks, trickled from an old brass faucet, a wooden scoop or be produced from a wall-mounted sculptural feature.

Other ideas

An alternative to the traditional fountain or spout is a low bubble fountain, usually installed where it can gurgle over a group of rocks or pebbles, a pitted antique cannon ball or perhaps out of the middle of an old millstone. Here, the well of water is concealed in an underground reservoir complete with its submersible pump. Bubble fountains are ideal for gardens used by children, since there is no tempting, dangerous depth of water visible.

Other, smaller features are limited only by your imagination: an old terra-cotta pot or urn laid on its side with water fed through a drainage hole, makes an excellent water cascade into a small pool or hidden reservoir. In a certain style of garden, a length of bamboo spilling water into a bronze bowl or formal pool adds exactly the right oriental touch. Cascades and waterfalls can tumble not just over a natural arrangement of rocks, but also over tiled steps or sheets of Plexiglas.

Often, those features created from seemingly discarded materials make the most successful designs, fitting naturally and smoothly into their environment □

▷ *Another simple but effective idea for the corner of the garden or patio is this wide, flat dish sunk into a bed of pebbles and shaded by leafy green plants such as* Alnus *and* Pachysandra. *The same effect might be achieved using any kind of natural container, such as an old sink, a stone trough, a sunken pot or an ornamental urn.*

WATERFALLS & STREAMS

For a large moving water feature to look at its best in the garden it should be used architecturally, either as a means of adding height or by giving the impression of additional length or width. Vitally important here is that you calculate the size of pump required to cope with the volume of water it has to move.

Designing a cascade

Apart from adding height, a waterfall, particularly in the form of a cascade, is an excellent device for linking one area of the garden to another or for creating a spectacular focal point. Natural-looking falls are difficult to get right and they need building up gradually using excavated subsoil from elsewhere in the garden (or bought in) and a selection of rocks and boulders arranged to appear as natural as possible. It will help if you can study how features such as this are laid down in the wild and experiment with different arrangements until it looks exactly right.

The right effect

It is one thing to get the boulders arranged correctly, and yet another to persuade the water to cascade over them satisfactorily: all

▷ *Judicious planting produces highlights of color along the course of a rocky waterfall: the yellow flowers of the water-loving Marsh Marigold* (Caltha palustris) *blend well with a purple-leaved* Acer *and a pink* Rhododendron.

▽ *Mossy banks and boulders have been used to create a natural winding stream through this shady woodland garden. It is an effect that is difficult to achieve and which really only suits a large site.*

◁ *A semiformal series of cascades adds breathtaking light and movement in a glade of Rhododendrons. Water falls from a great rocky height into a progression of stone troughs, combining natural rock with manmade features.*

too often it tends to disappear behind the rocks or just trickle miserably down them. The secret here is to line the back of the boulders with some synthetic rubber, taking great care not to tear it, and arranging it at the edges so that it is well hidden from view. But for a really good fall of water you have to install a lip of some sort at the top – a paving slab, flat stone or a piece of Plexiglas – which will produce a curtain of water. The final step is to surround the waterfall with moisture-loving perennials, shrubs and ferns.

Water cascades can be particularly effective in formal gardens, where they may take the form of a series of wide stone, brick, Plexiglas or tiled steps.

Streams and watercourses

A stream is an equally effective design feature, not just as an attractive winding watercourse but as a device for altering the apparent dimensions of your garden. If carefully planned, both the informal stream or more formal water channel can do wonders for disguising a boundary or awkward shape, dividing the garden into different areas or creating islands accessible only by bridges or stepping stones.

Whatever style you choose, a stream or watercourse is never sloped. Instead, you must use a pump to keep the water flowing: a sloping gradient only encourages the water to run away too quickly, leaving a dry bed whenever the pump is turned off.

The informal stream takes its lead from nature and you need to ensure that you do not incorporate too many unnatural twists and turns or strange shapes. To complete the effect, edge the sides with boulders, mosses, ferns and attractive stream-side plants, such as marsh marigolds, rushes and grasses.

For a more formal setting, you can create sharply defined, right-angled watercourses or channels, cutting across the plot to isolate the house, moat fashion, or install a circular design that leaves an island 'picnic' area.

In fact, you do not need water at all to design an effective 'stream'. You can, instead of using water, have an arrangement of stones and pebbles to suggest the flowing course of a stream. This is essentially a Japanese design principle (see p. 94), and it can work surprisingly well when edged with moisture-loving plants and crossed by bridges to create the impression of water below □

△ *This miniature landscape combines a tiny waterfall with rocks and trailing* Asparagus densiflorus *'Sprengeri' in the corner of a formal patio. The feature is highlighted by white-painted walls behind and the bright orange blooms of* Bougainvillea.

BRIDGES

Like stepping stones, which have already been discussed (see p. 120), bridges offer an invitation to cross and a temptation to find out what is on the other side. They provide a valuable element of mystery in a garden, whatever its size, and they also encourage the crosser to linger and appreciate the garden from a new aspect – nobody ever seems to hurry across a bridge.

For these reasons, it makes no difference whether a bridge spans a body of water, an area of pebbles or grass or even a planting area, the urge and the practicalities are the same: the provision of a safe, dry access and a useful viewing platform.

Styles of bridge

Bridges can be as simple as a low stone slab, a sawn log across a country-style stream or a wide, lumber-decked walkway just above the surface of a pool, perhaps continuing from an existing decked patio area. Decorated arched bridges are suitable, too, in the right setting, such as a large, formal garden, but they are expensive and complicated to build. An arch is really only necessary if boats need to pass beneath and in many ways a low bridge is preferable, for not only is it easier and less costly to construct, it also brings you nearer to the water and its inhabitants. In addition, lumber and brick are easier bridge-building materials to work with than stone or concrete: bricks look particularly good when linked to a building and can comprise low arches supported on concrete piers.

Whatever style you opt for, bear in mind that it is the simple designs that tend to work best. A bridge should not attract undue attention to itself and dominate the general effect of your garden design. Endeavor to use materials that blend with the rest of the garden: lumber can take the form of simple, sawn planks laid side by side or of railroad ties spanning the banks; there are simple preformed concrete bridges with a slight curve to them; or you can use a large granite slab to span the gap between two grassy, level areas on opposing banks.

Lumber can be stained in a wide range of colors, including blue, gray and even a rusty red color, if this helps it blend, while bricks tend to look better in the buff, gray and blue variations, particularly where they are going to be reflected in water. Any concrete footing or other constructional evidence needs to be smothered with attractive and fast-growing ground-cover plants.

Safety aspects

Like any walkway, a bridge must be safe to use and well constructed. Materials should be sound and firmly fixed and you should check all supporting banks, wood, concrete, brick and so on for signs of erosion annually. The walking surface itself should be nonslip and wide enough to stand on or cross comfortably; this may mean adding handrails made of lumber, rustic poles or stout rope, depending on style and preference. Another feature that is both practical and decorative is lighting – either spotlights slung beneath the bridge or, for a party atmosphere, lanterns strung above its length (see p. 164) ☐

△ Stout lumber planks stained blue and arranged in pairs make an interesting zig-zag bridge across a wide stretch of water. The change of direction gives a pause for concentration and affords a platform to view water plants.

▷ A slightly arched lumber bridge is softened by strong water-edge planting of Iris and Ligularia and has been provided with stout rope handrails which echo its curved design and prove that safety features can also be decorative.

▽ Across an informal stream a bridge may be as simple as a couple of well-weathered planks laid together to form a comfortably wide walkway. Here they link a small brick patio to a stone and lumber path.

▽ A large slab of stone or, as shown here, slate makes a useful simple bridge over a narrow stretch of water and can be matched to a path or stepping stones.

SCULPTURE

A PIECE OF SCULPTURE will add a special lift to the garden. It may be used to introduce a touch of excitement, as a device to startle you into looking carefully at your surroundings or it may simply be beautiful and ornamental. But because it adds so much to the overall atmosphere of the garden, any piece of sculpture needs choosing and positioning with care.

As a focal point, sculpture immediately catches the eye and the rest of the garden should be designed around it to maximize its impact. Do not think it needs necessarily to be stuck in the middle of a lawn, though, to be eye-catching; a fine piece often looks best at the end of a vista or in a corner of a patio, framed by trees or shrubs. Sculpture also makes a fine companion to a water feature; positioned by the side of a pool it will provide delightful reflections, while some pieces are designed to stand in the water, sometimes with water playing over them.

Types of sculpture

When choosing sculpture you need to take into account not only style but also its size and shape in relation to its planned position. You need to examine the piece to check it is well constructed and aesthetically pleasing in every way: do not be afraid to run your hands over it before buying to ensure that it feels as good as it looks. Also, it is vital to find out if the materials used are suitable for outdoors. New techniques have extended the scope of metal and lumber for use outside, and some stones are less inclined to crack than others when subjected to extremes of temperature.

Style is mostly a matter of taste. Abstract pieces look particularly good where their shapes and forms echo the structural nature of surrounding plants. The figurative element is still strong in modern sculpture, using the human form or animals as models, and it offers you the chance to make witty arrangements around the garden, such as a family of stone piglets rooting in a corner of the patio.

Final choice of course will be purely a matter of preference, but it can be difficult to decide whether a piece will be exactly right. Some suppliers or galleries will allow you to take a piece home for a few days on approval.

You will find that most pieces benefit from a backdrop of foliage, such as a tall shrub, a climbing plant smothering a trellis or plants with strong architectural features like large leaves or bold stems; others, quite naturally, are perfect for a watery setting. Where necessary, the base should be cut into the soil and disguised with grass or ground-cover plants. You can also derive great pleasure from the juxtaposition of certain plants and sculptures – a girl with a beautiful flowering azalea behind her perhaps, or a long-legged bird poised among stately flowering grasses.

Remember to choose to suit yourself. A good piece of sculpture can be an excellent investment but it is for you to live with and to enjoy □

▽ Surrounding plants will help provide a natural setting for your sculpture, like this girl by Glyn Williams who reclines among ferns and ground-cover plants. Care should be taken to prevent plants growing too vigorously and completely hiding the piece: they should frame it not smother it. This particular sculpture has been balanced on natural rock to raise it into its correct position.

◁ It is important that you position any sculpture thoughtfully so that it appears to form an integral part of your garden design. These sheep by Dutch sculptress Ire Bollen Slolwyk seem to graze naturally in the long grass beneath a shady tree.

▷ Large pieces of sculpture need a good background to show them off, particularly if they are of a light-colored material. This life-sized horse by Brian Taylor grazes against the dark backdrop of shady trees and is a real eye-catcher in a large, informal country garden.

▽ Sculptures make fine unexpected features as well as dramatic focal points. This brooding bird by the sculptor Chris Drury will only be spotted by chance under its shady canopy of trees along a waterside, woodland walk. The base of the plinth is hidden by long grass and wild ground cover to 'naturalize' the piece.

GARDEN ORNAMENTS

AS CAN BE SEEN on the preceding pages, original pieces of sculpture will add an exciting, and often architectural, dimension to a well-thought-out garden design. But there is also a need for more modest garden ornaments, which, although not unique or quite as stunning as a work of art, do have a role to play in injecting interest into a dull corner, for example, or may even become an attractive, eye-catching centerpiece. Garden ornaments are perfect for softening the appearance of paving, decks or pool edges and they combine well with freestanding tubs of plants.

Following the theme of using more natural features that blend well with their surroundings, those ornaments that look most in keeping are often mellow and well-weathered.

Types of ornament

Sundials are enjoying a revival of interest, both traditional stone types and more contemporary designs made of metal and Plexiglas. These can look superb set in the middle of a lawn or in a herb garden and suggest a more relaxed attitude to life. Similarly, ornamental or rustic-style birdbaths and feeders make a fine centerpiece; on a deck or patio, an arrangement of elegant urns or jars may be enjoyed simply for their shape and size.

These can range in size from one of huge dimensions made of rough terra-cotta to a collection of much smaller, finely crafted pieces grouped together for maximum impact. Bowls, Chinese ginger jars and amphora are all good, decorative materials – even cracked or damaged pieces can look good where you want a rough, weathered arrangement.

Other, more traditional, garden ornaments that can be used effectively, if sparingly, to create a specific mood or a surprise feature in the garden include a wide range of reproduction pieces (mainly made of reconstituted stone) and genuine antiques. Statuary, decorated urns, pillars, balustrading for steps and terraces and even ornate carved gateways and entrances can, with care, be incorporated.

Less expensive but often more exciting and unexpected are 'found' ornaments for the garden. These are objects you may find and enjoy for their unusual shape or texture: twisted driftwood, river-worn pebbles or even a chunk of rough, weathered stone.

As with any garden feature, you need to exercise a degree of caution here, since there is always the danger of overdoing the effect. This is particularly true of oriental accessories, such as bowls, mini temples and garden Buddhas, all of which can look perfect used sparingly in the right setting □

△ *The classic formal garden makes good use of decorative features, both inanimate and ornate plant forms. This tranquil green and white design using statuary and foliage plants is offset by the blacks and grays of paving and furniture. Between the tall, sheared hedges and a dense background of trees are twisty-stemmed standard trees, sheared box, domes and spirals and decorative urns. By blending stone, terra-cotta and leafy ornamental forms, exactly the right visual balance is achieved – an important consideration in a small garden. Here, clever screens of hedging and topiary have created an interesting area of light and shade that makes the garden appear much larger than it is.*

△ *Keep your eyes open for amusing or unusual garden ornaments which may be positioned on steps, tables or plinths to add life and interest to your design. These terra-cotta ducks make a striking center piece on a weathered lumber table beneath the shade of a freeflowering Impatiens.*

◁ A delightful garden ornament may provide the starting point for a planting plan. This
ornamental stone duck has been
half swallowed up by green and
gray foliage, using the soft wooly
leaves of Senecio cineraria and
Stachys lanata, and silver spiky
Lavandula contrasted with the
greens of Pittosporum tenuifolium
and Nepeta. Note how the plants
have been arranged in blocks of col-
or within which the stone ornaments form the center piece. By
softening them with the curling tiny-
leaved Nepeta, they make an integral part of the design and brighten
up the corner of the patio.

▽ Look out for unusual items
that can be combined with
plants and positioned to create a
focal point. On this sun-washed
patio an old birdcage makes interesting shadows against a bright,
white-painted wall. Left empty, its
wiry architectural form echoes the
decorative metalwork of its supporting table, linked by pots of
grassy Ophiopogon japonicum.

151

FINISHING TOUCHES

JUST LIKE INTERIOR decoration, garden design relies on those little personal touches and accessories to add originality and bring life to the basic structure and framework. Success at this stage is dependent on the patient and imaginative collation of seemingly random objects and effects: a colored wood stain, a collection of large pebbles or a stone trough or antique faucet converted into a small water feature.

You will find many of these elements in the photographs of gardens on the previous pages, and they represent the features that make those gardens unique and particularly appealing. It is not a good idea, however, to attempt to copy them slavishly – transplanting an idea exactly into a different garden is rarely successful unless it is properly adapted to its new setting.

There is also a talent in using and arranging materials in unexpected and pleasing ways: combining different pots, tubs and hanging baskets on a deck, patio or terrace; designing and building your own tables or seating around a large, well-established tree; or even the type of screening or soft furnishings, such as mats and cushions, that can be taken outside in fine weather as they are required.

Choosing and using containers

Container gardening (see p. 110 for planting and design details) relies as much on a good choice of tubs and pots as it does on the variety of plants you put in them. Generally, you should try to achieve a range of heights and sizes and a variety of materials and styles, too.

Arranging containers is mostly a matter of common sense and an instinct for basic design principles. Naturally, taller containers need to go toward the rear and white tubs show up better against a brick wall than do terra-cotta and so on. Groups of three always seem to make a pleasing arrangement based on a triangular shape.

In the normal course of your travels, keep your eyes open for any materials or objects that can be used profitably and attractively in the garden. An old marble-topped table, for example, a wrought-iron sewing machine stand or a washstand would make a perfect, sturdy table for al fresco meals (see p. 166) or collections of summer annuals or potted herbs □

▷ *This corner of a large patio has been well furnished with tubs, baskets, bowls and plants to provide an interesting arrangement around the elegant lounger.*

▽ *A decorator's eye has been at work in this small patio where a delightful wrought-iron, marble-topped table is the center piece for a pair of bay trees and an ornate trough, planted with Agave attenuata. The rough wall, painted a strong terra-cotta color, echoes the warm tones of the tiles and trough.*

POTS & CONTAINERS

The choice of containers available is vast, ranging from secondhand half-barrels, oriental jars, old stone sinks, ornamental chimney pots, an old wheelbarrow or even a large fisherman's basket lined with plastic.

Hanging containers also offer you the chance to exercise your creative instincts. Imagine how attractive scores of ordinary terra-cotta flower pots could look fastened with wires to a wall or trellis; bracketed baskets hung not just from walls but also from the trunks of large trees or a pergola; or terraces of pots on graduated shelves.

▽ *The unexpected can be a real eye-catcher. A tin bathtub has been painted brilliant blue and suspended from stout chains to provide plenty of planting space for a yellow and purple design of Lobelia, Tagetes and Crepis.*

△ *Cut flowers have their place in the garden too. Bright orange Gladiolus make a wonderful contrast with the deep blue of the swimming pool, their container concealed by an unusual and highly attractive pedestal basket.*

◁ *Oriental pots are a good foil for foliage plants, as this glossy green Alpinia purpurata proves in its black and gold container. You should be aiming at similarly harmonious plant and pot combinations.*

◁ *Pots and containers always look good arranged in groups of three. These handsomely decorated terra-cotta pots are fine companions for an exotic Cordyline australis 'Albertii' and leafy Griselinia lucida.*

LIVING IN STYLE

Increasingly, the garden is being viewed as an extension of the home, a pleasant environment in which to relax, exercise, eat and entertain. Such functional areas need to be carefully integrated with the more visual, planted aspects of the garden.

Yet leisure features must not only look good and blend with their surroundings, they must operate efficiently, too. Pools and hot tubs require sophisticated heating and filtration services; seating must be sturdy and comfortable; barbecues need to be unobtrusive when not in use but capable of coping with your outdoor cooking requirements. Luckily, the choice of styles is wide and there are ways of disguising and integrating more functional features.

Safety and comfort are also important considerations here, with adequate facilities for water and electricity supplies, good dry access from the house and some form of lighting for after dark use. Such features are never cheap so you should take care to plan them properly, ensuring that they will satisfy your needs for many years into the future.

SUMMERHOUSES & GAZEBOS

A SUMMERHOUSE or gazebo may seem like something of an extravagance – yet another place where you can sit and enjoy the garden. But the garden often needs such a structure, which, although undoubtedly decorative, can also be very practical as well.

In a large country garden, it makes sense to have a place to rest or shelter at the farthest limits of your site; while in a small garden, an attractive structure makes a fine focal point.

Creating a style

A summerhouse is usually constructed like a miniature house with a roof and windows. Styles vary considerably and one should be chosen to suit the space and setting allotted to it: a rustic log cabin perhaps, in a natural woodland garden; an ornamental pavilion in a formal garden; or a Chinese-style pagoda striking an oriental note. Depending on position, summerhouses may also be circular or octagonal with all-round vision or built on the lines of a chalet with a veranda and double doors.

The majority of summerhouses are made of lumber, giving them a softer, more natural appearance that blends well with a background of trees or densely planted shrubs. However, brick and stone can also be used.

Whether circular or square, with a plain or ornately pointed roof, a gazebo forms an enclosed and partially sheltered place where you can sit surrounded by flowers and foliage. They are generally made of metal with a natural or colored, painted finish, and some models are collapsible for storage.

Room with a view

A summerhouse or gazebo needs to be sited where it can enjoy a particularly fine or an unexpected view of the garden, perhaps adjacent to a feature such as pool or stream. You should also consider if the structure can be put to some secondary use: close to a swimming pool and fitted with cupboards, a refrigerator and a shower, a summerhouse makes an excellent changing room. Alternatively, with a desk and telephone point installed, you have a delightful summer office, while a dining table and chairs, lighting, books and toys suggest a charming garden dining area, cocktail bar, playroom or study □

△ The gazebo is not always a freestanding focal point in the garden. Here it has been smothered in ivy and clematis and linked to a pergola, where climbing plants can be encouraged to spread. Its stout stone columns and quirky tile roof make an interesting corner feature set against a dense background of trees, and it provides a shady place to sit when the sun is at its height.

◁ *The size and style of a summerhouse is restricted only by your imagination. A strong architectural structure has been built high above a white painted wall complex. With its mock classical columns, ornamental trellis and circular windows, it has a light, airy feel even in full sun. Inside, the cool effect is reinforced with a black and white tiled floor and green foliage plants that echo the mass of greenery to be seen through the open structure of the building. Painted white and pastel blue, and framed by conifers, it makes a stunning focal point as well as a pleasant place to sit.*

BALCONIES & VERANDAS

Balconies represent gardening at its most minimal: usually little more than a few square yards of suspended floor space but, potentially, a miniature landscape and certainly a most pleasant place to sit and enjoy the sunshine. Because balconies are small, they are best treated as an outdoor extension of an upstairs room – a bedroom or apartment living room, for example – with large glass doors that can be either hinged or sliding to allow the whole area to be opened up, yet still giving a view of the plants in bad weather.

Gardening on high

You could consider a balcony to be your summer breakfast room, a private retreat or, in an apartment, it may be the only piece of garden you have access to. While the elevated view is pleasant, balconies suffer the same problems as roof gardens (see p. 78), in that they are usually very exposed, catching the worst of any winds.

Screens, using permanent bamboo, lumber, glass or trellis, or tall plants grown in containers, retractable awnings or even toughened Plexiglas, will not only provide you with some very important shelter and privacy but will often create a real sun trap, perfect for relaxing in or using for ripening off miniature fruit and vegetable varieties.

Again, as with roof gardens, you must ensure that your balcony is strong enough to support your weight plus that of soil, plants with their containers and possibly furniture, too. Despite the fact that you will be obliged to use container-grown plants, you still have the option of growing small trees, shrubs, flowering and fruiting climbers, as well as your favorite herbs and flower and foliage plants.

When planning the planting of your balcony, it is important to bear in mind that it is essentially an external decorative feature attached to the building and that it must look effective from a distance as well as from indoors. Trailing and climbing plants can be particularly useful here, trained to disguise and soften the outline of the structure and to smother an otherwise dull expanse of wall. Another small but important point to remember is that you should provide all your plants and plant containers with deep saucers or trays – any spillage of water will not only be unpleasant for anybody walking beneath, it will also, if mixed with soil, cause unattractive and disfiguring stains on walls. A good, deep saucer will also ensure that plants have sufficient water to see them through the day in hot weather.

Ground-level verandas

A veranda or terrace is usually restricted to ground level, and consists of a covered or roofed area running the length of the house. A veranda is not simply a useful physical and visual link between the house and garden, it is an important practical feature especially in hot climates, or where the building faces the sun, giving a permanently shady area to sit.

The primary function of verandas, though, is to provide a comfortable view of the garden and, perhaps, of the landscape beyond. For this reason they tend to be slightly raised with a lumber, paved or tiled floor and steps leading down to the main garden area. Pillars or other supports along the length of the structure, sometimes paneled or screened to waist level, reinforce the impression that the veranda is an open window.

In general, verandas are not particularly wide, so your planting plan will need to be restricted to a few well-chosen containers of plants standing toward the front to catch maximum sun and light and, if space permits, container-grown climbers clothing the uprights and back walls. Because it is under cover and close to the house, you can supplement a table and chairs with built-in bench seating □

△ A balcony should be both functional and decorative, providing the maximum planting in the minimum of space. This stout lumber framework is not only a useful safety feature, it makes an attractive addition to the house entwined with flowering climbers and hung with baskets of plants.

▷ The veranda provides a shady place from which to view the garden, framed between its columns or supports. Interesting plants in containers provide a visual link between veranda and garden, and make a decorative feature on a paved or lumber surface.

▽ Even a highly ornamental framework benefits from the softening effects of creeping and climbing plants. Here, grapevines and honeysuckle scramble over an elegant wrought-iron balcony.

SEATING & FURNITURE

A S THE GARDEN and, in particular, the patio continue to develop into sophisticated outdoor living areas, they have begun to demand the same type of consideration when it comes to furnishings previously afforded to the dining or drawing rooms. While a picnic bench or inexpensive folding chair was fine for quick family lunches, full-scale entertaining, dinner parties and the like require something more comfortable to keep the guests in their seats. There is also, of course, a whole range of unashamedly luxurious lounging furniture ideal for soaking up the sunshine whether on a deck, lawn or beside a pool.

Built-in furniture

The increased availability of modular building materials, such as slabs, tiles and bricks, and a more creative attitude toward the use of pre-

served lumber out of doors, has encouraged the growth of built-in garden furniture. Seating, tables and other features are now commonly integrated into a wall or patio, or linked to a pool or planting areas. Like its indoor counterparts, this type of furniture is an excellent space saver in the small garden as well as being a useful device in a larger one, creating more formal, enclosed spaces. Stone or brick seating around a formal, raised pool provides a delightful opportunity to observe fish and plants close to, as well as giving you somewhere to relax and enjoy the sun.

On the patio, seats, tables and barbecue facilities can be designed and linked to create a complete outdoor-living complex, while lumber decks are flexible enough to allow matching wooden planters, seats and tables to be incorporated in the design, and even cupboards for storing barbecue equipment,

▽ *Furniture can be used to provide points of color within your garden design in the same way as flowers and foliage. These simple bandstand chairs have been given a couple of coats of glossy blue paint and positioned within a blue, yellow and mauve planting plan, including Verbascum and Epilobium. A neatly sheared hedge runs along the back of the border and curves around the seating area to provide a dark green background for flowers and furniture. The highlight of the seating enclosure is a fine hexagonal marble-topped table, and proves that table and chairs don't have to match to look good.*

▷ *Colored furniture can be used to make interesting contrasts on the patio or within the general garden design. Framed by the foliage of trees, shrubs, climbers and ground cover, deep red tables and chairs provide the only point of color among the lush planting. The dappled light of surrounding trees is echoed in the slatted construction of the chairs.*

▽ *Lightweight furnishings and a single color scheme are perfect for giving small roof and balcony gardens a spacious feel. Smart gray and white metal patio furniture echoes the wrought ironwork along the front of this city balcony. Predominantly green and white planting emphasizes the sophisticated effect, with a plain white awning above providing shade and shelter. Polygonum baldschuanicum has been trained to grow along all the vertical supports, while massed tubs contain white-flowering plants such as Impatiens, lilies and standard roses.*

cushions, tools and toys. Another advantage you find with lumber is that you can use it to build furniture around existing features – seating around a tree stump, for example, shelving around a tree for displaying plants or a table built into an awkward corner.

For occasional seating that blends perfectly with its surroundings, you can do no better than grow a living cushion of moss or low-growing herbs. The shape can be cut into a mossy bank with the soil-based seat supported on brick, stone or lumber. Low-growing thymes or chamomile are particularly appropriate, releasing a sweet scent when they are sat on.

Freestanding furniture

Freestanding furniture needs planning and positioning with care. On the practical side, it has to be comfortable to use and have a firm surface to stand on in the case of dining furniture, or a sunny stretch of lawn, deck or paving for loungers. Unless you are buying

These dramatic loungers are more comfortable than they look and make an interesting feature for a small, sunny, grassed area
surrounded by borders. Designer furniture like this
is worth looking out for if you want to make a bold
statement on your lawn or patio.

furniture as a set, always check that the chairs
are the right height for the table: nothing is
worse than having your knees wedged under
the tabletop or your nose only inches from
your plate.

Unless you are buying garden furniture that
can be left outdoors in all weathers (in which
case, be prepared to maintain it regularly),
storage is another important consideration.
Make sure that you have sufficient space in a
shed, summerhouse, garage or indoor cup-
board to provide cool, dry storage during
winter. For this reason, it is wise to investigate
stacking or folding chairs, and tables that
either fold up or can be quickly and easily
dismantled.

Maintenance

There is a wide range of traditional-style furniture available, much of which requires only
annual maintenance and can be left out year-
round. Hardwoods, such as mahogany and
teak, are attractive and weather resistant,
needing little maintenance. Softwoods, such
as pine, although equally attractive, have to be
treated with lumber preservative each year and
do not last anywhere near as long as the
hardwoods before deteriorating.

These days, the traditional 'cast-iron' tables
and chairs are more likely to be made of cast
aluminum, but any metal furniture simply
requires rubbing down and repainting whenever it starts to look weathered.

Furniture accessories

However good looking lumber, stone and
metal may be, they do not make comfortable
surfaces for sitting on for prolonged periods.
The answer here is a set of cushions, which
can, if chosen with care, make an eye-catching
addition, but will almost certainly have to be
brought inside at night or during rain showers.
Large cushions make comfortable seats in
themselves, thrown on a lawn or deck in fine

weather, for sitting or lounging. Fabrics will
need to be chosen with care to suit the style of
your garden, anything from stripes and traditional florals to distinctive oriental designs.

Ready upholstered furniture tends to
have molded plastic, or sometimes lumber,
frames, and is available in a wide range of
styles. Much of it is extremely luxurious, encompassing loungers, chairs and recliners
with matching tables, umbrellas, stools and
even drinks carts, which are convenient for
pool-side patios.

All furniture benefits from being positioned
in a well-sheltered spot, screened by banks,
hedges, walls or other types of screen (see p.
132). Tubs of plants and climbers on trellis or a
pergola will also provide shelter □

BENCHES

The garden bench, permanently sited where it can enjoy a good view of the garden, or at an obvious resting place, serves a very different function from most other garden furniture. It is primarily designed for resting on and enjoying the last warmth of the sun before sunset, for taking a short break from digging and weeding or for an early morning read of the newspaper before the bustle of the day starts in earnest. It is as much a part of the garden as the plants, which is why it is invariably positioned framed by shrubs or other foliage plants.

A bench can be as basic as a simple log slung between two tree stumps, or even a stone slab supported on brick pillars. More usual, though, is the traditional form of stout lumber seat with a backrest and arms, either sternly plain or delightfully decorative. Both styles can make a splendid focal point at the end of a long walk.

△ The garden bench can be as simple as a slab of stone or lumber beside a narrow path and half hidden by ground cover and a vigorous trailing plant such as this Fuchsia. The base of this one has been supported on blocks and the backrest slightly tilted to provide comfortable seating at the right height.

◁ There is no reason why furniture shouldn't strike a whimsical note within the formal garden. These 'art deco' benches have been positioned at the end of a large lawn against a dark green backdrop of trees and shrubs.

▽ The traditional bench is positioned within an alcove or bower, which is easily created by placing foliage-covered trellis behind and tubs of flowering Petunias on plinths on either side.

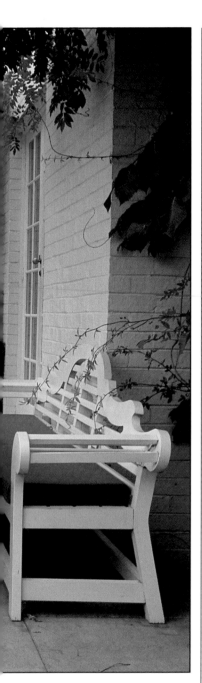

△ It's worth seeking out exactly the right style and type of furniture for your patio or veranda. The effect of an elaborate, white-painted wooden table and benches is the perfect match for the overhead structure which shades them. Fabric-covered cushions make seats more comfortable and can be brought inside at the end of the day.

◁ Lumber lends itself to a variety of effects for your patio furniture. The old-fashioned lounger chair is an attractive piece in its own right. Stained a soft blue, it looks stunning on a patio of pastel pink tiles and glazed pots.

LIGHTING

WITHOUT A comprehensive and well-thought-out system of outdoor lighting, you simply will not be getting the best from your garden. Quite apart from the fact that lighting will extend the garden's use after nightfall, allowing you to sit and enjoy a warm summer's evening or to dine outdoors, you can use lights to accentuate certain features to be enjoyed all year round.

Two important features – safety and balance – recommend that lighting is not treated as an afterthought. If carefully planned and installed at the early stages, you can ensure that you have a safe and sufficient supply for your needs and that the overall effect is attractive, subtle and well balanced.

Effective garden lighting

Successful garden lighting relies not on overall floodlighting but on a combination of smaller lit areas, which can be individually controlled to create a variety of localized effects or, used together, to light the whole garden. Preplanning will also help you to integrate lighting fittings so that they do not intrude.

The different types of outdoor light suggest a variety of uses: spotlights for highlighting trees, fountains, sculptures and other special features; lamps for paths and bridges; and underground well lights for general uplighting. The patio will benefit from bulkhead lamps fitted to walls, overhead lanterns hung from a pergola or ground-level spiked spotlights in surround-ing planting beds. Parties demand something special, and you may like to add candles, outdoor fairy lights or bamboo flares to your lighting plan.

A path is best lit in a soft, indirect fashion, with patches of illumination along its course, rather than as a hard passage spotlit from above. Freestanding downlighters will form soft pools of light or you can illuminate the occasional plant for the same effect. Bridges can be safely lit with lamps fastened beneath the structure or with lanterns strung overhead.

Designing with light

Apart from the strictly utilitarian aspects of garden lighting, some really stunning effects are possible. Plants, for example, will take on a completely different character at night, with spotlights emphasizing their size and shape dramatically. Directional spotlighting will accentuate shape and throw intriguing shadows onto nearby walls or fences, while downlighting through branches and leaves will create a dappled effect.

Water features really come alive when lit at night. A fountain or waterfall is best lit from below, as is a pond or other stretch of still water – nothing is worse than shining a glaring light directly onto the water's surface.

With all these effects, you need to exercise caution if you are considering colored lights. Reds and oranges are best avoided, but blues and greens can be used to light flowers, foliage and water successfully □

◁ *Sculpture and water are two of the best garden features to highlight at night to create eye-catching effects. Here, the two have been combined with a pair of leaping dolphins above a large, formal pool.*

▷ **Inset** *Trees look particularly effective when lit from below, silhouetting the branches and foliage against the night sky. Light fittings should be disguised whenever possible; here, a spotlight is concealed in long grasses. Colored lights need to be used with caution but a partial green filter has brought out the greenness of the leaves without losing the outlines of the branches.*

▷ *In the ideal garden lighting design, lights are positioned at various points around the garden or patio to achieve a subtle atmosphere rather than a single overall glare. Uplighters have been hidden inside plants and downlighters used to spotlight a seating area on this large patio. Spiked flowers and an ambitiously lit awning contribute to the total effect.*

EATING AL FRESCO

W HEN THE WEATHER is warm and the garden is looking good, the last thing you will want is to be indoors, particularly at meal times. One of the pleasures of owning a garden, or even a very small yard patio or balcony big enough for a table and a few chairs, is being able to enjoy breakfast in the freshness of early morning, a sunny lunch under the shade of a large umbrella or a dinner party as the sun sets on a balmy evening. Comfort is important, so as well as being sunny, your chosen area will also need some form of protection from intense sun, winds and light showers.

The outdoor kitchen

If the patio or terrace is your outdoor dining room, then the barbecue is your al fresco kitchen. There is really no need to go inside to a hot stove when a barbecue can cope with nearly every occasion, from an impromptu informal lunch to a full-blown dinner party with all the trimmings. Without doubt, food tastes better outdoors and it certainly tastes different when cooked on a garden grill or barbecue – acquiring that distinctive smoky flavor as the fat sizzles on glowing charcoal or, in the case of artificially fueled barbecues, natural lava rocks.

Barbecuing is a wonderfully informal style of cooking that has, nevertheless, developed into quite a cuisine. It is no longer just a fun way to cook sausages or steaks for those with scouting tendencies, but the perfect method of grilling kebabs, chicken, chops and fish, as well as foil-wrapped vegetables and fruits.

The ideal accompaniments to these types of food are different sorts of bread, dips and salads, which all suit the new, healthy lifestyle that recommends good, simple food and fresh ingredients cooked quickly and with the minimum loss of nutritional content. As a bonus, this style of cooking has generated the invention of all manner of delicious sauces and marinades using new herb combinations.

Freestanding barbecues

If your barbecuing is to be a success, it is important to choose the right type of barbecue for your needs. First and foremost, it should be large enough to cope with the amount of food you are likely to want to prepare. Struggling to feed ten people on a grill designed for two is no fun and you probably will not even bother to use it very often.

There is a barbecue to suit any size and situation, from a tiny hibachi, which you just stand on the patio or raise off the ground on a bench, to huge, freestanding, catering-sized models with stands, wheels, double grills, shelves and even a built-in wine rack. You must make sure you have sufficient space to use your barbecue safely and to store it away afterward. This factor may influence your choice, since many are attractive enough not to look out of place permanently on view in the corner of the patio.

Built-in barbecues

For a really integrated look, you may prefer to build in your barbecue, slotting the grid into a stone-, brick- and lumber-built structure, designed to blend with its immediate surroundings. This is the perfect opportunity to create an outdoor cooking complex, complete with integrated shelves, cupboards and tiled work surfaces for food preparation. You might also like to consider a built-in chimney to cope with the smoke.

Generally, position will be dictated by proximity to a convenient seating area, since food needs to be served as soon as it is cooked, and it also helps if you can keep an eye on the grill from the table. Shelter from prevailing winds should also affect the siting, both for your own comfort and the efficient operation of your barbecue.

Powered barbecues

The type of barbecue you choose may also influence its position. Traditionally fueled charcoal barbecues can be located where you please, although it is a good idea to provide a covered fuel store nearby. There is, however, an increasing number of powered barbecues available that save a lot of time and effort yet still produce food with a good flavor.

Gas- and electric-powered barbecues operate by heating natural lava rocks to produce that familiar smoky flavor. Where the charcoal grill requires arranging, refueling, lighting and then waiting for the charcoal to reach the correct temperature, the gas or electric barbecué lights at the touch of a button and needs only approximately 5 to 15 minutes before you can start cooking.

This is, of course, a more expensive method of outdoor cooking and, for electric models you will have to have access to a heavy-duty extension lead. Gas models necessitate maneuvering and storing heavy gas cylinders □

◁ *What could be more delightful than to enjoy a meal under the shade of a large tree and surrounded by a screen of attractive plants? The larger the table, the better, for remember, fresh air gives people big appetites whether it be for a barbecue, a cocktail or a relaxing glass of wine. A cloth and fine china will quickly turn the occasion into a celebration.*

▽ *A gas- or electric-powered barbecue is quicker and cleaner to use. This one has been cleverly connected unobtrusively for gas, avoiding the need for a bulky cylinder on the patio. It also helps if you can disguise your barbecue with tubs and containers of bright annuals and glossy evergreens.*

SWIMMING POOLS

SO MANY PEOPLE would love to have their own swimming pool in the garden yet do nothing about it, either suspecting that their site is too small or fearing that it would ruin the overall garden design. There is no denying that a swimming pool is large and intrusive and therefore not easy to landscape successfully, but with a little careful thought it can be done.

Siting and design

Before you start planning the shape, style and color of your swimming pool, its position will be dictated by certain practical considerations. You require access to electricity and drainage, for example, and you also require some type of weatherproof housing for a pump and filtration system. Shelter is essential, not just for privacy but to protect you from prevailing winds and, if the pool is not sited near the house, facilities for changing and showering, too. For many gardens, a summerhouse is the answer, or you may be able to enclose the whole area within a poolhouse.

Both for convenience and for safety, though, a swimming pool is best sited close to the house, where any children or pets can be supervised – even so you should consider some type of enclosure (a wall or fence) with a lockable gate.

Basically, the pool can be any shape and size within the limits of space and budget, although too elaborate a design will be expensive to construct. Keep shapes open and simple: circles, ovals and rectangles work best, or a combination of different geometric shapes. Often, the hard lines of a pool can be softened by incorporating a small splash pool.

Unless the pool is to be enclosed within its own area in a large site, you will have to experiment with shapes and sizes within the confines of your existing garden. As with an ornamental pool or pond (see pp. 88 and 140), refine the shape using string or a length of

△ *A spectacular view of Sydney harbor was too good to miss when this indoor swimming pool was designed. The pool water apparently flows straight toward the harbor, disappearing* into a small trough concealed beside the great picture windows. The overall impression is that sky, sea and pool are one, as the designer intended.

△ Swimming pools can incorporate decorative features such as falls and fountains providing they do not allow plant matter to pollute the water. A cascade links a large formal swimming pool to a wide, raised ledge, complete with a statue and tubs of plants.

◁ The swimming pool lends itself to formal or informal designs to suit its location. This informal, lagoon-style pool creates curved contours, naturalized by an island bed of dense evergreens, rocks and cooling fountain sprays that play over the surface of the water.

▽ In this geometrical pool in a small patio garden, plants are restricted to containers and a stone lion stands sentinel on the paving slabs, which take their lead from the structure of the house.

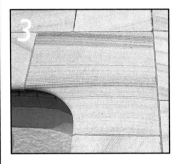

1 *The vivid blue ceramic tiles that line this pool, and the rough russet-blue of its surrounding brick, provide interesting contrasts of color and texture.*

2 *Three materials have been successfully blended together: a curving Belgian block edge links the blue mosaic to an informal stone-paved patio area.*

3 *For a much sleeker effect, sandstone slabs have been used to edge a plain blue pool with attractive rounded corners.*

△ *A natural lagoon shape can be adapted for an indoor pool. This one has been surrounded by irregular stone slabs and raised beds of exotic palms and ferns to encourage a tropical atmosphere. Hanging baskets of plants from the rafters of the pool house add interest overhead and the building is subtly lit for night-time use. Lighting is an important feature of any pool, indoors or out, to maximize its use.*

hose, and view the effect from every possible angle, including any upstairs windows.

In a small garden, where a swimming pool may be taking up most of the available space, an informal, lagoon-style pool may be your best option. Here, irregular, but not too exaggerated, curves can be surrounded by a backdrop of rocks and plants contained by retaining walls or raised beds. For more formal shapes, you will find that ovals are successful in rectangular plots and circles looks good in square ones. Squares and rectangles look best if sited asymmetrically within the garden so that they are viewed obliquely, avoiding the impression of an expanse of water.

Disguising the pool

Careful planning and design are required to integrate a pool successfully into a garden. This may involve screening with trees, walls, hedges or fences, landscaping the surrounding garden or making a natural feature of the pool itself.

The color of the pool lining will make a big difference to the way it blends in: turquoise and sea green, for example, will shine brilliantly in sunlight, and while this may be appropriate for a Mediterranean- or subtropical-style garden, it will often appear out of place in a more temperate environment.

Often, the soil excavated during construction can be redeployed to landscape the surrounding areas. Care is needed here to make sure that relief areas follow the natural contours of the land.

A screen will help to disguise a pool, or even hide it totally from view. Walls are expensive to build but they provide excellent shelter, and it may be possible to utilize an existing walled area of the garden. Trellis, bamboo screens and fences should be planned in conjunction with tall or climbing plants to soften any hard outlines. Alternatively, use evergreen foliage or tall hedges.

Planting around swimming pools needs careful thought, since the water must be free of dead leaves and other vegetable matter. Also, plants too close to the water's edge could be killed by the chemicals used to sterilize the water. Apart from a background of evergreen trees and shrubs, plants can be contained in raised beds or in pots and tubs round the pool margins – providing you with an ideal opportunity to brighten up what can become a rather cold and clinical area.

The immediate pool surroundings must be of a nonslip material that is easy to clean and durable. Again, take your lead from nearby surfaces and features, using brick, stone, lumber or ceramic tiles as appropriate □

◁ A swimming pool can be perfectly integrated into the natural landscape, as this one proves. It resembles a forest pool, edged with great boulders and a pebble beach, and incorporating a small waterfall. The dense screen of surrounding plants makes useful shelter.

▷ The swimming pool should be designed to meet your needs as well as match its location. This rocky lagoon-style pool was designed and constructed for disabled users and the water is reached by means of a ramp which spirals through shallow water to the deep end.

HOT TUBS

As an invigorating bath in which the body is massaged by high-powered jets or bubbling water, a hot tub is an ideal place to idle away a pleasant hour or two or to relax in after the tensions and pressures of the day. Hot tubs are usually made from hardy redwood, cedar or any similar lumber resistant to moisture and to splintering. A circular design with straight sides is the most popular, fitting well into a rectangular or curved patio area and looking equally good whether sunken or slightly raised. Other shapes, such as squares, rectangles and even hexagonals, are available if these would suit your space better.

Inside a hot tub are seats, which bring the hot water comfortably up to chin level. To circulate the hot water and to keep it scrupulously clean, a system of pumps, filters and heaters is employed, and the water is either blown or bubbled out through jets in the side.

Because you naturally want it handy for use, a tub is usually sited on the patio or decked area adjacent to the house, or installed in conjunction with a swimming pool. But there is no reason why a tub should not be sited in any well-sheltered and private area of the garden.

Spas

Although working on the same principles as hot tubs, spas are made of fiber glass and are, therefore, considerably cheaper to buy. Because of their construction, though, they do require more careful disguising, but once sunk into a patio or terrace or hidden by a raised platform and surrounded by plants, they can look every bit as inviting. Again because of their construction, spa shapes tend to be less geometric, which can make them easier to integrate into the garden.

Siting considerations for a spa are exactly the same as for a hot tub – convenient access to an electrical supply and a private, sheltered location where you can enjoy the water in comfort without being overlooked. To this end, consider some form of lumber or bamboo screen, or a pergola (see p. 136) fitted with awnings. Or for a more natural effect, use a living wall of large foliage plants, hedging bushes in containers or raised planting beds.

Surroundings for hot tubs and spas should be chosen to match nearby surfaces, but lumber looks particularly good, especially with a tub where it can be built at different levels and adapted to include extra seating, storage and planting spaces. Other materials such as brick and tiles can be used, but the prime requirements are that they can be comfortable to walk on and nonslip □

△ Integrated into the main design of a swimming pool complex, a hot tub or spa makes a striking as well as an enjoyable feature. A circular spa breaks up the shape of the rectangular pool and has been surrounded by lumber decking to integrate it into the overall design.

◁ The hot tub is the perfect companion for lumber decking if it can be sunk into the decking itself or surrounded by tubs of green plants to soften its outlines. Screens and an overhead pergola shade the tub from wind and sun.

DESIGNING WITH PLANTS

No attempt has been made in this chapter to supply you with a
description and recommendation of individual plants: this will depend
on your own preferences and local availability. Instead, we have
given guidance on the use of individual plant types as design material
and advice on how to combine and contrast different plant shapes
and colors.

Availability of plants

It is advisable to check the local availability of plants before you set your heart on a
particular variety. Although most of the species mentioned in this book are readily
available in North America, some, especially in the aquatics section, may be difficult to
find; also, plants sometimes become temporarily in short supply owing to poor weather
conditions.

Asking at your local garden centers and nurseries will soon pinpoint which plants are
going to be difficult to find. A more widespread search among stockists countrywide is
relatively easy thanks to source books such as *Gardening by Mail: A Source Book* by
Barbara J. Benton (Tusker Press 1986). This will provide you with an extensive guide to
all the nurseries in the United States.

Alternatively, you could join a specialist or national horticultural society, such as the
American Horticultural Society, which organize regular plant sales, annual seed lists,
newsletters and bulletins for members.

TREES

TREES REPRESENT the backbone of your garden plan and for this reason they should be planned first. With the variety of shape, color and seasonal interest on offer, they make a vital contribution year-round and, as a series of woodland walks or attractive glades, you could design a complete minimal-maintenance garden of trees with shade-loving perennials and spring bulbs among grassy paths.

More often, though, trees form the starting point for a more varied planting, with individual species or groups of trees serving practical as well as decorative roles. Apart from the privacy they afford, they also give shade, which is particularly important in hot climates where a dense canopy may make a patio more comfortable. You can also create dappled shade using lighter foliaged trees.

As a decorative feature, trees are unsurpassed, offering interest in the form of shape and color in bark, branch, blossom, leaf and berry, often in the same specimen and certainly encompassing all the seasons. Those trees that are particularly 'garden worthy', in that they provide varied effects throughout the year, are useful for planting as specimens – placed where they make a focal point – and you need to ensure that the effect is not obscured by other trees or large features.

Shape and color

Consider the general shape of trees in your plan. They can be conical, round, weeping, flat topped or fastigiate (tall and thin). For more formal effects, you can shear trees into artificial shapes or, as with fruit trees, train them espalier-fashion against a wall or fence.

Color is an important aspect, not just for the glorious drifts of spring blossom of a Japanese cherry, crab apple or hawthorn, but also for the wonderful range of foliage color, from the breathtaking yellow of *Gleditsia triacanthos* 'Sunburst' or *Catalpa bignonioides* 'Aurea', the deep green large leaves of the Foxglove Tree (*Paulownia tomentosa*), lacy gray Cut Leaf Alder (*Alnus incana* 'Laciniata') or the fresh evergreen Strawberry Tree (*Arbutus un-*

△ A splendid Juglans regia shades a secret green garden enclosed by tall hedges. Its base has been smothered by ground cover in this predominantly green design, but the main planting is restricted to the edges of the area where plants will receive more sunshine.

◁ Trees grown in series rather than as single specimens produce a continuous canopy of foliage and make a charming overhead feature. These alders create a shady, leafy walk and echo the shape of informal and sheared hedging forms below. Remember that this dense effect will keep out a certain amount of rain and produce drier areas below.

▷ The country garden path between mixed herbaceous planting becomes an avenue when bordered by standard Acer pseudoplatanus 'Brilliantissimum'. The small stature of the trees and their lovely fresh foliage are in contrast to the larger backdrop of deeper green behind.

edo) to the exquisite autumn color of a Japanese maple or a yellow tint from the Paper Birch (*Betula papyrifera*).

Trees can offer so many delights: the long, elegant leaves of the willow, the extraordinary lime-green, fan-shaped foliage of a *Ginkgo biloba* and the spiky clusters of the blue cedar (*Cedrus atlantica* 'Glauca'); or the early summer flowers of *Laburnum* or Lilac are as good as any shrub. Magnolias are some of the most beautiful trees in the world and are available in great variety.

In winter there is the deep green of the evergreens contrasting with the skeletal forms of the deciduous trees and those with bright, red winter shoots, such as *Salix alba* 'Chermesina', the bright berries and the fascinating variety of bark colors and designs, like the peeling, orange Paperbark Maple *Acer griseum* and gray marbled *Parrotia persica* □

SHRUBS

SHRUBS PROVIDE the overall form and shape of the garden and create the framework against which all other features are planned. Within this role, they satisfy many other garden requirements by providing screens, acting as dividers, supplying permanent evergreen interest, seasonal variety, color, scent and shape, and most require little maintenance. Wonderful effects can be created by using shrubs that contrast in form, color, spread, habit and leaf structure. Use good design sense with your shape and color blending and you will produce a superb effect, providing you are careful not to overdo the final look with too many varieties planted too closely together.

Beware of combinations of shrubs that would not normally grow in the same habitat, since they will always look uncomfortable together: roses, for example, and rhododendrons. A tough mountain plant does not mix well with one more used to scrambling over a Mediterranean cliff top.

A basic framework of evergreen shrubs, such as *Fatsia japonica*, *Cotoneaster* and Rhododendrons, will hold the garden together and provide interest in autumn and winter, but do also consider a selection of deciduous varieties. These tend to be faster growing and produce some spectacular, if often short-lived, effects. Many of the popular flowering deciduous shrubs, such as *Magnolia*, *Forsythia*, *Daphne* and *Philadelphus*, have only a short period of flowering glory, so if you want better value, especially in a smaller garden, look for the more unusual cultivars that have good leaf variations, like variegated *Choisya*. Where shrubs are close to a patio or deck, you may wish to consider strongly scented varieties, such as *Mahonia*, *Philadelphus*, *Daphne* and *Choisya ternata*.

Many trees are suitable for growing as shrubs and are, indeed, often sold as such. Given time, they become large trees, but if sheared and trained they make excellent additions to a collection of shrubs. *Cornus alba* 'Sibirica', for example, produces red winter color and is best suited to large gardens where specimens can be grouped to accentuate the color advantage. The small Japanese maple (*Acer palmatum* 'Dissectum Atropurpureum') is also perfect for creating a small, tree-type feature, since it is extremely slow growing.

Other trees can be grown as half-standards – *Malus* 'Red Jade', *Catalpa bignonioides* 'Aurea' or *Eucalyptus gunnii* – and cut back to

△ Many shrubs will produce delightful flowers. One of the most valuable is the Hydrangea, *a genus of 80 deciduous and evergreen species.* Hydrangea paniculata *'Floribunda' (left) produces loose panicles of greenish white blooms among dense green leaves. The flat, lilac corymbs of* Hydrangea acuminata *'Bluebird' (inset) can be particularly beautiful.*

ROSES

Roses are clearly in a class of their own, and for many no garden would be complete without them. Not only do shrub roses produce a beautiful selection of flowers, many with delicious fragrances and breathtaking colors, some, like *Rosa rubrifolia*, *R. moyesii* and *R. rugosa*, have attractive foliage, too. Consider a hedge of *R. rugosa* 'Rubra', guaranteed to provide pleasure from early summer right through to autumn with its spicy scent and, later, bright oval hips, and you will appreciate what excellent value roses can be. There are other roses offering similar benefits: ramblers like *R. sempervirens*, a hardy evergreen, or the richly scented hybrid 'Stanwell Perpetual', producing an informal hedge of seemingly endless blooms.

△ *Climbing roses make excellent cover for garden walls or trained up the side of a building and will produce a mass of blooms in summer. To emphasize their effect, play down the color of surrounding plants, as has been done in this clever pink and green design.*

▷ *Shrub roses can be used to create many lovely different effects, like this semidouble form* Rosa *'New Dawn', whose simple white flowers look stunning against the glossy, dark green hedge. The single rose has a wilder, more natural appeal (far right) –* Rosa canina, *Dog rose, with a delicate pink flower with yellow centers offers the advantage of interesting foliage, too.*

△ The rose bower or arbor, usually a simple but decorative lumber or metal structure, offers the opportunity to design special features incorporating climbing roses. Use them to create walkways, archways or a thick hedge of flowers and foliage. This modern climber, Rosa complicata, makes a spectacular display.

▷ *A fully hardy shrub with attractive leaves and fine flowers is a valuable asset. Hydrangea arborescens produces bright green leaves and flat white flower heads, which bloom from mid to late summer. The flowers are often so heavy that they droop on their stems; they fade to a bronzy brown when they are finished. Providing varied and long-term interest, this makes a good shrub for small gardens.*

▽ **Bottom** *Consider the background of larger specimen shrubs to ensure you display them to best advantage. A white-painted and fairly ornate frontage brings out the best in this* Leptospermum scoparium, *which needs that brightness to set off its delicate pink flowers and light-colored foliage.*

▽ *Shrubs with variegated foliage can be used sparingly for special effects such as brightening a dark corner. This variegated* Choisya ternata *'Sundance' has been planted in a simple lumbered container to enliven a corner of this patio area.*

keep them small. Other effects include topiary where, like trees, shrubs are sheared into strong, sculptural forms.

Designing with such a variety of shrubs needs special care, since the end result will influence the look of your garden for many years. Shrubs tend to look best in loose arrangements of varied groups and random shapes, rather than in neat, regular, nursery-style beds. Larger, more rambling country gardens can swallow individual plants, so here shrubs should be used en masse, perhaps as many as five or seven plants in a group, to create a more visible effect. In smaller gardens and more intimate areas, you may wish to grow a particularly fine species as a special feature. In this case, take care to choose one that has some outstanding attributes, such as large leaves, bright flowers, scent or good foliage.

For an entirely different effect, some shrubs can be encouraged to scramble or climb into a trellis to provide a strong background for other plants, Japanese Quince (*Chaenomeles*), *Ceanothus* or *Hydrangea petiolaris* are all useful shrubs for this (see *Climbers*, p. 180).

You could easily design a whole garden based on shrubs, a blend of striking forms and color in foliage and flowers that would need little maintenance, apart from occasional pruning. If well planned, the result could be stunning and perfect for anybody who had little time to spend on maintenance. Taken a step further, some shrub families are so diverse it is almost possible to use them as an exclusive themes: *Cistus*, *Myrtus* and *Cotoneaster* would offer this type of scope.

Difficult conditions

Some shrubs also make superb subjects for container growing, which allows less hardy varieties to be moved indoors or overwintered in a cool greenhouse. Containers can be positioned on patios or on decks, by pools or close to planting beds as special features. *Viburnum*, *Daphne*, *Escallonia* and *Mahonia* all grow well in containers, as do the half-hardy *Olearia*, *Fuchsia* and the very beautiful flowering *Abelia grandiflora*. These plants can be brought out when in flower to give the garden, patio or deck additional points of interest or to brighten specific areas.

If chosen with care, many shrubs will perform well under difficult conditions, helping to maintain interest and to create an attractive garden environment where one might otherwise not be able to exist.

Coastal locations are often a problem because few plants will survive salt wind, while roof gardens and balconies also suffer from exposure, with little between them and the

worst of any breezes. Shrubs that can withstand strong, cold wind, and make effective barriers, include *Olearia*, *Cotoneaster*, *Pyracantha*, *Pittosporum*, *Hebe*, *Grevillea*, *Escallonia* and Myrtle. Similar problems are often experienced in cold, sunless sites and here *Aucuba*, *Fatsia japonica*, *Escallonia* and *Berberis* can be used to save the situation.

Hot, exposed areas bring different problems, with baking, dry conditions that spell almost instant death for many specimens. Here, you need to find plants that would survive these types of conditions in the wild: some examples include *Carpenteria*, *Ficus*, *Ceratostigma*, the Australian Bottlebrush (*Callistemon*), Rosemary and *Bougainvillea*, all of which would provide shade and shelter for other plants.

When purchasing shrubs, look for the occasional semimature specimen in a large pot. Three or four of these may be slightly expensive but they will add an immediate air of maturity and get the garden off to a good start. Make sure you give plants plenty of organic matter around the roots when planting and keep them well mulched and watered. You may need some type of irrigation system in hot, dry climates. If you are concerned about the appearance of the garden before the shrubs have matured a little, you can plant more than you need and then thin out, which is expensive, or use annuals or herbs to plug the gaps until the shrubs are larger □

△ In the woodland garden, Azaleas will produce spectacular early color and dramatic fresh green foliage against a background of more sober trees. Form and color vary tremendously, from large, dense, bush-forming shrubs to those with a lighter, spreading habit, with single and double blooms in reds, pinks, purples and oranges.

▽ Try to include a few scented varieties of shrubs close to the house or patio. Lavender is a traditional favorite and will attract bees and butterflies. *Lavandula spica*, shown here, will make a low hedge or clump of silver gray leaves and pale lilac flowers.

CLIMBERS

PERENNIAL CLIMBERS are an important element of good garden design, whether trained to smother a trellis, pergola, wall or fence as a screen, or used to provide vertical interest. Climbers are also useful for linking one foliage feature to another, for disguising features you would rather not see, and for quickly transforming your raw design into a garden.

Variegated and evergreen climbers are ideal for covering, screening and disguising, giving extra color and interest at every level year-round. Ivies are an obvious choice. They are vigorous growers and self-clinging but have mostly insignificant flowers. However, they come in a splendid choice of foliage from cream blotched *Hedera canariensis* 'Canary Cream' to yellow-edged *H. helix* 'Golden Jubilee' or *H. h.* 'Atropurpurea', which is purple in winter.

Grapevines are another group of popular woody climbers with a good range of foliage shapes and colors but, unlike the ivies, which are shade lovers, most grapevines prefer plenty of sunshine, and if given the right conditions some will bear fruit. The fastest growing and a good screening grapevine is 'Black Hamburg', which also provides delicious grapes. One of

▽ *Fast-growing and dense-covering flowering climbers can be used to create charming displays of leaf and bloom in the summer. Honeysuckle (Lonicera) will happily clamber over walls and fences and along bridges, and should be positioned close to paths or patios where its heady scent can be appreciated in full.*

the hardiest of the grapevines, and producing a spectacular display of autumn color, is the Crimson Glory Vine (*Vitis coignetiae*). The Virginia creepers can also be relied on for good autumn color, while the *Rhoicissus* is evergreen but tender.

Other climbers are grown for their splendid flowers and scents, particularly when trained over a pergola or bower or positioned close to a patio where the blooms can be appreciated at close quarters. Few sights can rival the pendulous, scented racemes of *Wisteria sinensis*, the blanket of flowers produced by any of the *Clematis*, one of the climbing roses or, in gardens with a Mediterranean climate, the showy bracts of *Bougainvillea*. The exotic-looking Passion flower (*Passiflora*) is a semihardy evergreen that is prone to frost.

For scent, you cannot beat the honeysuckles and jasmines, which are both attractive plants. More unusual perennial climbers include the moderately hardy and vigorous Chinese Gooseberry (*Actinidia chinensis*), the extremely hardy hop (*Humulus lupulus*) and the semihardy *Thunbergia grandiflora* □

▽ *Some of the grapevines are valuable not just for their attractive green leaves in summer, over a pergola or trellis, but also for their splendid autumn tints – Vitis coignetiae, for example, turns a magnificent deep red, purple and gold (bottom).*

△ *Flowering climbers make spectacular displays when trained to scramble among trees as well as manmade structures. This Clematis 'Jackmanii' has brought a green-gold Elm, Ulmus hollandica 'Wredei', out in purple blooms.*

◁ *Trained to cling to a simple wire trellis, a large flowering climber like this Clematis 'Jackmanii' is very decorative.*

▽ *A dense curtain of variegated climbers like Hedera helix 'Goldheart' will brighten a dull wall or fence.*

HERBACEOUS PERENNIALS

HERBACEOUS PERENNIALS provide you with an ideal opportunity to experiment with combinations of forms and textures in the garden. Being semipermanent, they represent low-maintenance features yet, if desired, they can be split up and moved around or replaced as the fancy takes you. Their seemingly endless range of shapes and colors is perfect for introducing fresh interest into a planting design and for trying out new ideas.

As with other plant groups, a basic framework of a few reliable evergreens is useful for maintaining the general shape of the garden throughout the year, and these should be chosen for the variety of their foliage as well as for their seasonal interest. Some of the best contrasting foliage forms are to be found among the spurges, *Euphorbia. robbiae* is particularly useful, with smooth, rosette-forming green leaves. It will tolerate dry shade but grows extremely vigorously in moist soil.

The evergreen *Helleborus* is another useful group with attractive green leaves and, often, winter flowers. *H. corsicus* (also known as *H. argutifolius*) is a strong and hardy plant with toothed leaves and has the bonus of greenish yellow flowers. A lovely wild form for woodland areas is the Christmas Rose (*H. niger*), which produces beautiful large, waxy white flowers. Another useful and natural-looking group of plants which flower early is *Ligularia*, flourishing on the margins of a pool or bog and making a striking display of gold or yellow flowers. Consider also *Tellima grandiflora*, a native of North America and producing large clumps of attractive leaves year-round; or *Tiarella cordifolia*, from the eastern part of North America, with hairy, maple-shaped leaves that turn from green to a more bronzed color in winter.

For variety among the greenery in winter, include other 'evergreen' colors such as *Lamium maculatum* which has silver-striped leaves; Lamb's Ears (*Stachys lanata*) producing silver, wooly foliage; or lungwort (*Pulmonaria*), a valuable all-seasons plant with white-spotted green leaves and mauve-blue flowers.

For the best and most subtle contrasts and effects, herbaceous perennials should be selected for their variety of leaf shape and size and for their soft, natural flower forms rather than bright, showy blooms: this will enable you to blend and balance the shades more easily. You will find that some of the wilder forms have the prettiest leaves and softest-colored flowers. Goat's Beard (*Aruncus*), for example, has large, feathery plumes of white flowers and attractive fernlike leaves.

Spiky, half-hardy evergreen *Phormium* with its swordlike leaves, giant *Gunnera* with leaves like enormous green parasols, dramatic *Crambe cordifolia* with dark green leaves and a fuzz of tiny white flowers, feathery *Astilbe* and lime green *Alchemilla mollis* give you some idea of the range and variety available.

It is particularly important when planning for herbaceous perennials that you remember the first rule of bed and border design: large varieties to the rear, shorter ones to the front. The aim is to create a continuous flow of foliage and blended colors from the ground upward in solid blocks of leaf and bloom. If you can choose sturdy, self-supporting plants you will minimize maintenance □

▷ *Planted in blocks of single colors, perennials can achieve some interesting contrasts of form and texture. These pink Lychnis coronaria make a stalky foreground for light pink Phlox paniculata.*

▽ *The aim of the herbaceous border is to provide a solid block of interesting shapes and colors. Perennial plants offer plenty of scope to experiment with combinations like this bright red, orange and yellow one, using Alstroemeria, mixed Lilies and bright red Verbena.*

△ Perennials do not have to be grown in long, straight borders and look equally good in large formal blocks of contrasting shapes. Clumps of Miscanthus sinensis 'Gracillimus' and the pink daisies of Echinacea purpurea have been planted in gaps between the bricks of this patio area.

△ Plan your herbaceous borders carefully to achieve the best effects – placing the delicate pink Papaver orientalis in front of the deep purple Limonium perezii is a touch of genius.

▷ Where plants produce spectacular effects, give them a prime position so that they can be enjoyed in full glory. This tree peony, with its light green leaves and oversized white blooms, makes a dramatic feature beside the front door sheltered behind a low, neatly sheared hedge.

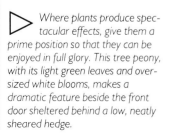

GRASSES & BAMBOOS

GRASSES AND BAMBOOS, with their tall, slender stems and graceful foliage, provide a welcome relief in shape and texture from the normal habit of the majority of garden plants. They are architectural plants almost to the point of being an art form, creating vertical interest, variety and contrast within a planting design with their many different-colored stems, plumes and tassels. They do, however, require plenty of space and should be allowed to form dense clumps or thickets. Thinning out the seedlings will ensure stronger, more healthy plants.

You can rely on bamboos to add an exotic touch to the design and they are available in a surprisingly wide variety of forms, from the dwarf *Sasa*, growing only a few inches from the ground, to the giant *Phyllostachys* and *Bambusa*, reaching 6–10 m (20–30 ft) high. They are useful evergreen plants, not just for creating an oriental feel in the garden but also for providing exotic shelter for a summerhouse or gazebo, or for creating exciting play areas.

Bamboos require moist but reasonably cool conditions and will grow well close to water providing that their roots are not actually submerged. In general, they die back after

flowering and look rather unsightly, but since most will not flower for many years, they give good service as part of an integral garden plan. All bamboos can be pruned, Japanese style, to create stronger, bigger stems, but this treatment is usually reserved for *Phyllostachys*, which produces decorative stems.

It is not simply their elegant, graceful habit that makes bamboos such an excellent plant for garden design, they can offer a tremendous variety of textures and colors in leaves and canes, too. *Phyllostachys aureosulcata* has a yellow-striped stem, while *P. nigra* has green stems the first year which then turn a dramatic black. Both produce the feathery, fluttering foliage familiar in Japanese and Chinese, settings where they are contrasted with rock, stone and water.

The *Arundinaria* family of bamboos is equally handsome, with its slender, colored stems and glossy foliage, but it does tend to be more invasive, and so needs plenty of room and occasional thinning. Hardy *A. japonica* is the largest, making dense thickets of dark green canes and ribbonlike leaves that will thrive in half shade providing the soil is kept moist. The Golden Leafed Bamboo (*A. viridistriata*) is perhaps even lovelier, with light green and yellow-striped foliage; *A. nitida* produces a tall, dense thicket of purple-marked canes and light, gray-green leaves.

Another highly attractive hardy bamboo is *Sasa palmata*, which has large leaves perfect for making an impressive show in group plantings. It can be too invasive in small gardens and it is better grown in a pot where it makes an excellent specimen plant, but it does require a lot of water during the growing season. Equally invasive, but worth cultivating for its purple-green canes, is Kuma Bamboo Grass (*Sasa veitchii*).

There are many other grasses worth growing for their long stems and elegant foliage but because they are deciduous, they need to be chosen and positioned carefully to avoid an unsightly dead area in winter.

The giant of the grasses is *Miscanthus sacchariflorus*, which grows in large clumps of thick stems reaching 3 m (10 ft) and has

◁ Arundinaria murielae *makes a tall, elegant clump of long green canes and bright green foliage. Raked gravel around the base and an arrangement of rocks are useful not only to cover the bare soil beneath but to impart a distinctly oriental flavor.*

△ Bamboos and grasses, because of their contrasting, narrow, spiky habit make excellent companions for plants with flat broad leaves. They produce a wide variety of different and always interesting effects.

1 A green fountain of Spartinia pectinata *is grown against a lush clump of* Hosta lancifolia.

2 The feathery brown seed heads of Stipa gigantea.

3 Delightful stripes of a large, clump-forming and invasive Phalaris arundinacea 'Picta'.

fluttering narrow leaves. It makes a good contrast with some of the large, lush plants such as *Gunnera* or *Rheum*, and also serves as an effective windbreak. Other *Miscanthus* grasses are valuable for their dramatic impact, varied color forms and delicate flower heads. Many grass species make excellent subjects for blending and contrasting with herbaceous perennials and can be selected specifically for both dry and moist conditions.

Consider the interesting variety of shapes and shades in damp areas with the popular Canary Grass (*Phalaris arundinacea* 'Picta') producing large clumps of bright green and white-striped spiky leaves, and *Stipa gigantea*

with arching leaves that turn bronze and red in autumn and remain throughout the winter. Another moist soil lover is the Sweet Galingale (*Cyperus longus*), which produces tall, arched stems of dark green leaves and drooping clusters of red-brown flowers.

For dry, sunny areas, the grass family *Festuca* is one of the most interesting, making compact cushions of spiky blue. *F. glauca* is powder blue and will grow in full sun; *Avena candida* is another useful blue grass. Completely different again is *Achnatherum* (also now more correctly known as *Stipa calamagrostis*) with its narrow green leaves and feathery cream flowers □

△ *A variety of grasses and bamboos makes a superb setting around a small pool and pebbled patio. Arundinaria murielae and Miscanthus sacchariflorus have been used to soften the edges of lumber walkways and provide a feeling of height and lushness around the water. Both will thrive in the moist atmosphere at the water's edge.*

FERNS

FERNS ARE VALUABLE for their tolerance to shade and their lovely feathery fronds that always seem to add an exotic junglelike touch to the garden. They require little soil but plenty of humus or sphagnum peat and, while some will tolerate sunshine, most will be happiest in moist shade. The only maintenance necessary is an annual cutting away of the dead fronds and an occasional topdressing.

Ferns can be either deciduous or evergreen and come in two types: those that produce a circle of fronds around a central crown, as with the Royal Fern, and those, such as *Polypodium*, that spread in all directions via a creeping root system.

Among those that grow on slightly drier soil are *Polypodium vulgare*, a familiar wild fern that makes good, spreading ground cover, and the Buckler Fern (*Dryopteris filix-mas*), which seems able to survive most conditions and produces fernlike fronds of deep green.

There is also a selection of ferns that like to be in more than moist conditions – in a bog or at a pool side, for example, where their roots can take advantage of the constant supply of water. Most beautiful of these plants is the Royal Fern (*Osmunda regalis*), which is a slow grower but worth waiting for because of its bright green fronds that turn orange and then copper in the autumn. Other bog, pool and stream lovers are the Sensitive Fern (*Onoclea sensibilis*) and the aptly named Ostrich Feather Fern (*Matteuccia struthiopteris*), which produces curving feathery fronds and looks particularly good when planted in clumps.

There are many other ferns that can be grown in moderately normal conditions providing you do not let them dry out. Hart's Tongue Fern (*Phyllitis scolopendrium*) adapts well to both moist and drier conditions and has bright green fronds; *Adiantum venustum* makes delicate lacelike fronds, and is a relation of the familiar Maidenhair Fern (*A. pedatum*). This has two interesting variations: the Japanese *A. p. japonicum*, which puts out pink fronds and stems in spring, and *A. p. klondyke*, which produces black stems.

Blechnum ferns are lime haters; *B. pennamarina* being a useful, small evergreen for shady areas, *B. spicant* is slightly taller and a brighter green suitable under trees. *Polystichum setiferum* 'Acutilobum' is a particularly beautiful deciduous fern with delicate foliage rivaled by the pretty *Cystopteris fragilis*, which must be grown in moist shade.

Those fascinating giants, the tree ferns, can be tamed to your garden in cool climates by growing Dicksonias or Cyatheas in pots and taking them outside in warm weather.

Most ferns have a delicious fresh green aroma when pressed between the fingers but there is at least one, *Dennstaedtia punctilobula*, that is worth growing for its refreshing scent of new-mown hay. *D. punctilobula* increases quickly by underground runners and can be too invasive among less vigorous plants in shaded areas of the garden □

1 Ferns are wonderful plants for softening hard landscape features. Nephrolepsis cordifolia, the fern shown here, is also a native of the southern hemisphere but, like tree ferns, can be grown in pots outside for the summer.

2 Ferns will grow in both dry and moist situations and are invaluable for soft ground cover. They are particularly good for path edges where their green fronds can break up an unwanted straight line. This hardy fern is Adiantum pedatum 'Asiatic Form'.

3 The lovely fern Osmunda regalis – the Royal Fern – makes a wonderful specimen plant in damp shady places or near a small pool. The handsome large leaves in the background are those of Peltiphyllum peltatum.

◁ Tree ferns are not entirely hardy in northern climates but can be grown in milder areas, where only light frosts are experienced, or in containers. Mainly native to Australia, New Zealand and South America, they look best planted near or around ponds or even swimming pools.

▷ Soft, luxuriant, decorative foliage is a very useful ingredient in garden design, as ferns such as this Matteuccia struthiopteris amply demonstrate. This very hardy fern is another form suitable for water-edge planting.

△ Rock and ferns are familiar companions and combine well, particularly where the garden rises steeply and you can create the effect of a rocky outcrop planted with ferns. Planting them like this allows you to appreciate their foliage more easily.

WATER PLANTS

A POOL OR STREAM, even a small tub or sink of water, provides the opportunity to grow a collection of water-loving plants, a group distinguished by their lush forms and extravagant variety of foliage shapes and colors. Apart from the water lilies, which have a cool translucence and the foil of deep green, saucerlike leaves to temper their brilliant colors, most water-loving flowers are soft and natural, creating gentle drifts of color that look delightful reflected in the water's surface. This effect can be highlighted with the occasional bright-flowered plant, but keep these to a minimum because of the magnifying and doubling effect of the water.

The true aquatics are those that grow on or below the water's surface and are planted in submerged baskets of rich, silty soil. Most spectacular of these are *Nymphaea*, the water lilies, of which there are many both hardy and more tender tropical forms. For even the smallest water garden there is a dwarf form of *Nymphaea*, *N. pygmaea alba*, which is ideal for small ponds or tubs. *Nymphaea* offers a particularly wide choice of blooms in glowing reds, whites, pinks and yellows, and large, flat leaves in shades of red and green. Of the tropical water lilies, *Victoria amazonica* is hard to better, with leaves gaining a size of up to 2 m (6½ ft) in diameter and with creamy white, sometimes pink-tinged, flowers as large as 20 cm (8 in) in diameter.

Other aquatics include the tiny kidney-shaped leaved Frogbit (*Hydrocharis morsus-ranae*), which spreads over the water's surface and bears white flowers like miniature water lilies, and the rampant oxygenating plants, such as the Water Violet (*Hottonia palustris*) with its mass of pale mauve flowers and ferny foliage, Water Crowfoot (*Ranunculus aquatilis*), producing a carpet of white and green, and the red and yellow *Myriophyllum spicatum*.

A pool or stream edge is the perfect place for growing some of the dramatic water-edge plants, such as the huge *Gunnera manicata* with its huge umbrellalike leaves, spike-leaved iris, shade-loving *Petasites japonicus*, the ornamental rhubarb, *Rheum palmatum*, and the bright green parasol foliage of *Peltiphyllum peltatum*. These are balanced by softly colored flowers: the lilac-blue of the hostas, fluffy pink and red *Rodgersia* and yellow *Lysimachia*. Brighter splashes of color among the greens, grays and blues of the poolside are provided by the orange daisies of *Ligularia*, the bright yellow of the Globe Flower (*Trollius europaeus*) or the brilliant red of *Geum rivale*.

Further architectural forms are supplied in the damp soil beside a bog, pool or stream by the shade-loving ferns (see p. 186), bamboos (p. 184) and the spiky shapes of reeds and rushes, such as the classic common bulrush (*Scirpus lacustris*), sporting fat brown pokers on the end of long green stems, the green-and-white-striped Zebra Rush (*Scirpus tabernaemontani* 'Zebrinus') or the cream-striped *Acorus calamus* 'Variegatus' □

△ Many water-edge plants can offer both interesting foliage and attractive flowers. The Pickerel Weed, Pontederia cordata, will make a splendid display of glossy, heart-shaped leaves with lighter markings and in late summer will produce soft, purple-blue spikes of flowers.

△ The purple loosestrife, Lythrum salicaria, is a common sight beside natural ponds and streams with its vivid purple spires. Packed close together, they intensify the effect of the color. This is a plant that will grow almost anywhere and tolerates many conditions, except full shade.

◁ *Any size of water feature offers the opportunity to grow an interesting selection of water-loving plants. Growing plants in or beside the water, or in surrounding tubs and urns, gives further scope for contrasting shapes and sizes. A small pool edged in lumber decking has successfully contrasted the bright green arrow heads of Sagittaria sagittifolia, spiky Typha angustifolia and the deeply cut leaves of Fatsia japonica.*

1 Nymphaea alba is a classic water lily native to Europe with attractively marked leaves and pure white flowers with yellow stamens.

2 Nymphaea 'Masaniello' is distinguished by its large overlapping green leaves and stunning, starry blooms with pink-flushed golden centers.

3 Nymphaea 'Marliacea Chromatella' is extremely hardy and free-flowering but can be difficult to establish. It has attractive, light green leaves and yellow flowers.

GROUND-COVER PLANTS

GROUND-COVER PLANTS are not only valuable for hiding any bare areas of soil, they also make an attractive base for taller plants and help keep weed growth to a minimum. It makes sense then to select a good range of evergreens for year-round cover, although there are many deciduous varieties that provide flowers in summer or good leaf color in autumn.

Low maintenance is one important aspect of ground-cover plants in garden design. Another is their use for linking larger plants to create a flowing continuation of foliage from ground level upward. These plants can also be encouraged to spread over steep banks or over walls in the manner of climbers and, indeed, many natural climbing plants can double as ground-cover ones.

The diverse range of these plants falls into several principal groups. First, there are the clump formers, which are mainly herbaceous perennials or annuals that form dense mounds of foliage around a central rootstock. *Alchemilla mollis* is one of these – a deciduous plant worth growing for its large silver-green leaves and mass of yellow flowers. The Hellebores are also clump formers, the best for ground cover being the evergreen shade lovers such as *H. corsicus* and *H. foetidus*.

Another group tends to make carpets of foliage. These are usually herbaceous plants, shrubs and alpines, like the evergreen *Au-brieta*, which covers banks, walls and rockeries in gray-green leaves and pink or purple flowers by means of surface runners or a prostrate growing habit.

Many shrubs, like some of the prostrate forms of *Cotoneaster*, are hummock-forming ground-cover plants producing a dense mat of green preventing weed growth, or the evergreen *Viburnum davidii*, which is capable of producing an excellent coverage of deep green, glossy leaves, attractive flowers and, sometimes, berries too. Other shrubs, such as low-growing roses, can also be used as ground cover because of their drooping stems.

Many of the climbing plants that can be grown as ground cover will produce, without any form of support, a tangled mass of growth to smother all in their path. Honeysuckle (*Lonicera*) will perform this way and is perfect for creating sweet-smelling banks or raised beds. Other climbing and rambling plants will naturally spread over the ground, rooting at intervals, and make effective ground cover. Surprisingly, *Clematis* is a good example if given the room to spread. The creeping *Hydrangea petiolaris* and everlasting pea *Lathyrus* are useful flowering deciduous creepers, while Virginia Creeper (*Parthenocissus*) and Japanese Crimson Glory Vine (*Vitis coignetiae*) are well worth considering for their green summer cover that turns to rich reds and oranges in autumn □

△ Low-growing alpines make an attractive display when planted in a stone trough and raised on a bench or plinth to make a miniature rock garden nearer eye level. Aim for a good variety of plant shapes and colors and different containers for a larger, more ambitious effect.

△ Plants which live naturally in poor, stony soil are excellent for 'softening' rocks and boulders with an eye-catching carpet of green leaves or tiny flowers. Saxifraga oppositifolia ' Rosea' is invaluable as ground cover.

△ **Top** *Many of the plants which thrive in hot, dry, rocky conditions have strong or spicy scents, and benefit from being grown beside a path or patio where they may be brushed against to release their fragrance.* Lavandula spica 'Rosea' *and* Ruta graveolens 'Jackman's Blue' *make good companions with their lilac and yellow flowers and gray-green foliage.*

△ Alchemilla mollis *is an excellent ground-cover plant which enjoys well-drained garden soil. It produces good, dense cover of palmate leaves and yellow-green flowers – a fine plant for sloping banks.*

◁ *Look for good ground-covering plants that will provide interest for most of the year and exciting combinations of foliage shapes.* Euphorbias *are useful both for their light green feathery foliage and bright yellow flowers.* Pulmonaria saccharata *is an evergreen with white-spotted, green leaves.*

BULBS & TUBERS

BULBS AND TUBERS are the low-maintenance gardener's dream: a self-contained unit that is easy to grow, which often looks at its best when nothing else is stirring and is capable of growing almost anywhere. Quite apart from the convenience, bulbs, tubers and rhizomes produce a spectacular variety of beautiful blooms for additional season displays or they can be naturalized in wilder areas between grass. The only favor they ask is that their foliage be allowed to develop for about six weeks after flowering has ended. This will give them the chance to build up food reserves for next year. Bulbs are usually left in the ground, but some can be dug up as soon as the flowers are dead and hung in a dry, dark place until ready for planting again. They will, however, be weaker in consequence.

When planted in beds among other plants, it is useful to mark their position with sticks or something similar to ensure that they are not accidentally sliced by a careless spade or fork later in the year when the foliage has died back. It is in grass, however, that bulbs are really in their element, especially the spring-flowering *Crocus*, snowdrops (*Galanthus*), *Scilla* and *Narcissus*, providing a delightful natural display under trees, along banks or in wild meadow areas.

The easiest way to plant bulbs in grass is to lift a flap of sod and plant several at a time before replacing the section. Bulbous plants are also excellent subjects for pots and containers, where they should be planted with their tips protruding and kept in a dark, cool place for about eight weeks after planting. When they start to grow, take them out and place them where they will be seen to best effect – on a deck or patio, beside a pool or near the house.

Most bulbs do well in containers, but particularly effective are the tulips and hyacinths, *Narcissus*, *Crocus* and *Chionodoxa*, or tiny *Muscari*. It is also worth considering some of the bulbous and tuberous plants that flower in summer and autumn for planting in containers: plants such as the lovely Summer Hyacinth or Spire Lily (*Galtonia candicans*), which produces tall spires of creamy, bell-shaped flowers in midsummer, or any of the splendid members of the *Lilium* family. The Diamond Lily (*Nerine bowdenii*) flowers in autumn and produces attractive, green, strap-like leaves and rich pink flowers.

Apart from the lilies, iris is one of the largest families of plants to come from bulbs or corms. The family offers an enormous range of sizes, shapes and colors, combining spiky leaves with exotically formed, lipped blooms, from the magnificent bearded iris to the tiny South African Baboon Flower (*Babiana stricta*).

In the wild or natural garden, consider the wood sorrels (*Oxalis*), which produce low-growing tufts of clover-shaped leaves and dainty pink, white or mauve flowers, or the brightly colored anemones and shade-loving cyclamens. All these plants are excellent for underplanting shrubs and trees, brightening the grass in a woodland setting and, because they are low growing, for incorporating in a rock garden. Other flowering plants suitable for a rocky yet moist location include the Winter Aconite (*Eranthis hyemalis*) and the dwarf forms of ornamental onions (*Allium*) □

▷ Summer-flowering Crocosmia *'Lucifer'* is a striking subtropical plant that will survive cold weather conditions if planted in well-drained soil. Its strong, green, sword-shaped leaves and profusion of red-gold, tubular flowers make a spectacular display in the herbaceous border and are useful for cut flowers. Clumps may be lifted and divided every three or four years and plants are generally free from pests or disease, making them a good, low, border plant.

1 The pure white, scented trumpets of Lilium longiflorum makes it a charming pot plant for extra interest on the patio in summer.

2 For an unusual display of flowers and foliage, Eucomis bicolor has loose green leaves and curious shaggy heads of pink flowers.

3 Tulips can be relied on for bright spring colors in tubs and window boxes. Tulipa kaufmanniana, for example, is attractively striped in red and yellow.

4 Most stately of the spring-flowering bulbous plants is Fritillaria imperialis *'Aurora'*, an attractive plant for beds and borders.

5 Fritillaria persica produces dramatic blood-red, almost black, spires of flowers.

6 The clear blue flowers of an Agapanthus *'Headbourne Hybrid'* can be appreciated at their best en masse.

PLANTS FOR SHAPE

FOR A GARDEN to look its best it must be well thought out and properly balanced in both shape and color. The range of colors and effects at your disposal is astonishing, perhaps even a little too diverse, for without careful planning the end result can appear muddled and confused. As a general rule, never plant on a whim, but instead take the time to draw up a detailed planting plan, as described on pp. 61–70. Also, take care to keep larger specimens to the back of any planting areas, graduating down in size to ground-cover varieties at the front. The spread of plants is another consideration: position them a little closer than normal for a lush, dense effect, but not so close that they crowd each other and do not flourish. If you are worried about gaps while plants are maturing, plant more than you need and thin out later (which is expensive) or mulch the soil with wood or bark chips to keep weeds to a minimum.

FORM & TEXTURE

Plants used for their shape are often strong on foliage but are nonflowering or have only insignificant flowers. There are some, however, such as rhododendrons, that offer a spectacular display of both. It is vital to select and blend your plant shapes carefully because they, in effect, form the weave of the cloth on which the bright flowers are only the trimmings, and a combination of different sizes and shapes will create a far more subtle and relaxing impression than a medley of hues.

On browsing through the gardens featured in this book, you may have noticed that certain plants appear many times, although used in different ways: architectural plants such as hostas, *Ligularia*, *Phormium*, grasses and *Fatsia japonica*. Gradually, your eye will become more attuned to the qualities that make them appeal to a designer and you will begin to see how a spiky plant, such as a reed or grass, looks just right beside one that has leaves more dish or hand shaped.

Much of this is simple common sense and a talent for selecting contrasts, but there are guidelines you can follow in order to achieve the best possible effect. Balancing height is obvious: not just taller plants to the rear, but also a good range of plant heights throughout the design. It also helps to position denser shapes to the rear, reserving the lighter, more delicate species for the front of your plan.

▷ *Gunnera manicata is one of the largest plants that can be grown in the garden and is much valued for its huge umbrellalike leaves. It will make great clumps beside a lake or pool in the damp muddy soil in which it grows best. It needs careful positioning as it does not like to be moved once established.*

△ *Plants with dramatic foliage make good focal points in dull corners of the garden. The deeply cut leaves of Rheum palmatum 'Atro Sanguineum' are highly ornamental, producing feathery plumes of pink flowers. It is easy to grow in rich, moist soil and a sunny position.*

△ *The Plume Poppy, Macleaya cordata, is a large plant suitable for producing striking clumps of attractive leaves and tall panicles of flowers in beds or borders. They make good background planting or shelter for other smaller plants. They seldom require additional support.*

△ Plants with sword-shaped foliage are useful for contrasting with broader leaved types. Phormium cookianum 'Tricolor' also has yellow-striped leaves to provide contrasting colors.

A mistake often made is to overplay the effect with too many groupings and too many dominant plants. Understatement is always the best policy, using a few beautiful, strong forms against a background of more restrained plants. This is even true in the tropical garden where you may be trying to capture a jungle atmosphere – a solitary banana plant among less dramatic, architectural types is often enough to create exactly the right effect.

Remember that shrubs and trees have interesting foliage and are capable of producing fine forms, too. Fast-growing, large-leaved plants, shrubs and trees will quickly create a mature look and provide a superb background for other varieties. The Japanese maples, Catalpas, Populus lasiocarpa and many others can always be relied on to make a focal point of leafy shapes and branch forms from spring through winter.

There are many shrubs with large, or particularly well-formed, leaves that will create a full and fascinating spectacle – magnolias, Rhododendron, Viburnum, laurel and some Hydrangeas. Climbers are also invaluable for providing vertical interest, and leaf shapes; even within a single family such as ivies (Hedera), shapes can include points, ovals and hearts. The vines, particularly Vitis coignetiae, can have stunning foliage forms; look, too, at the shapes made by Aristolochias or the fruiting Actinidia chinensis and Passifloras.

Once you have planned a strong framework of dramatic shapes, creating focal points and areas of special interest, you can begin to fill in the gaps and link them with a flow of smaller foliage plants. They may be making less of an obvious statement, but they should be equally attractive and well balanced. It is important to contrast shapes on the vertical as well as the horizontal planes: taller plants among those

△ Don't forget that herbs and vegetables can make interesting flower and foliage combinations too. The soft, wooly leaves of Salvia officinalis provide textural contrasts alongside a curly headed savoy cabbage and a border of bright Tagetes 'Cinnabar'.

◁ Ornamental cabbages provide not only eye-catching shapes and textures, but also stunning color variations. This bright pink, frilled variety is particularly handsome.

forming mounds or with spreading habits. Remember that ground-cover plants can be used vertically – trained to smother walls and banks, for example.

The overall effect should flow from one plant to another to give the impression of larger blocks or shapes that are useful for emphasizing existing architectural forms in the garden. Low-growing plants could be used to tumble downward in sympathy with a flight of steps, softening the edges and drawing attention in the right direction.

Contrasting and complementary foliage shapes such as these will create a good solid background to your design, linking features and providing long-term variety. For added interest you should also consider the shapes of plants and fruits as they appear and add their attractions to the overall design. Again, save those with a particularly striking appearance to use as focal points. The glorious impact of clematis or rhododendron blooms deserve to be enjoyed unimpeded, as do the more fragile forms of orchids or lilies.

Flowers and fruits

Flowers come in an even wider variety of shapes than do leaves: trumpets, bells, balls, pom poms, racemes, stars and frills, and in double and single forms. Again, you should be looking for variety of shape, contrasting heavy hanging racemes or a strong spike of tiny flowers with larger, more exotic blooms or the cloudlike effect of a free-flowering, clump-forming plant. Consider the contrast between the heavy head of a sunflower, the pokers of *Kniphofia*, light, fluffy *Gypsophila*, the massed balls of *Hydrangea*, feathery Celosias or the aptly named bottlebrushes (*Callistemon*).

For a year-round garden, it is also necessary to balance the effect of berries, seedheads, pods, catkins, fruits and cones. All add interest and variety to the total design, and require careful preplanning.

Habit

It is not just the individual elements of your plants that contribute shape and form to the garden; their very habit creates a certain look and attitude and will influence the atmosphere of your design. Plants can be tightly upright like a bulrush, pendulous as in the example of *Ilex aquifolium* 'Pendula', fastigiate (columnar) like *Taxus baccata* 'Fastigiata', or weeping like many of the cotoneasters.

Plants can also be given artificial shapes by shearing or training. Topiary forms of trees or shrubs may provide amusing or sculptural shapes within your design, but the Japanese have refined the technique to an art. In the

◁ Look out for clever combinations of form and color. The large, deeply cut and purple-tinted leaves of Rodgersia pinnata pick up the pink flush of its delicate lacelike flowers.

▽ A blend of interesting, low-growing foliage plants can be used to brighten up the base of a tree trunk. In this semiwild garden, gray Artemisia ludoviciana, and a striking variegated thistle, Silybum marianum, add light and variety to an otherwise dull area.

oriental garden, plants are sheared to emphasize the patterns of energy seen in nature – an approach that requires imagination, understanding and practice. More formal plant training, such as fan and espalier forms, has its origins in the centuries-old fruit orchards of northern Europe, where fruit trees were trained against any suitable wall for warmth and protection, as well as to take up as little space as possible.

Texture

Plants not only offer variety of shape but of texture, too. As always, you should aim for a selection of different effects within a grouping. Even the bark of trees varies enormously, from the rough and deeply scored oak to the peeling or shiny and smooth *Prunus serrula*. Foliage can be thick and shiny, like many of the evergreens, or light and fluttering: *Ginkgo biloba*, for example, probably the most ancient surviving tree, has delightfully shaped, soft green leaves.

Alpine plants, and those that enjoy a rocky environment, tend to have fleshy swirls and whirls of foliage or elaborately jointed stems, looking not unlike the legs of an insect; those from hot, dry locations are often soft and wooly. Most unusual of all are the very varied shapes and textures of the cacti and succulents: great swollen stems, hairs, spikes and bulbous appendages being common, as well as a great range of unusual flowers. You will find other textures in the garden: silky tassels, soft, downy undersides and moist, translucent surfaces. All of these can be pressed into service in order to create a fascinating variety and year-round unending interest □

△ *Exciting and varied designs can be devised employing exclusively foliage plants. In this blend of large and small leaf shapes, great purple Rumex combines with light, yellow green and gray foliage to provide an extravagant, colorful border that spills over a rough stone path, making an exciting change from the usual selection of bedding flowers.*

HOSTAS

Hostas, also known as the Plantain Lily, are exciting plants for designers with their wonderful variety of deep-veined, almost quiltlike, markings and foliage shades. They make superb ground cover, combining foliage in blues, greens, grays and variegated options with softly colored flowers that appear in summer.

The largest and most dramatic of the hostas is *H. sieboldiana*, which has large, gray-green leaves and lilac flowers; *H. s.* 'Elegans' is gray-blue and more deeply veined. Variegated forms, such as *H. ventricosa* 'Variegata' with its yellow border, need to be used with care to avoid too strong a contrast, and is better blended with a plain green like *H. lancifolia*.

▷ *The strong blue foliage of* Hosta sieboldiana *'Glauca' and its tight, clump-forming habit make it a real eye-catcher among a mixed arrangement of green foliage plants.*

1 Hosta lancifolia *has a dense habit with neat mounds of pale green leaves.*

2 Hosta crispula *has striking wavy, white leaf margins set off with pale lilac flowers.*

3 *Hostas are very suitable to pot cultivation providing they are regularly watered.*

4 Hosta sieboldiana elegans *makes a large clump of blue green leaves and lilac flowers.*

5 *The vigorous habit of* Hosta ventricosa *makes it an ideal specimen plant.*

SEEDHEADS

Do not overlook plants that produce good seedheads after flowering. The garden where every stage of a plant's lifecycle produces something of interest is naturally easy to maintain and full of variety. The dry, skeletal nature of seedheads is their chief attraction, which contrasts well with the fleshier lushness of leaves and flowers.

Seedheads are also valuable for providing interest at the end of summer when little is in flower and deciduous foliage plants are beginning to die back. Many heads will last right through the winter, supplying strong visual elements for the garden, as well as suitable material for arranging in the house.

◁ The Eryngiums are oustanding for their spiky teasellike heads in metallic shades of silver and violet in late summer. Both lilac E. maritimum (far left) and steely blue E. agarifolium (left) will shine out in the herbaceous border. If you cut the flowers before they fade, they will make good winter flower arrangements.

▽ The globe artichoke, Cynara scolymus, produces dramatic pink-tinged heads which look as delicious as they taste. They are just as effective in flower borders as in the vegetable lot.

◁ Heads can be as neat and colorful as the blue spiny pompoms of Echinops vitro (far left); or form brushlike teasels like Dipsacus laciniatus whose prickly, green flower heads have pink fringes. Both make an excellent contrast against a display of more lush, flowering forms.

△ The spectacular Heracleum mantegazzianum grows twice as tall as a man and produces massive white umbrels on top of stout stems of spiky green leaves, and interesting seed heads later.

◁ The deep-cut dark green leaves of Acanthus spinosus make a fine feathery background for its tall, white and purple flower and seed spikes which appear in summer.

PLANTS FOR COLOR

COLOR, WHETHER USED in a restrained or exuberant way, cannot fail to be a dominant element of your garden design. There has been a move away from the garish effect of a jumble of overly bright or artificial shades, and today gardens tend to feature a strong but gentle basic color scheme, using the more startling colors as occasional highlights or bright accents.

Single-color gardens are also enjoying a new popularity (see p. 206), where the plants are limited to just one or perhaps two colors, providing a unified and often stunning effect. As a general rule with this type of design, it is best to use only green or silver plants as a background to your chosen color in order to maintain a natural, relaxing atmosphere. Bear in mind that it is not just flowers that provide a large variation in color but also foliage, stems, bark, fruit and berries, giving you a choice of reds, greens, blues, mauves, blacks, browns, yellows and golds. Thus, you can plan for variety and interest throughout the seasons without overloading the palette.

Another consideration when planning your garden color scheme is where you will be using them: do not restrict colors to only one level across the garden, but plan a fuller effect from ground level upward. Silver *Cerastium* (an excellent specimen for winter color), brilliant yellow-flowering *Potentilla* or white-spotted *Pulmonaria* are an indication of the variation that can be achieved at the lower, ground-cover levels. Above, use the foliage and blossom colors of trees and large shrubs or encourage fine-colored climbers to scramble over trellis, walls and fences.

With such a choice it may initially be difficult to formulate any kind of working plan for plant color. What will help, however, is to establish a good background of trees and shrubs using flowers where possible from your chosen base color. Existing features, surrounding architecture, the landscape beyond the garden and other materials such as paths, fencing and brickwork will provide the inspiration for deciding which colors to use.

Within these very specific and personal limitations, there are color combinations that work and those that do not: for example, silver/blue/white, gray/pink/blue and purple/blue/yellow always look good together, as do red/blue/white for drama, orange/yellow/cream for warmth or cream/yellow/white for a light, sophisticated look. Try not to mix red and yellow, orange and blue or red and purple.

There are, of course, other combinations that you can use successfully: a blue/gray garden is very cool, for example while all-white can be exceedingly beautiful.

Flower color

It is the softer, more pastel-colored flowers that blend well and these are often found on the simpler, wilder plants. This does not mean that their flowers are any less beautiful: few highly bred varieties are as lovely as an iris, a soft lilac *Wisteria sinensis* or a delicate orchid. These subtle shaded plants should be positioned in large massed groups where the flowers can form great drifts of color, either among a background of foliage or melting one into another – mauve into blue, pink into white and so on. Use the brighter colors – your quick-flowering annuals and plants with scarlet, orange and purple flowers – more sparingly as highlights.

There are many shrubs and trees, such as the flowering cherries and *Rhododendron*, that can provide useful high-level flower color, especially in spring and early summer before the rest of the garden is ready to bloom. Bear in mind, too, that bulbs are a valuable source of early color (see p. 192). Against these, you can plan a succession of perennials flowering in your chosen colors, with the occasional annual as a bright 'top-up' color in containers or in any gaps that need filling while plants grow to mature size.

Foliage color

In general, foliage color is longer lived than that of flowers and so provides a more lasting effect. But do not think that you have only a limited choice of hues – many shades of green, bronze, silver, yellow and creams are at your

△ *Tubs and containers are useful for a quick display of summer color and you can have great fun experimenting with different combinations of colorful annuals. A tall bushy* Salvia coccinea *is a perfect match for the massed flowers of low-growing* Impatiens holstii *'Scarlet Baby' which covers the sides of the stone container.*

▷ *Remember that stems and leaves can be as strongly colored as flowers.* Lobelia fulgens *'Queen Victoria' has stunning dark, almost purple black foliage and scarlet flowers which look spectacular against the dark green of a large, interesting, foliage plant, like the castor oil plant,* Ricinus communis. *Add a deep purple* Verbena *'Sissinghurst', a pure white miniature rose to lighten the effect, and a matching red nasturtium (*Tropaeolum majus*) and you have a vibrant arrangement of color and form.*

◁ *A light summer hedge of sweet pea,* Lathyrus odoratus *'Spencer Mixed', produces eye-level bright colors and the bonus of sweet scent and good flowers for cutting. Train* Lathyrus *up netting, along wires or up free-standing wigwams of stakes to make a colorful vertical display.*

disposal, as well as spotted and striped variegated versions.

Many of the trees, shrubs and ground-cover plants used primarily for their foliage color are deciduous and will not give year-round interest. But there is a large number of 'evergreens' that will. Many shrubs and trees, such as several types of *Eucalyptus*, *Senecio* 'Sunshine', the helichrysums, *Santolina* and various *Verbascum*, will produce eye-catching silvers or gray among the more somber greens.

Gold- or yellow-leaved plants can add a glow and lighten an otherwise dull or shady corner. Again there are many to choose from: *Catalpa bignonioides* 'Aurea' is outstanding here. Choose also from *Taxus baccata* 'Dovastonii Aurea', a golden yew, yellow forms of *Hedera* or the hardy, slow-growing *Aucuba japonica*.

Plants with red, purple or pink foliage need to be used more sparingly but they can add exactly the right contrasts. Consider *Photinia*, *Cotinus coggygria* 'Atropurpureus' and *Pieris formosa* 'Forrestii'. Plant names to look out for here often include 'Purpurea' or 'Purpureum', which indicates a red/purple colouring.

Variegated foliage plants are another category that can add interest to the garden if used with restraint. If mixed with green foliage, they can look very good indeed. There are many species with variegated forms that are also evergreen: *Fatsia japonica* 'Variegata', *Salvia officinalis* 'Tricolor' and *Iris foetidissima* 'Variegata' are only a few of the many that have silver, white or cream variegation. *Vinca major* 'Variegata', *Thuja plicata* 'Zebrina' and several *Ilex* and *Elaeagnus* produce golden yellow variegation.

On the subject of foliage color, green itself must not be forgotten. It comes in so many shades from fresh lime to a deep, glossy forest green that it is not so much one color, but several. Always easy on the eye, and the perfect background for other plants and flowers, you can use it without fear anywhere in the garden, from ground cover to climbers.

Stems, fruits and berries

Other parts of the plant will make their contribution to your color scheme and need to be planned for. Stems, bark, fruits and berries are useful for the contribution they make in late summer through to winter, when you may need a little cheery interest in the garden. The Dogwoods (*Cornus*) have bright red stems that look best grown in groups where the color will be intensified. Look out for trees with unusual bark colors, such as the Paperbark Birch (*Betula papyrifera*) which has a white/pink/orange peeling bark, the Snow Gum (*Eucaly-*

ptus niphophila) with its gray/orange marbled effect and the fine rowan with orange/pink bark, *Sorbus aucuparia* 'Beissneri'.

Trees and shrubs are also a source of fruits, not just red or orange berries but bright blue ones, too, like those of the Asiatic Sweetleaf (*Symplocos paniculata*) or the yellow-brown capsules of *Koelreuteria paniculata*. The Baneberries (*Actaea*) are another good source of berries, mainly white, pink or shiny black fruits. Or, for vertical interest, find room in the garden for a fruiting climber: in full sun, the Chinese Gooseberry (*Actinidia chinensis*) will produce large hairy brown fruits that are also fine to eat □

▷ *Plants which produce a mass of tiny flowers create a colored cloud effect which is useful for offsetting deeper, more concentrated colors. Gypsophila is used for this very effect in wedding bouquets and indoor flower arrangements; here G. paniculata 'Bristol Fairy' surrounds scarlet Verbena × hybrida 'Blaze'.*

▽ *Single-bloomed plants on long stems create a much lighter, looser effect, particularly when positioned against a background of light greenery. This often works well where flowers produce mixed shades like the pinks of this Cosmea bipinnatus 'Mixed'.*

◁ There is great satisfaction to be had in the successful blending of matching shades. Only their flower shapes and contrasting foliage show where the soft blue of Perovskia atriplicifolia blends with Agapanthus.

▽ White can often be as vivid as a color and is used to best effect to lighten darker areas or in a single color scheme. The tall spikes of this clump of Lysimachia ephemerum could not be more different from the billowing flowers of Phlox paniculata 'Snow Queen'.

△ *Many of the yellow-flowering plants produce a buttery shine when grown in sunlight. This yellow viola or pansy has shiny green leaves too, and is useful for illuminating dark corners in an informal garden. Grown against the lobed, red-green foliage of an Oxalis, it is made to look even brighter.*

▷ *Yellow is used against a dark green hedge and a background of trees. Verbascum lightens the background with its tall, yellow, flowering stems rising well above the top of the hedge. In the foreground, a bright yellow Coreopsis hybrid makes a dense blanket of yellow beside a dark green, large-leaved yellow Lupine. Feathery Solidago 'Golden Mosa' offers yet another contrast in size, shape and form with its long, lemon yellow stems of tiny clustered flowers.*

▷ **Far right** *A totally green and yellow design maintains a fresh sunny atmosphere even when skies are gray. The use of yellow provides a wide range of materials at your fingertips from the large flowering spikes of Ligularia to ground cover Mimulus luteus and the interesting flower shapes of Hemerocallis 'Golden Chimes' and the evening primrose Oenothera. The tall teasels of Dipsacus laciniatus produce interesting green shapes within the design.*

SINGLE-COLOR SCHEMES

Using a single-color planting scheme can be particularly striking in a small garden, where multicolored plants might look confused and overcrowded. It can make a pleasant feature as part of a larger garden, too, in an area sheltered by walls or screens.

Green is perhaps the only color you can use exclusively in the garden, and there is certainly enough variety in foliage shapes and forms (there are even green flowers) for you to be able to put together an exciting design. Other colors, including white, gray or silver, need an evergreen background to set them off.

Well planned, a single-color scheme can keep some elements of its chosen hue all year round, using not only flowers but leaves, branches and berries. Many trees and shrubs have colored foliage or bright fruits, while a large number of plants are available in variegated form – useful if you have selected white or yellow for your plan. Striped or spotted edges to leaves can pick up on your color and so provide much needed interest.

Bear in mind that a limited color scheme is even more in need of variety of plant form. Aim for a good mix of different shapes with the occasional large or unusual specimen acting as a focal point.

When considering which colors to choose, white is always popular, offering a good choice of plant material to select from, and it has the effect of adding light to a shady or small garden. Yellow works in a similar way, but it is warmer and therefore ideal for a colder site. Reds and blues are more difficult and are too strong to use exclusively. Think about using these colors within a two-color scheme, the reds softened by white, for example, or the blues blended with pinks and mauves.

△ *Yellow flowers blend well with white and gray to create a sulfurous effect. Achillea taygetea combines all those shades in the one plant, the white, wooly flower heads opening to a brilliant yellow against the feathery gray-green foliage.*

AUTUMN COLOR

In the carefully orchestrated garden, autumn can be one of the best and most vivid seasons, with a spectacular blaze of reds, yellows, oranges and browns against the deep green of evergreens that are going to carry the garden through the winter.

Some plants come to maturity in autumn and flower then; others have started flowering in midsummer and will carry on long after the main summer season is over. The Scotch Flame Flower (*Tropaeolum*) is one of these – a mid- to late summer flowering climber that produces bright red, tubular flowers.

It is always worth planting a selection of autumn-flowering bulbs, which, like their spring cousins, provide a fine display when other plants are underground or dormant. The Diamond Lily (*Nerine bowdenii*) is particularly attractive with its pink flowers; the autumn crocus, *Colchicum autumnale*, is lilac pink; the winter daffodil, *Sternbergia lutea*, a vivid yellow.

The maples (*Acer*) are superb and varied and should be positioned where their fine autumn display of stunning foliage colors can best be appreciated. A. *palmatum* is perhaps the loveliest, with its feathery scarlet leaves, while A. *griseum* produces an orange peeling bark as well as red autumn foliage color.

For best value, look out for plants that yield attractive autumn fruits, not just good foliage color. The rowan is an obvious choice, but you should not overlook *Euonymus europaeus*, which has red-pink fruits peeling back to reveal orange seeds, and of course holly berries, rose hips and snow berries □

△ *Well-shaped trees with good autumn color, like the Japanese maples, make an excellent focal point in a small garden or in the corner of a large one. Acer palmatum 'Ozakazuki' pro-* duces spectacular scarlet foliage in autumn, and is a perfect specimen tree for the patio or small garden.

△ *There are many shrubs that produce exciting late-season color with their leaves or berries. A number of Pyracantha species are popular for their bright berries. Here they have been contrasted with an equally attractive berry-producing Cotoneaster.*

◁ *The browns, russets and yellows of semi-woodland in a large informal garden can make a subtle, but very attractive, display. These horse chestnuts, reflected in a wide stream, illustrate the point particularly well.*

8

DESIGN GUIDE

The surfaces and materials used to surround and construct your garden have a strong influence on its general atmosphere and final appearance. From the previous chapters you have gained some idea of the variety of effects you can create using stone, lumber, bricks and plants to make screening, boundaries, paths, paving and ornamental features. Here you can explore further some of the styles available, both ready to buy and to design and build yourself.

You will notice that it is not always the materials used that give a particular feature its individuality and style, but often the way it is constructed or positioned. The best effects will be those that you adapt and devise for your own circumstances rather than features you simply copy from other gardens. Existing surfaces and local supplies may give you a clue as to which materials to choose; the overall theme of your garden will set the style. The rest is up to you and your imagination to link, shelter or decorate individual areas.

WALLS & FENCES

Depending on the degree of privacy and shelter you require, walls and fences can create a total boundary enclosure or be constructed so that they allow tantalizing glimpses of the view. Both walls and fences can incorporate peep holes, slats or other types of aperture to allow a carefully controlled view of the landscape or garden.

Fences

Fences are easier and less expensive to construct and install than walls, but you must be prepared to give them an annual coat of wood preservative. This can be a time-consuming job, especially where you have allowed plants to climb the fence and these will have to be carefully disentangled beforehand. Also, bear in mind that some preservatives are harmful to plants. Some ready-made types of fence are specially treated to withstand decay for up to 30 years but they are, naturally, more expensive and you will find choice of styles limited.

You can give fences a far more solid appearance by creating the impression of thickness and depth. Overlapping lumber panels can be installed in a double layer or, alternatively, upended railroad ties of varying heights make a rugged, informal fence. Similarly, use overlapping pales bolted together to form an unusual, sturdy looking barrier.

Lightweight fences tend to come in the shape of woven or wired panels. Commonly used materials include grass, brushwood, reeds and bamboo, wood strips as well as plastic. If you are enclosing a curved or irregularly shaped area, then consider using close-woven stake panels; reed or grass panels usually look best supported in lumber frames, which also provide support and rigidity.

Walls

There are many different types of wall and your final choice should be influenced by the style of surrounding structural features. For a more mellow, weathered appearance, use second-hand bricks or specially prepared new ones.

Walls do not have to be formal. In the right setting, and where you do not need a great height, a dry stone structure, made with unmortared, uneven stones, can look perfect. This type of construction looks particularly good if you plant the crevices between the stones with plants.

Even more formal walls need not be made of brick but can, just as easily, be built with a rendered exterior and a rubble center. Cap the top with tiles to keep out the rain □

WALLS

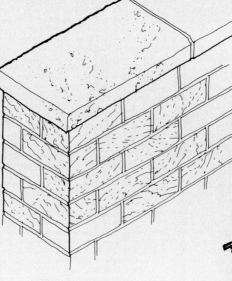

Brick wall construction
Coping should overhang the wall to protect the brickwork from erosion by rain.

Choose the mortar color and joint profile to suit the type of brick. Dark mortar and recessed joints, for example, will set off light bricks.

The texture and appearance of the wall are determined by brick, coping and mortar joint details.

Block walls
Coping may be made a feature by using attractive tiles or slates.

The face of blockwork can be rendered for texture and then painted to provide color interest.

Retaining walls
Lumber railroad ties may be used as a stepped, retaining structure. Spaces between the ties should be planted with overhanging plants.

Construct dry stone retaining walls with pockets of soil to allow masonry to be invaded by plants.

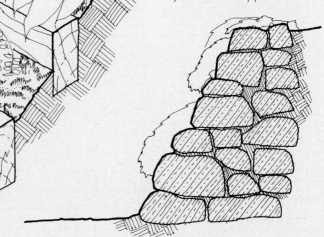

FENCES

A solid appearance is created by depth and shadow.

A lumber frame and reed panel core give a lightweight fence.

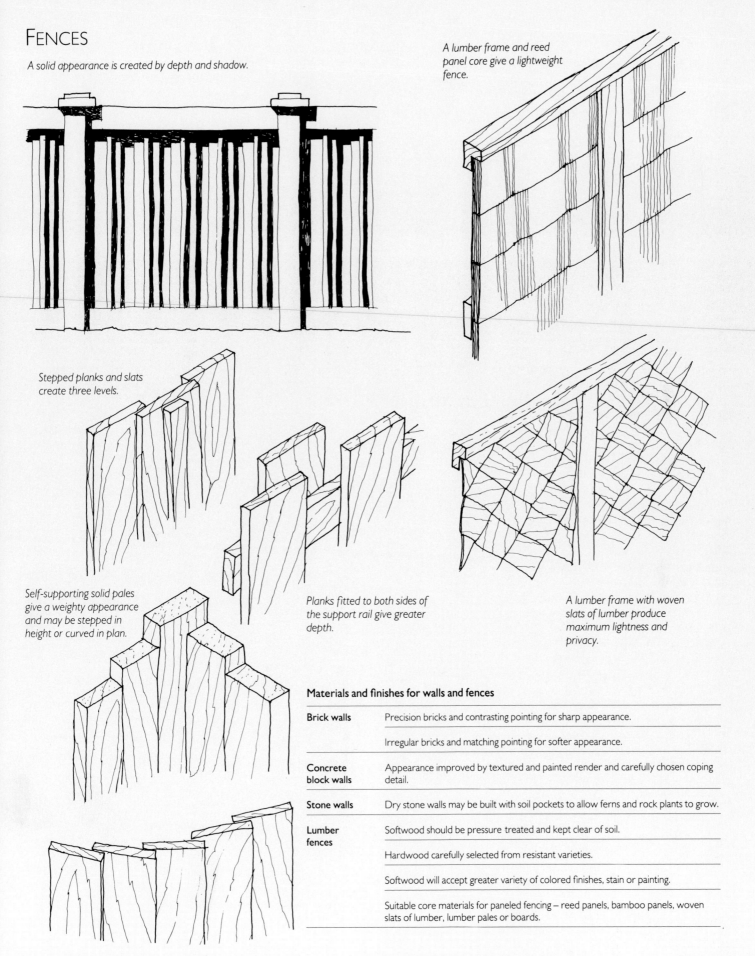

Stepped planks and slats create three levels.

Self-supporting solid pales give a weighty appearance and may be stepped in height or curved in plan.

Planks fitted to both sides of the support rail give greater depth.

A lumber frame with woven slats of lumber produce maximum lightness and privacy.

Materials and finishes for walls and fences

Brick walls	Precision bricks and contrasting pointing for sharp appearance.
	Irregular bricks and matching pointing for softer appearance.
Concrete block walls	Appearance improved by textured and painted render and carefully chosen coping detail.
Stone walls	Dry stone walls may be built with soil pockets to allow ferns and rock plants to grow.
Lumber fences	Softwood should be pressure treated and kept clear of soil.
	Hardwood carefully selected from resistant varieties.
	Softwood will accept greater variety of colored finishes, stain or painting.
	Suitable core materials for paneled fencing – reed panels, bamboo panels, woven slats of lumber, lumber pales or boards.

GATES & ENTRANCES

Like the walls and fences that usually support and surround them, gates can be solid and sturdy for privacy and security, or lightweight and less substantial, providing a view of what lies beyond them. It is a good idea to consider whether the view beyond is actually worth revealing before making your choice.

Solid gates for privacy can be made to blend by matching them exactly to the style of surrounding fences. If you prefer to make a feature of them, choose a contrasting material, such as wrought iron or ornamental lumber set into a suitably sturdy supporting frame. Here you need to take care that a feature gate is in style with other garden elements or it may look uncomfortably out of place. Scale is a consideration here, too, since a gate used as a focal point should not appear to dwarf its surroundings; if, on the other hand, it is too small, it will have no impact.

There are many ways you can design a 'peep-hole' type gate: close louvered gates have an attractive, broken image, for example, and can create a dramatic lighting effect when the sun shines through the slats. More solid types of gate can incorporate holes and windows – square, diamond-shaped or circular – either completely plain or divided up by windowlike panes.

You can also create an almost invisible gate effect by using vertical steel dowels or bamboo canes that barely obscure the view and merely serve to enclose an area.

Sometimes gates are used to mark an important entrance as well as to frame a view, and here the gate surround will be as important as the gate itself, perhaps topped with a straight or curved roof or arch. Where privacy is not a consideration, you may decide to do away with the gate altogether and simply create a framed archway – but bear in mind that you will be accentuating a view of the garden looking in as well as one looking out from the garden side. Again, the materials you use should be governed by other features in the garden: a stout, rough-lumber construction, elegant stone or a lightweight framework of bamboo □

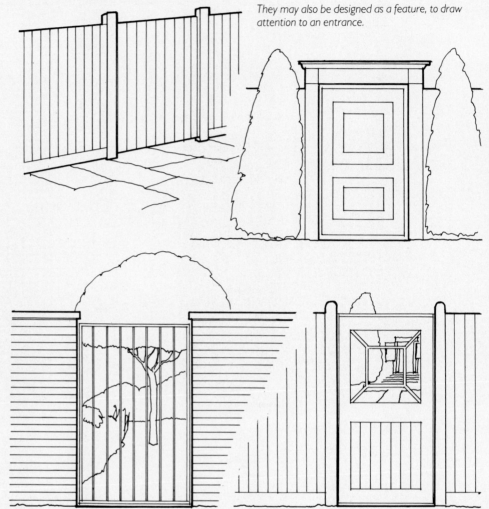

Gates may be discreet to disguise an entrance.

They may also be designed as a feature, to draw attention to an entrance.

A gate may give a glimpse of a landscape beyond.

It may also frame the view of the other side.

Size and proportion
Gates relate in height to the distance from the observer.

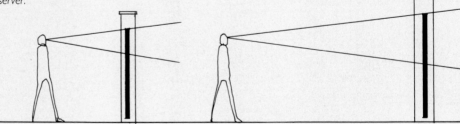

Viewed from close to, a low gate has a similar appearance to a taller gate viewed from a distance.

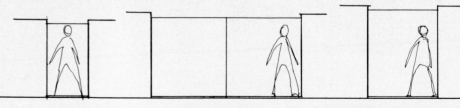

A simple entrance.

A principal gate for people and vehicles.

An important entrance.

Gate styles
The gate may announce the character of the landscape beyond.

Gates can reflect the character of buildings and landscape while controlling access to them.

Gates can take on the form of adjoining hedges and fences, and they can be operated by controls on the gate itself or by a remote signal.

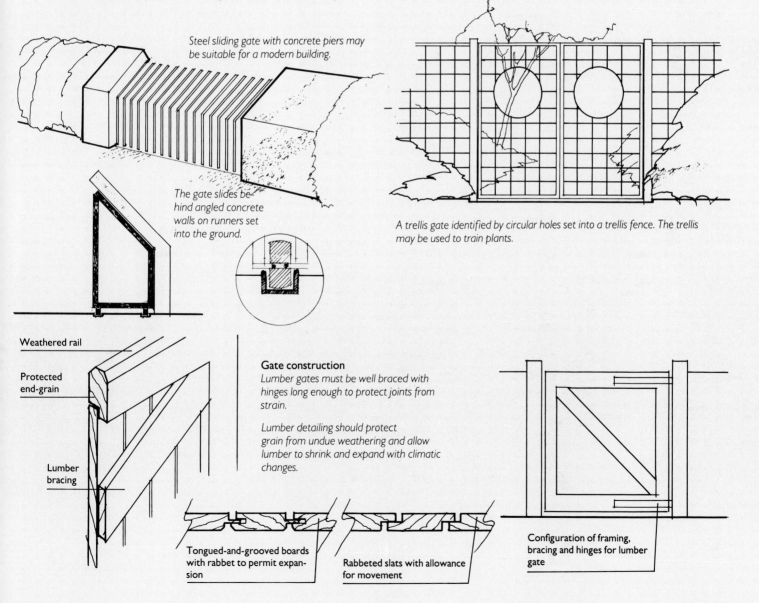

Steel sliding gate with concrete piers may be suitable for a modern building.

The gate slides behind angled concrete walls on runners set into the ground.

A trellis gate identified by circular holes set into a trellis fence. The trellis may be used to train plants.

Weathered rail

Protected end-grain

Lumber bracing

Gate construction
Lumber gates must be well braced with hinges long enough to protect joints from strain.

Lumber detailing should protect grain from undue weathering and allow lumber to shrink and expand with climatic changes.

Tongued-and-grooved boards with rabbet to permit expansion

Rabbeted slats with allowance for movement

Configuration of framing, bracing and hinges for lumber gate

TRELLIS & SCREENS

Trellis and screens tend to be less substantial than boundary fences and, because they are easily transported and simple to erect, make perfect temporary screens around an area while you are waiting for a hedge to grow. They can also be used as an attractive vertical surface surrounding an eating or bathing area and are a commonly used device for dividing up the garden into individual 'rooms'.

Trellis

Lumber trellis is available in a range of simple ornamental designs, including square, diagonal and diamond patterns, or featuring highly decorative motifs with attractively turned supporting posts. The more ornate types need sensitive placing if they are to look in keeping with the rest of the garden.

For a simpler effect, and perfect for gardens with an oriental atmosphere, bamboo trellis can also be considered. This may be available drilled and nailed with galvanized nails, to ensure it holds together, with traditional bound twine disguising its construction. Being light, bamboo trellis is ideally suited to roof and balcony gardens, if sheltered.

Screens

Screens are also available in a wide range of styles. They can be permanently fitted around a hot tub or barbecue area and sheltered from the worst of the weather by a covered pergola or awning. Temporary summer screens can be brought inside and stored over the winter period. This is usually the case with fabric screens, where a simple framework of lumber with stretched plain canvas or brightly colored fabric to match cushions, umbrellas or other outdoor furniture, can be laced or clipped into place using press studs.

Other types of screen include horizontally slatted louvers. These can either obscure or reveal what lies beyond, depending on where you view them, and they look particularly effective when laid in panels so that the slats run in different directions.

Toughened glass or Plexiglas screens are useful when you need shelter from wind but do not want to cut out the view. These can be set into a framework so that they are virtually invisible or you could decorate the frames and make more of a feature of them. They are perfect for the balcony or roof garden where you wish to maintain maximum visibility yet need extra protection □

Trellis

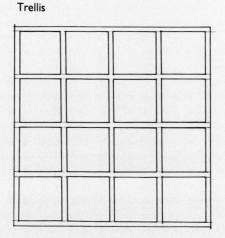

Square lumber trellis.

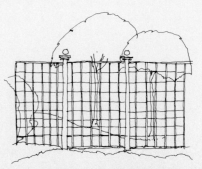

A trellis screen can define a space without obstructing the views beyond.

Diamond pattern trellis.

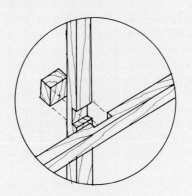

Construction details can add refinement to a simple trellis.

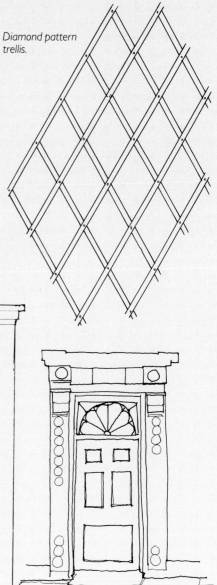

Trellis may be designed to pick up an architectural motif from a building.

Louvers

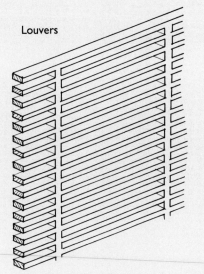

Louvered screens allow light to penetrate while obscuring views or maintaining privacy.

A pattern of alternating louver panels allows a play of light and shade that changes with the sunlight.

Glazing

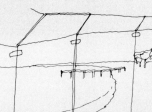

Glazed screens are effective for maintaining views in exposed situations.

Frames

Panels may be solid or open.

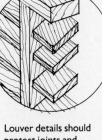

Louver details should protect joints and slats.

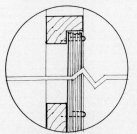

Frame detail to allow screen material to be replaced.

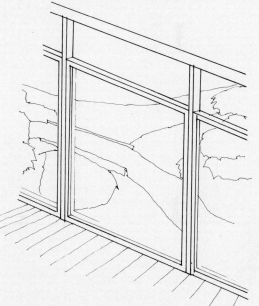

Transparent screens may be constructed with no visible framing, or as glazed panels within a frame.

Canvas

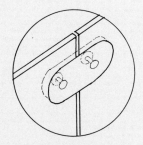

Canvas may be used as a seasonal protection on permanent screen supports.

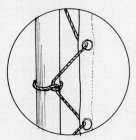

A canvas screen may be laced on to a supporting framework.

Glass panels may be jointed with plates, which obstruct virtually none of the view.

PERGOLAS

A pergola must be strong and sturdy enough to take the weight of heavy climbing plants and to withstand the worst of winter weather with possible gusting winds and heavy snows. Lumber supports should be well bedded in concrete or support spikes buried in the ground. Lighter weight structures may need support in the shape of tensioning cables attached to a nearby wall or large tree.

The simplest type of structure consists of a basic frame with beams set along the top using stout lumber or old railroad ties, but an attractive variation on this uses beams set into the cross beams to create interlocking housed joints. Allowing the cross beams to protrude beyond the basic framework always looks more attractive than cutting them off flush, and it allows you to hang baskets of colorful plants from the overhangs.

Lightweight versions

Bamboo pergolas are useful for a much lighter effect. The canes can be spaced close together or widely apart, nailed for stability and then bound with twine for a traditional finish. But if you are just looking for minimal plant support and are not interested in building a substantial structure, wire can be stretched under tension between two stout walls to create a tunnel of flowering climbing plants. The wire used must be a stainless steel type or plastic covered.

Where the pergola is supporting a screen or overhead shelter for a patio or other area, you may also want to add temporary screening material, such as cane mats or reed panels, to the sides.

Different finishes

Depending on which materials you choose, pergolas can be finished in a range of ways and colors. Softwoods can be painted or stained, not just in the standard wood shades but also in soft blues, rusty reds or even in white or gray, which produces a soft, well-weathered effect. Each coat applied produces a slightly darker shade so it is advisable to take the process slowly to ensure you do not overcolor the wood and finish up with something garish.

Hardwoods should be painted or simply oiled once a year to maintain their natural sheen and color. Reed screens and bamboo poles can be treated with clear matt or satin varnish, depending on the finish you want □

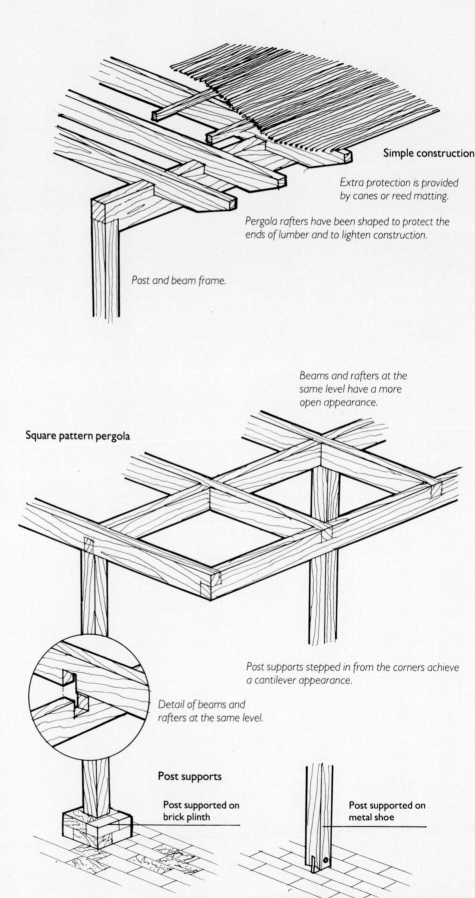

Simple construction

Extra protection is provided by canes or reed matting.

Pergola rafters have been shaped to protect the ends of lumber and to lighten construction.

Post and beam frame.

Beams and rafters at the same level have a more open appearance.

Square pattern pergola

Post supports stepped in from the corners achieve a cantilever appearance.

Detail of beams and rafters at the same level.

Post supports

Post supported on brick plinth

Post supported on metal shoe

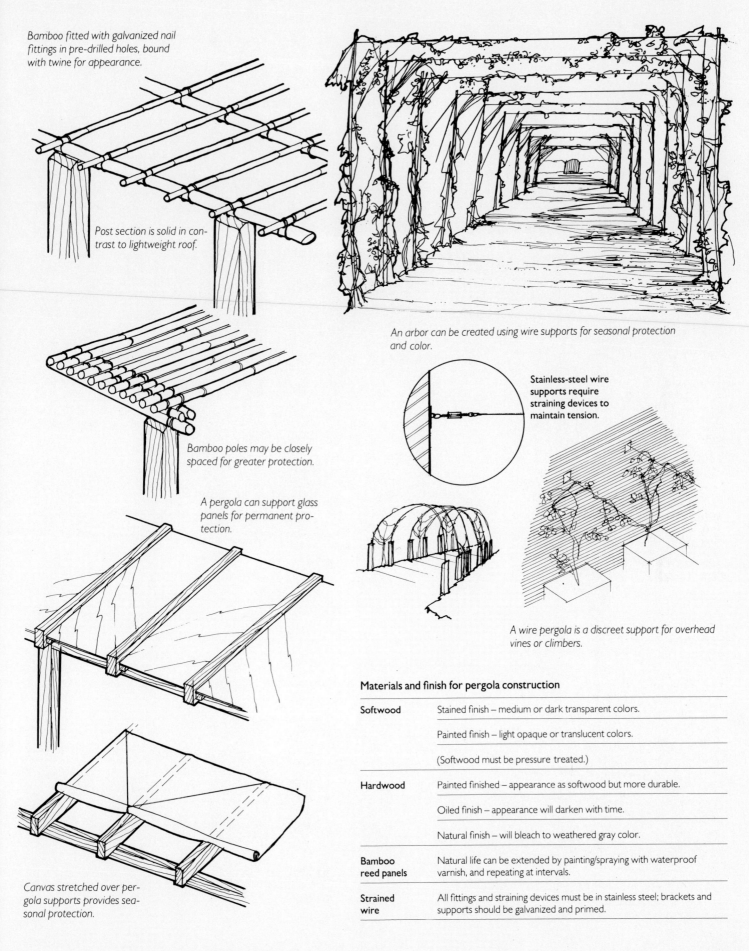

Bamboo fitted with galvanized nail fittings in pre-drilled holes, bound with twine for appearance.

Post section is solid in contrast to lightweight roof.

Bamboo poles may be closely spaced for greater protection.

A pergola can support glass panels for permanent protection.

Canvas stretched over pergola supports provides seasonal protection.

An arbor can be created using wire supports for seasonal protection and color.

Stainless-steel wire supports require straining devices to maintain tension.

A wire pergola is a discreet support for overhead vines or climbers.

Materials and finish for pergola construction

Softwood	Stained finish – medium or dark transparent colors.
	Painted finish – light opaque or translucent colors.
	(Softwood must be pressure treated.)
Hardwood	Painted finished – appearance as softwood but more durable.
	Oiled finish – appearance will darken with time.
	Natural finish – will bleach to weathered gray color.
Bamboo reed panels	Natural life can be extended by painting/spraying with waterproof varnish, and repeating at intervals.
Strained wire	All fittings and straining devices must be in stainless steel; brackets and supports should be galvanized and primed.

217

BRIDGES & WALKWAYS

A bridge or walkway does not just take you from one side of a water feature or planting area to the other, it also provides resting and vantage points and it should represent an attractive feature within the overall garden design. Because of this, it must not only be safe and practical to use, it must look good, too.

Bridges

To build a simple bridge, the choice of materials is vast, providing you can find something large enough to span the area and which is safe to stand on. A couple of planks, a block of stone, cast concrete or an old granite curbstone can all make a delightful, informal bridge across a small stream. Alternatively, you can use two substantial pieces of lumber with slats between to form the walking surface.

Slatted hardwood is particularly versatile and can be fastened together and laid lengthwise or horizontally with the edges cut square or in strips of varying length in order to give a little shaping.

The idea with a simple bridge is that it runs just at ground or water level, making a natural line from one bank to the other. The arched or ornamental bridge is a very different project and requires careful construction and installation. Concrete and stone arches can be purchased ready made, while lumber bridges are usually made to order to your own design. With safety in mind, a handrail is a sensible addition. Lumber poles, bars or thick ropes can all serve this purpose.

Walkways

A walkway may be an extension of a decked area and so be constructed from matching lumber to make paths or bridges. The beauty of a walkway is that, like a simple, informal bridge, it runs close to ground level, making it unobtrusive and an attractive design feature. Planks can be staggered or laid in blocks with the wood running in different directions. Alternatively, construct a narrow gangplank-type walkway with handrails across rocks or a water feature.

Like anything made of lumber in the garden, the wood can be finished in different ways to make it look a natural part of the garden (see *Pergolas*, p. 216 and *Decks*, p. 226) □

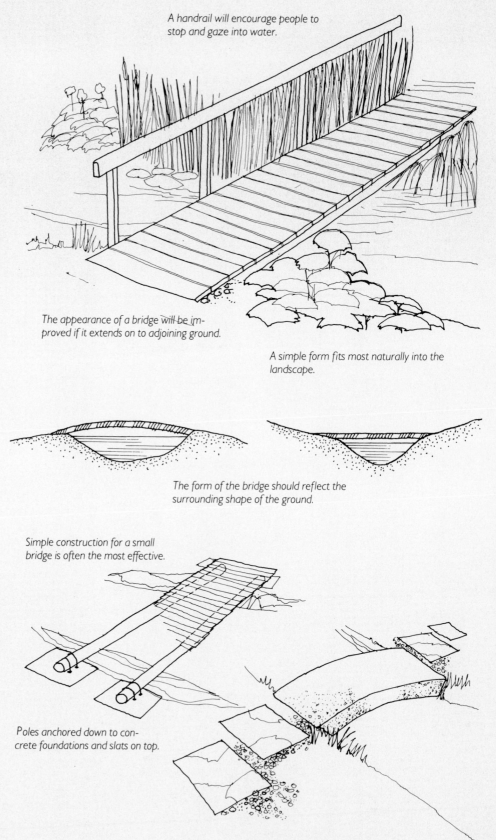

A handrail will encourage people to stop and gaze into water.

The appearance of a bridge will be improved if it extends on to adjoining ground.

A simple form fits most naturally into the landscape.

The form of the bridge should reflect the surrounding shape of the ground.

Simple construction for a small bridge is often the most effective.

Poles anchored down to concrete foundations and slats on top.

A stone or cast concrete bridge is ideal for a small stream.

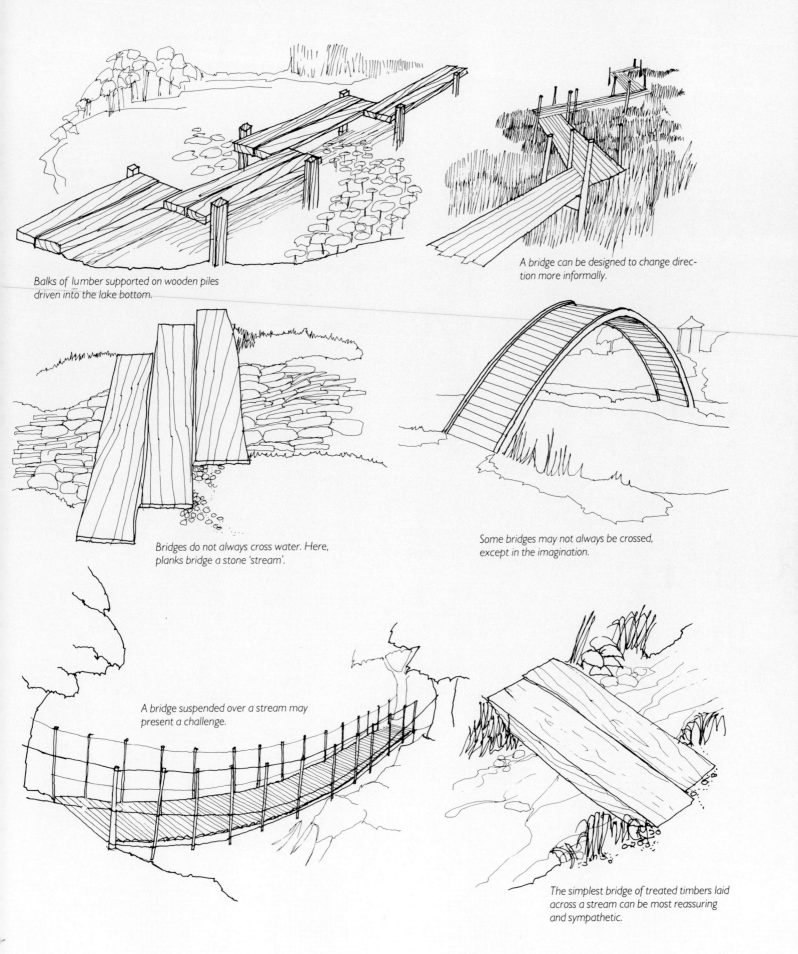

Balks of lumber supported on wooden piles driven into the lake bottom.

A bridge can be designed to change direction more informally.

Bridges do not always cross water. Here, planks bridge a stone 'stream'.

Some bridges may not always be crossed, except in the imagination.

A bridge suspended over a stream may present a challenge.

The simplest bridge of treated timbers laid across a stream can be most reassuring and sympathetic.

STEPS & TERRACES

The shape and size of your steps determine the way they will be used: for a leisurely, unhurried pace, they should be wide and shallow with a long tread and a shallow riser; small, steep steps will take you quickly from one level to another. Materials vary, too, from lumber, stone and brick to precast concrete, which can be delivered as a customized unit, built to your specifications and ready to install. With the other materials, however, you can be more inventive, introducing different combinations or changes of direction.

Steps can be as simple as grass or gravel notches cut into a slope and reinforced with boards, or they can be of a freestanding lumber construction linking different levels in a system of decks. Both can look good in an informal garden but, for a more formal, classical effect, you can use stone or brick leading down from a paved terrace to the main garden or linking areas in a more geometric design.

As with all constructional elements, steps should blend with the main theme of the garden and, generally, be made from natural or well-weathered materials that are easy on the eye. It is possible, however, to introduce decorative elements and so make them more of a focal point. Examples of this could include contrasting a series of rough lumber steps made from railroad ties with a brick pattern between, or by adding a decorative handrail of lumber, bamboo poles or even stout colored rope. This type of addition is not just decorative. For safety, handrails on steps or balustrades around terraces are a necessity where the change of level is more than 60 cm (2 ft), unless access to the edge is restricted by water or particularly dense planting.

Another way of creating interest in a steep or long flight of steps is by incorporating a viewing platform – it need only be a slightly wider step – at the point at which the steps change direction, but it will encourage users to pause and view the garden from a new angle.

Terracing is where a slope is cut into a series of level platforms rather than steps, and can be grassed, planted, paved or used to create a water terrace. The slope between the terraces is generally retained by vertical or angled walls, and the different levels can, themselves, be linked by steps or a waterfall. When constructing a terrace it is important that you average the slope by cutting and filling – this way you should not have the bother and expense of removing or importing any extra material □

STEPS

For comfort, external steps should be shallower and wider than internal ones.

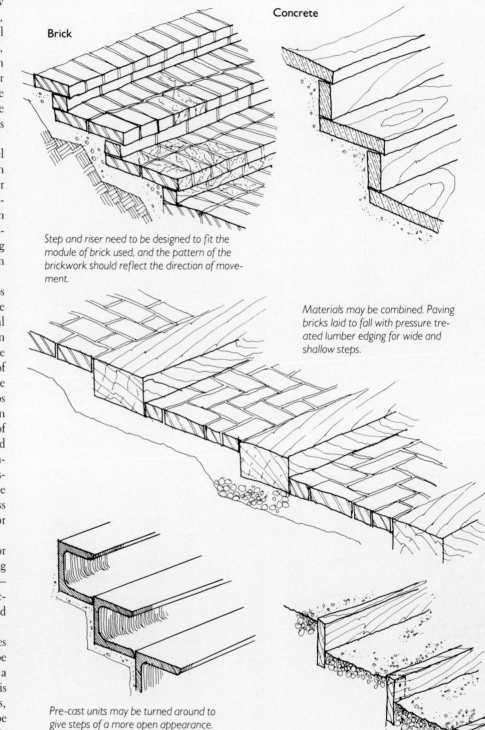

Step and riser need to be designed to fit the module of brick used, and the pattern of the brickwork should reflect the direction of movement.

Materials may be combined. Paving bricks laid to fall with pressure treated lumber edging for wide and shallow steps.

Pre-cast units may be turned around to give steps of a more open appearance.

Simple steps in a soft landscape have been achieved by using pressure treated lumber boards pinned into the ground to retain gravel.

TERRACING

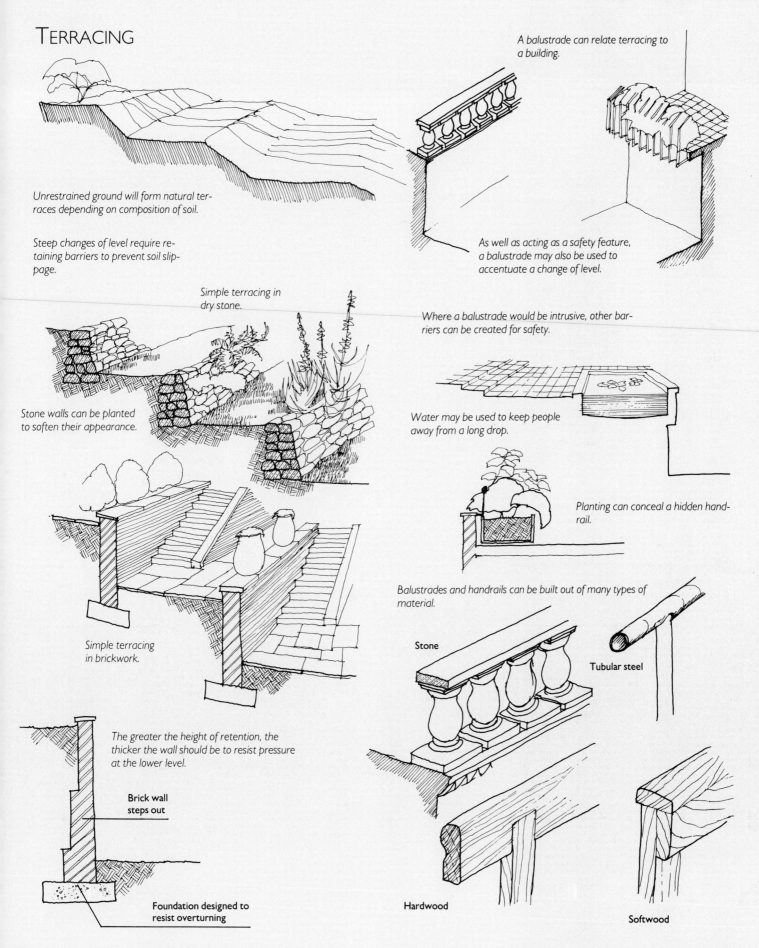

Unrestrained ground will form natural terraces depending on composition of soil.

Steep changes of level require retaining barriers to prevent soil slippage.

Simple terracing in dry stone.

Stone walls can be planted to soften their appearance.

Simple terracing in brickwork.

The greater the height of retention, the thicker the wall should be to resist pressure at the lower level.

Brick wall steps out

Foundation designed to resist overturning

A balustrade can relate terracing to a building.

As well as acting as a safety feature, a balustrade may also be used to accentuate a change of level.

Where a balustrade would be intrusive, other barriers can be created for safety.

Water may be used to keep people away from a long drop.

Planting can conceal a hidden handrail.

Balustrades and handrails can be built out of many types of material.

Stone

Tubular steel

Hardwood

Softwood

CONTAINERS

Garden containers, whether for plants or water, will constitute an essential decorative element of your garden design. As important as shape, size and texture, which have already been dealt with (see p. 110), is that they be practical, sturdy and weatherproof. Naturally, if the container is to be used as a water feature it will need to be waterproof but, generally speaking, good drainage is vital. Another point to bear in mind when adapting containers for use in the garden, is that any weatherproofing or decorative treatment you apply must be nontoxic to plants.

Types and care of containers

Containers tend to fall into three categories: those you buy ready for planting; 'found' containers, which may have to be adapted in some way to their new role; and homemade troughs, boxes and planting blocks, constructed from stone, brick, concrete or lumber, and used perhaps as part of a paved or decked area or planting complex.

Bought containers range from terra-cotta urns, reconstituted stone troughs and planters to painted slatted tubs, baskets and painted or glazed ceramic ware. Your supplier should be able to advise you if the containers of your choice are frost resistant.

Cheaper and, in many ways, more exciting are found and homemade containers. These include painted oilcans, half barrels, old boxes, sinks troughs, pails and baskets, all of which can be easily adapted to make attractive and versatile plant containers.

Whatever type you go for, spend a little time making sure your container is correctly planted so that plants will flourish. Begin with a good layer of small stones or crocks to encourage drainage: this layer should be as deep as about 15 cm (6 in), depending on the type of plant. Next, fill with a potting mix of the correct chemical composition for the plant. The new soil level should match that of the old pot or bag the plant was in. Finally, both as a decorative touch and to reduce evaporation, finish off with a layer of pebbles or moss on top of any exposed areas of soil.

Aftercare is just as important as correct planting and, because containers offer a restricted environment, you need to pay strict attention to feeding and watering. In the hot summer months, standing tubs on a bed of damp pebbles will help keep the soil moist, as well as help drainage in wet winter areas □

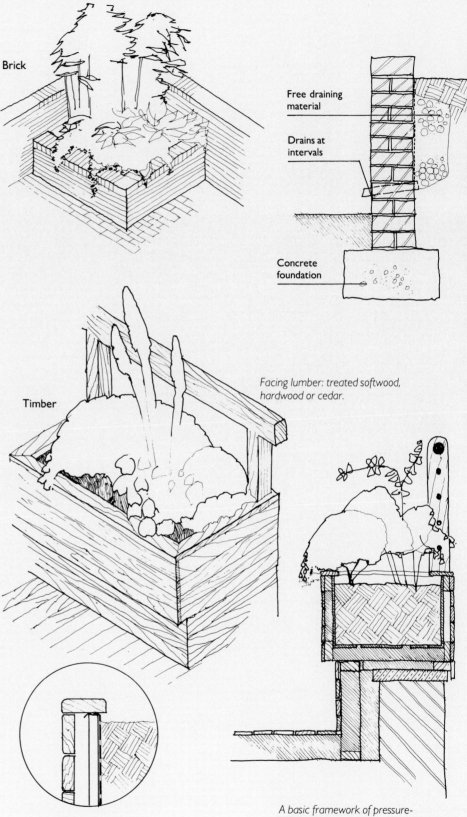

Brick

Free draining material

Drains at intervals

Concrete foundation

Timber

Facing lumber: treated softwood, hardwood or cedar.

Liner taken under edging lumber, soil kept below top of liner to avoid damage to face lumberwork.

A basic framework of pressure-treated lumber and waterproof ply is lined with polyethylene, with drainage holes drilled in the bottom.

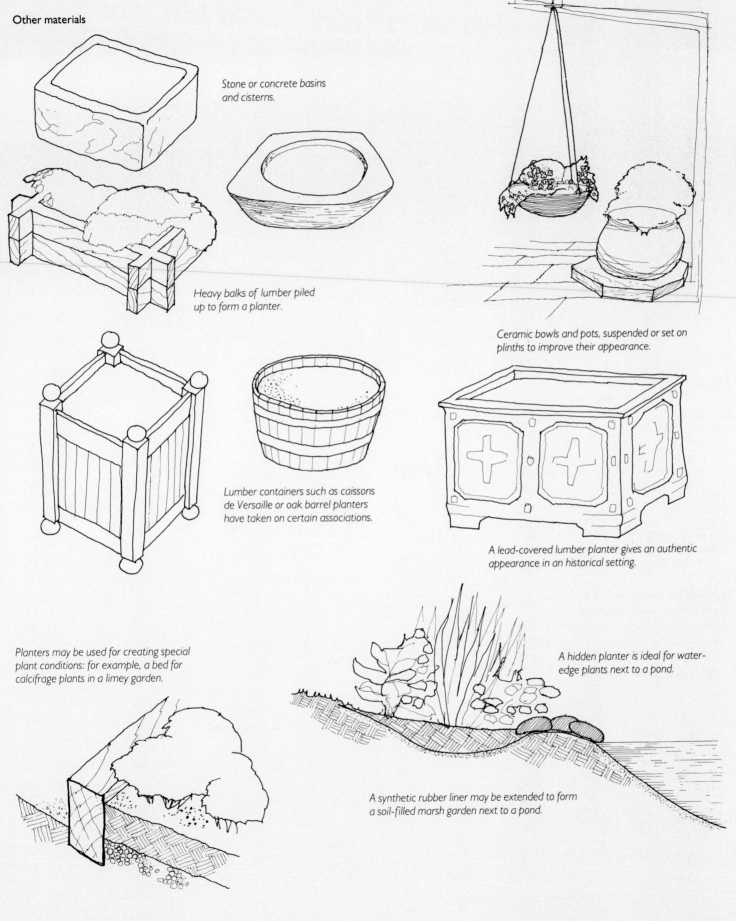

Other materials

Stone or concrete basins and cisterns.

Heavy balks of lumber piled up to form a planter.

Ceramic bowls and pots, suspended or set on plinths to improve their appearance.

Lumber containers such as caissons de Versaille or oak barrel planters have taken on certain associations.

A lead-covered lumber planter gives an authentic appearance in an historical setting.

Planters may be used for creating special plant conditions: for example, a bed for calcifrage plants in a limey garden.

A hidden planter is ideal for water-edge plants next to a pond.

A synthetic rubber liner may be extended to form a soil-filled marsh garden next to a pond.

223

DECKS

Strong supports and an attractive surface are the secrets of a successful deck, whether it is designed to sit just off the ground or comprises a large platform extending over water or a sloping site. Fittings can be concealed by using rustproof nails or made a feature of by attaching brass cups and screws to hide the nail heads. A practical point to bear in mind when designing your deck sections is to build in removable panels to provide access to any services below, such as plumbing for a pool or hot tub or electrical cables for garden lights.

The joists should support the walking surface clear of the ground and they need to be placed close enough together to give proper support to the surface lumbers – a slight spring to the deck is acceptable. Gaps between the planks should be large enough for water and dirt to run through but not so wide that narrow heels are likely to become caught.

The type of lumber you choose to construct the surface of your deck will influence its style and looks. New planks give a very smooth, neat appearance and they look good when arranged in intricate herringbone and basket weave patterns; thicker, stouter lumber and second-hand sections will be rougher and less formal. It is important to remember that where a deck will be walked on with bare feet, you must use perfectly smooth, splinter-free wood, with rounded rather than square corners. This is essential around hot tubs and pools.

The way you lay the wood is important, too. Continuity of direction over changes of level will give a fluid and very natural passage; changing direction creates a different effect – a visual break and the opportunity to create patterns within the arrangement of planks.

Also, give some thought to how your deck is going to relate to its surroundings. It could, for example, be set on the same level as other types of surfacing material, such as stone or brick, to provide an interesting change of texture. If, however, the deck is raised a few feet, or even a few inches, it will appear to float over adjoining surfaces such as paving, grass or water.

Finally, you can use your deck as a disguising feature by building it around a raised swimming pool or setting into it a sunken hot tub or spa, planting beds, concealed storage chests or lumbered, sheltered seating areas. The all-important last step is the finish of the wood, and the chart opposite will give you some ideas of the very wide range of colors and finishes available □

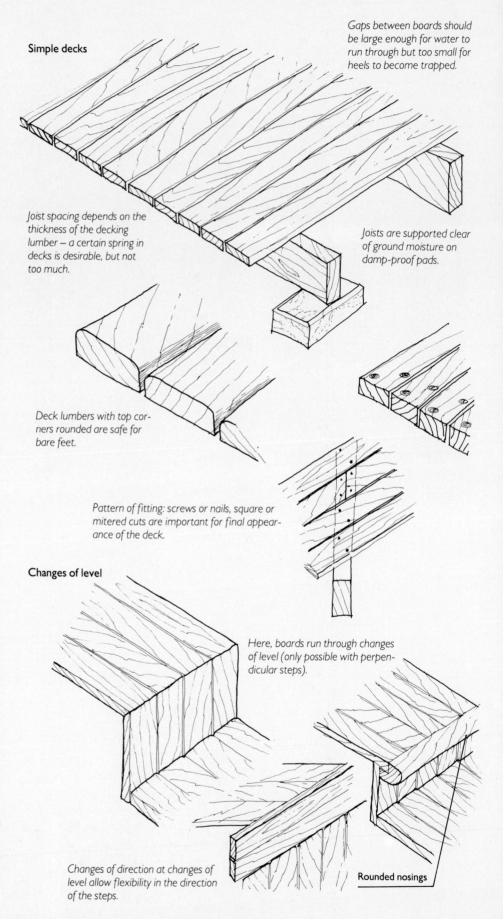

Simple decks

Gaps between boards should be large enough for water to run through but too small for heels to become trapped.

Joist spacing depends on the thickness of the decking lumber – a certain spring in decks is desirable, but not too much.

Joists are supported clear of ground moisture on damp-proof pads.

Deck lumbers with top corners rounded are safe for bare feet.

Pattern of fitting: screws or nails, square or mitered cuts are important for final appearance of the deck.

Changes of level

Here, boards run through changes of level (only possible with perpendicular steps).

Changes of direction at changes of level allow flexibility in the direction of the steps.

Rounded nosings

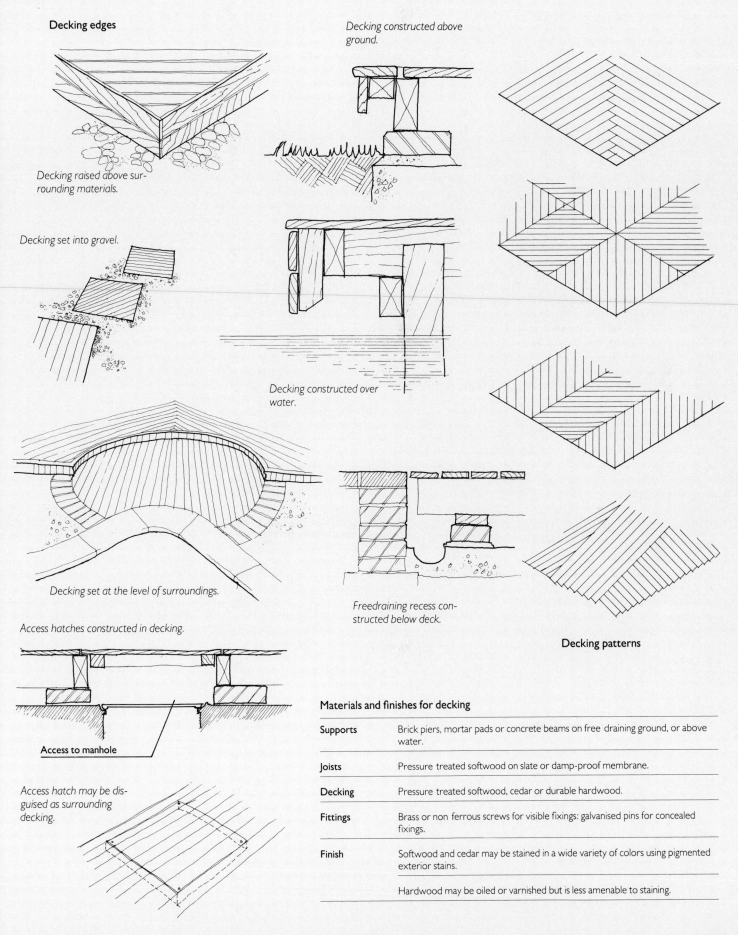

Decking edges

Decking raised above surrounding materials.

Decking set into gravel.

Decking set at the level of surroundings.

Access hatches constructed in decking.

Access to manhole

Access hatch may be disguised as surrounding decking.

Decking constructed above ground.

Decking constructed over water.

Freedraining recess constructed below deck.

Decking patterns

Materials and finishes for decking

Supports	Brick piers, mortar pads or concrete beams on free draining ground, or above water.
Joists	Pressure treated softwood on slate or damp-proof membrane.
Decking	Pressure treated softwood, cedar or durable hardwood.
Fittings	Brass or non ferrous screws for visible fixings: galvanised pins for concealed fixings.
Finish	Softwood and cedar may be stained in a wide variety of colors using pigmented exterior stains.
	Hardwood may be oiled or varnished but is less amenable to staining.

225

PATHS & PAVING

Paths and patio areas need a firm, level surface that is easy to keep clean and reasonably dry. Choice of materials here is wide, including new or secondhand bricks and paving stones, concrete units and lumber.

If you are looking for a plain, unobtrusive, natural-looking surface, Belgian blocks or paving slabs can be laid over large areas and softened with tubs of plants or even creeping plants positioned between the slabs. Brick and concrete paving units lend themselves more to being laid in decorative patterns and you can buy them in a range of colors and interlocking shapes and sizes. It is also possible to order bricks and concrete units in a special color if you want to match them to an existing building or other feature.

Simple designs, such as borders, herringbone and weave patterns, are easily acceptable to the eye and, if carefully planned, can be used to make a stunning focal point or a more subtle link between features.

Some paving materials are designed not to be comfortable underfoot: cobbles, for example, can be used to create an interesting change of texture or to indicate a no-go area.

Combining materials, particularly within a patio area, often works extremely well and you can use this technique to make patterns and designs of complementary surfaces. Bricks make excellent dividers for areas of larger paving slabs, or stout railroad ties can also be used as edging or dividers. Another option is to lay different paving materials in alternate blocks to form a checkerboard effect.

Stepping stones

In effect, stepping stones are a discontinuous path and, as such, can be made from similar materials: simple flags, large, flat stones or sections of sawn logs. These can lead from a path or paving area across grass, planting beds or water, where they can be just at water level or raised above. But safety is an essential requirement of any type of stepping stone, and it needs to be safe to stand on, firmly fixed and nonslip.

Stepping stones laid straight from one point to another are not usually visually exciting. Much better is to lay them so that they describe some sort of pattern when seen against their background of water or grass □

Flexible brick paving

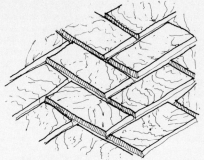

Paving bricks for flexible paving usually have chamfered edges.

Paving bricks are laid on a bed of sand on a consolidated granular bed and leveled with a flat-plate vibrator.

Joints may be brushed with a dry mix of cement and sand – pointing is not necessary.

Edge restraint necessary for large paving areas.

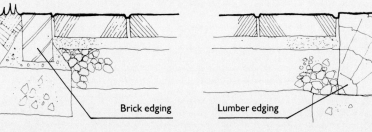

Brick edging   *Lumber edging*

Rigid brick paving

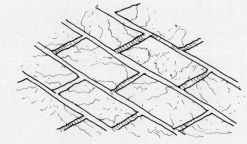

Paving bricks for rigid paving may be thinner – 1½ to 2 in (4 to 5 cm) and they usually have square edges.

Paving bricks are laid on a bed of mortar on a solid base – a lean-mix concrete – and pointed with mortar, which may be colored to match or contrast with bricks.

Rigid paving may be continuous to the edge.

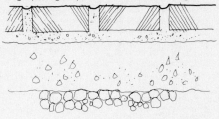

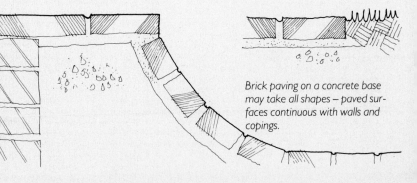

Brick paving on a concrete base may take all shapes – paved surfaces continuous with walls and copings.

Stone and concrete paving

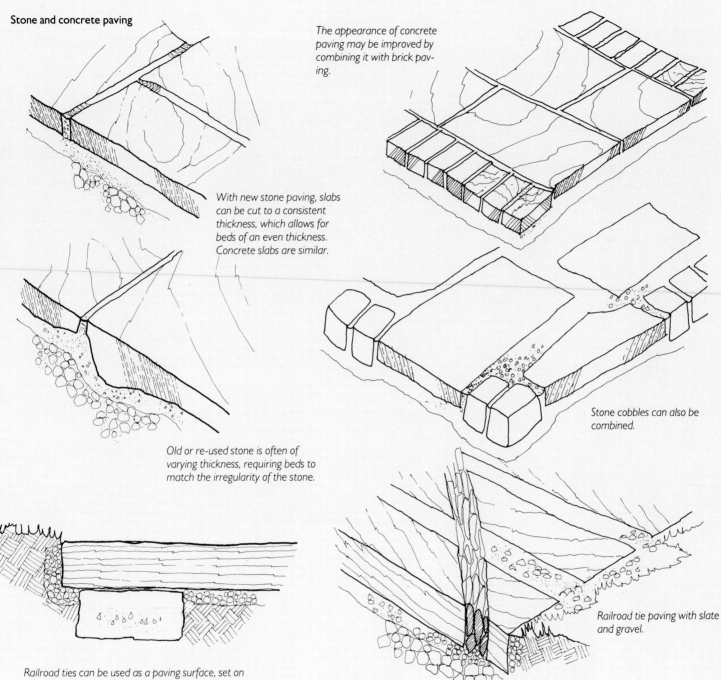

The appearance of concrete paving may be improved by combining it with brick paving.

With new stone paving, slabs can be cut to a consistent thickness, which allows for beds of an even thickness. Concrete slabs are similar.

Old or re-used stone is often of varying thickness, requiring beds to match the irregularity of the stone.

Stone cobbles can also be combined.

Railroad tie paving with slate and gravel.

Railroad ties can be used as a paving surface, set on concrete and surrounded by freedraining material.

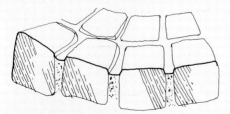

Cobble stones and Belgian blocks may be used alone or in combination with other materials.

Different paving materials, construction and appearance

Brick	Flexible paving on consolidated granular bed, consistent texture and color.
	Rigid paving on concrete base, pointing gives a sharper appearance.
Stone	New stone on granular or solid base will take time to develop a weathered appearance.
	Reused stone paving on granular base has immediate weathered look.
Concrete	On granular base, consistent coloring may be set off by using contrasting material.
Lumber	Railroad ties or oak planks set in free draining material. Care must be taken that surface does not become slippery.

227

STEPPING STONES

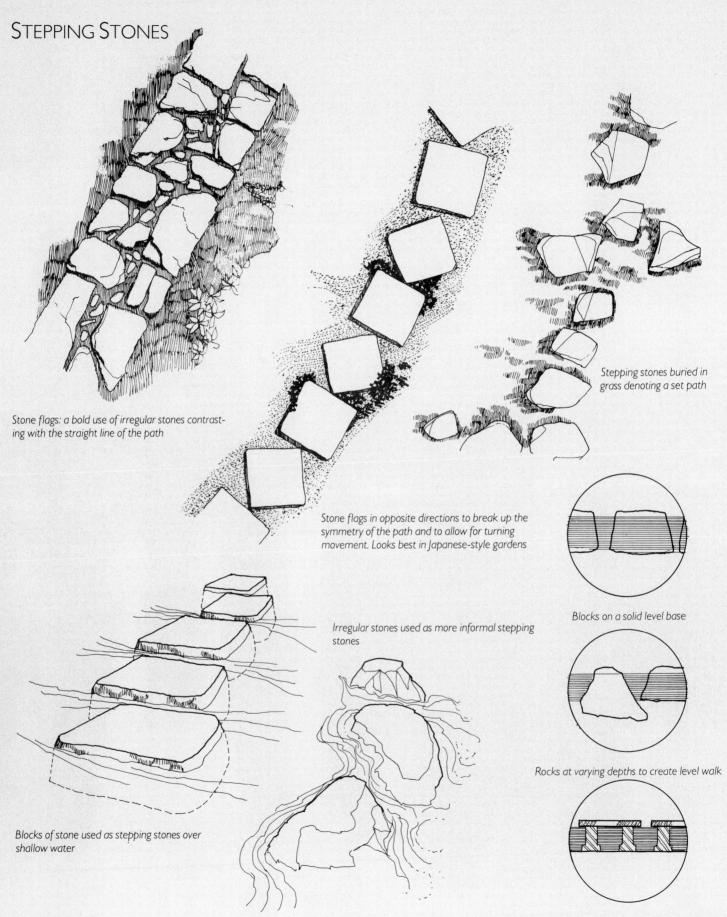

Stone flags: a bold use of irregular stones contrasting with the straight line of the path

Stone flags in opposite directions to break up the symmetry of the path and to allow for turning movement. Looks best in Japanese-style gardens

Stepping stones buried in grass denoting a set path

Irregular stones used as more informal stepping stones

Blocks on a solid level base

Rocks at varying depths to create level walk

Blocks of stone used as stepping stones over shallow water

Stones or slabs supported on brick piers

APPENDIX

This section is intended as a useful plant reference to be used in conjunction with the rest of the book, and it relates directly to the *Designs & Themes* chapter starting on p. 71. The Plant Lists will provide a quick, but by no means definitive, guide to suggested plants that can be used in city and country gardens, dry, shady or moist situations and so on. *The Zonal Guide* on pp. 238–9 will indicate which plants are suitable for your particular area.

Since success with plants is fifty percent choosing the right ones for your own situation and fifty percent careful handling, detailed advice on choosing and maintaining your specimens is also included.

Failure to observe these basic guidelines will lead to frustration, disappointment and not inconsiderable expense, since replacing failures can become a costly practice.

Most of the gardens in this book are designed to be as labor and maintenance free as possible, making it even more important to get plants off to the right start and to position them where they will happily flourish.

Choosing Plants

When selecting nursery plants for any design, be it large or small, don't judge them purely on their looks as appearances can be deceptive. For instance, many young plants can look very much alike when lined up at the local garden center, dwarf and slow growing conifers being barely distinguishable from forest trees. However, within a few years the forest trees could be up to roof height, while the dwarf, slow growing varieties are likely to have put on only a few inches. Similar mistakes can be made with habit where two cedars, identical at five years old, may grow to between 90 cm (3 ft) and 18 m (60 ft) spread at maturity. Where trees and shrubs are involved, and the ground is obviously going to be occupied for many years, it is particularly important to choose the right plant for the job. Mistakes in size, scale or suitability may make it necessary to grub them out, so losing several seasons' growth.

Practical considerations

A systematic approach is the most successful when it comes to drawing up a short list of plants for inclusion in the garden. The following headings are a useful reminder for assembling the necessary information.

Naming

First identify your plant: most have at least two names: a latin/botanical name and a popular name.

By all means use the popular name for your own identification, but these vary so widely from area to area, you must establish its internationally accepted latin name before you buy to avoid mistaken identity. The latin name is made up in two parts. First the 'genus' which is like its surname, say *Cotoneaster*. The second part or forename – *horizontalis* – denotes the 'species'. Where several plants share the same 'species' name, variations are often distinguished by a cultivar name, as with *Cotoneaster horizontalis* 'Variegatus'.

Type and role of plants

It is helpful to establish the useful lifespan and speed of growth of plants:
● Herbaceous perennials will flourish for anything from one to 50 years. Always check.
● Some perennials are treated as annuals or biennials.
● Most shrubs have a useful life of 15–25 years and longer.
● Some trees, like laburnum, have a relatively short lifespan of 25–30 years. The majority, however, will outlive the planter.

Plants are often chosen purely for their decorative value and cosmetic effect. This is shortsighted: always consider other possible functional uses – otherwise you risk missed opportunities. When choosing trees, always take into account their potential for: screening, shading and shelter. Shrubs provide great scope for the marking of boundaries and internal divisions, as well as hedging and visual screening. Provided they are tall and thick enough, they are also excellent for reducing noise and dust levels from nearby roads and industry. Trees and shrubs, together with many ground-covering herbaceous perennials, will reduce soil erosion and so contribute to soil stability on banks and slopes. You won't be able to grass anything with a gradient of more than 1 in 3, but banks up to 1 in 2 can be planted with trees, shrubs and ground cover. Land steeper than this needs terracing. Flowering and foliage annuals and biennials may also be used for screen and shelter, particularly when grown in containers.

Hardiness

As discussed under zoning, always check on the hardiness rating of plants. This gives an indication of a plant's ability to survive the local climate. Where plants are grown in a zone cooler than their hardiness rating, be prepared for the extra work this will involve.

Garden worthiness

Some plants can offer more than one attractive feature: fine leaves, lovely flowers, interesting shape or good autumn color, and these are of great value in the small garden. Use them as a focal point for year-round interest.

Safety

Safety is an important consideration, particularly if the garden will be used by children.

Many plants have fruits poisonous to humans or animals; shrubs like kalmia and taxus have poisonous foliage. Trees and shrubs like *Ilex*, *Crataegus*, *Rosa* and *Berberis*, with their vicious spiky leaves or thorns, are best avoided near paths or walkways. Don't plant trees like *Robinia* and *Ulmus* that are noted for dropping their branches in high winds, where they could prove hazardous. Others, like *Prunus cerasifera*, are noted for dropping their leaves or fruits and making driveways slippery.

Aesthetic qualities

Where plants are being assessed mainly for their appearance, one of the chief points to consider is their season of interest. It is important to know not only when they flower or bear fruit, but also how long they maintain a decent display and which are scented. Plants with a long season of color and interest are preferable to those with a fleeting, short-lived show, unless the blossom is particularly eyecatching or occurs at a time when few other plants are looking good. Some trees and shrubs provide more than one notable display each year – perhaps a good show of blossom in spring and then a bonus of colorful fruits or foliage in autumn.

Evergreen foliage is of particular value when it comes to creating year-round interest. In an effort to avoid winter bareness, many leading designers aim for a 2:1 ratio of evergreen to deciduous plants. Variegated as well as monocolored red, blue, gold, purple and gray summer foliage will provide a long season of color. Autumn tints in fiery red, flame, yellow, orange and crimson shades can be outstanding just before leaf fall. You should also make use of fruiting and berrying plants to take the season well into autumn and winter, and the colored stems of *Cornus* and *Salix* varieties or and the attractive bark of *Betula*, *Prunus* and *Rubus*, wherever winter color is lacking. Don't ignore the potential of bare winter branches: *Acer japonica*, *Betula*, *Corylus avellana* 'Contorta', *Salix matsudana* 'Tortuosa' and *Rhus* are all useful here.

Size

The ultimate height and width of plants should be considered in relation to their setting as well as to other plants, not forgetting to take growth rate into account. Use temporary quick growing plants to fill in around slower growing, longer lasting permanent plants rather than plant these too close, which only results in overcrowding and weak, disease-prone, spindly growth. Trees are almost invariably planted too close together. They may look, and be, all right for the first few years, but if they grow too large, close to buildings, drains, gutters and services they may become dangerous and cause damage to foundations. As a general rule, don't plant any tree nearer to a building than a distance equal to its ultimate height.

Habit and shape

Trees Most develop a characteristic shape and outline: some are tall, narrow and columnar and well suited to confined spaces and small gardens. Others grow into large, spreading or round-headed trees needing plenty of space and ideal for providing dappled shade. A few trees have a natural weeping or domed habit, making them useful as specimen or feature plants. Choose with care from the extensive range of dwarf and slow-growing trees for smaller effects.

Shrubs Use tall, narrow species for accent plants; bushy for mixed borders; dumpy, mounded, prostrate and creeping shrubs for ground cover and in a rockery.

Climbing plants and wall shrubs These maximize the space available in small gardens, where they soften, camouflage and generally add interest to walls, fences and buildings. Be wary of those which attach themselves to supports by means of aerial roots or suction pads. They should not be grown on old or crumbly walls where they are likely to damage the mortar and weaken the structure. *Hedera*, *Parthenocissus* and *Hydrangea petiolaris* are notorious in this respect and are always best grown on a trellis set some 5 cm (2 in) out from the wall.

Nonwoody plants Again habits vary enormously. For example, rosette-forming grass-like tufts range from the small edging *Festuca glauca* to the tall exotic *Cortaderia* (pampas), ideal as a focal point. Select from the tall and spiky plants like *Althaea*, *Kniphofia* and *Lupinus* for good back of the border plants, also useful for contrasting with bushy cottage-type garden favorites like *Helenium* and *Rudbeckia*. From among the carpeters and creepers are many excellent rock, wall, pocket, container and edging plants.

Trained forms Many trees and shrubs can be trained or sheared to create sculptural forms or special effects.

Bush trees These include fruits, and are trained as bushy plants with a short main trunk of 30–60 cm (12–24 in) from soil level to the lowest branches. This makes for ease of pruning.

Standards Where extra height is required, trees are trained with a ball of foliage above a tall, single stem. This is a popular form for container grown plants like bay (*Laurus*) – as well as for fruiting and ornamental trees grown in beds or in grass.

Pyramid trees and shrubs These are wider near the base and taper to a point at the tip and are popular for planting in containers near doorways.

Fan-shaped trees Trained so that branches radiate from a short trunk and are ideal for covering walls and fences.

Espaliers Also popular for wall coverings. Typically, they have a main central stem with twin branches trained horizontally in tiers on each side.

Plant positioning and habitat

When selecting plants, choose them on a sound ecological basis, for the secret of success is to match plant requirements with site conditions. In short, the closer the site approximates a plant's natural habitat, the more easily it will adjust to its new surroundings and the easier it will be to maintain.

Climate

The need to match a plant's hardiness to climate are discussed under zoning (see p. 238).

Shade and sun Although many plants are fairly adaptable and may tolerate a variety of different conditions, most have strict preferences for sun or shade. For practical purposes, the site should be assessed according to the level of light intensity and commonly categorized as: full sun; partial shade – with some direct sun as in east- or west-facing borders; dappled shade – as under a canopy of leaves; and permanent shade – no plant will grow where shade is excessively heavy. See lists for plant suitability. As a rough guide, flowering and fruiting plants need more sun than foliage plants such as *Hedera*, *Euonymus* and *Taxus*, which can tolerate permanent light shade. Variegated foliage keeps its contrasts best in good light. Gray-leaved plants and those with thick or needlelike foliage can usually stand more sun than those with large, thin, green leaves, such as ferns.

Wind Plants vary considerably in their ability to stand up to wind with its chilling and drying effects. Assess the likely degree of exposure to wind of all planting positions and make your selections accordingly. Exposed coastal positions, and those on high ground, call for the most wind-resistant plants of all. Choose from plants such as *Olearia* and *Rosmarinus*.

Soil

When assessing your plants, the main points to watch here are soil texture, moisture content and depth – plus acidity/alkalinity (pH). All garden soil must be drained if subsoil water is going to get away, otherwise there is a risk of waterlogging and suffocation of plant roots. Even when very heavy soil is well drained, water can be slow to disperse after prolonged periods of rain. Under these conditions, consider bog or moisture-loving plants. On the other hand, if the soil is sandy or gravelly and quick draining, select a range of drought-tolerant plants. Sometimes there is an inadequate depth of soil and you may have to consider container plants as an alternative. Bedding plants need a minimum 10–15 cm (4–6 in) of good topsoil; herbaceous perennials 15–20 cm (6–8 in); shrubs 30 cm (12 in); and trees 45–60 cm (18 in–2 ft). Where the soil is alkaline, or limey – with a pH of between 7 and 8 – you will not be able to grow acid lovers like azaleas, camellias and rhododendrons unless, again, you resort to containers of suitably composed soil. Other sites can be adjusted by adding fertilizers or by liming.

Plant quality

When buying plants by mail, choose a well recommended supplier. Better still, go where you can inspect your plants before parting with money and where you can check them thoroughly for the following points:
● Freedom from pests and diseases.
● Container grown plants should be well developed – with shoots and branches in proportion to the roots.
● Look for evenly balanced, well rounded plants. Avoid any which are lopsided or badly damaged.
● Containers should be intact – with roots just showing out of the bottom. Avoid any which have thick roots pushing their way through the container – a sign of neglect.
● Be wary of wilted, sickly or dried plants.
● In the case of balled plants, avoid any which have a badly crumbling rootball.
● With bare root plants, steer clear of those which are withered and shriveled or any which are bursting into premature growth □

PLANTING HINTS

Buying plants for a new garden, or just filling in the gaps left by the casualties of last winter's frost, can be an expensive business, so it is a good idea to tackle the job in a sensible and logical manner.

Planting plan and program

Working to a preplanned design helps to make sure that nothing is overlooked and can save you time and money, by pinpointing avoidable mistakes. In fact, whenever more than five or six plants are set out at any one time, it is a good idea to prepare a proper 'planting plan'; while for an ambitious project where many different plants are included, it really becomes a necessity. It need not be elaborate; a simple layout plan showing the position of each plant together with a list of names will suffice. In addition, on large projects where planting is to be carried out in stages, you should work out a planting program, paying due regard to what needs planting and when. This will allow the workload to be organized in a more practical manner.

Ordering and buying

Get plants ordered in good time to be sure of having them on hand when needed. Otherwise, you run the risk of missing good weather while waiting for plants to arrive, and valuable opportunities to push ahead with planting can be lost.

Pegging out

Using stakes, at least mark the positions of the main plants. Any minor rearrangements can then be made without having to move the plants around and risk damaging them.

Timing

One very important aspect of timing is to ensure that bare root and balled plants are out of the ground for the shortest possible time. To avoid a setback, get them planted as soon as possible after delivery. Although container-grown plants can be set out at almost anytime, providing weather and soil conditions are suitable, there is an 'ideal' planting season for most plants. The actual dates will depend on the type of plant and locality. Autumn is the traditional planting time for most trees and shrubs – including conifers and other broad-leaved evergreens. However, in cold climates and on wet soil, planting is best held back until spring. Many perennials, spring-flowering bulbs and spring bedding plants are also set out in autumn.

Spring is the other popular time for planting trees, shrubs and climbers. However, in general, spring-planted stock is more difficult to establish. Plants must be kept well watered during their first season to increase their chances of survival. Summer-flowering perennials, rock plants and bulbs can all be planted in spring, and this is also a good time for setting out aquatics and bog plants or summer-flowering bedding plants.

Taking delivery

When taking plants home from the garden center, don't stick them on a roof rack or in an open trunk, leaving the foliage exposed. Put them inside the vehicle, out of the wind, or protect them with windproof wrapping. This should be removed immediately on arrival.

If plants are delivered before the ground is ready, unwrap and give them a good watering. Plunge the roots of bare root plants in clean water for an hour or two to soak. It is then good practice to 'heel in' all bare root and balled plants – ie plant them in temporary quarters. Excavate a hole for individual plants or a shallow trench where a number of plants are involved. Both must be large enough to take the roots comfortably. Dormant deciduous plants are usually set obliquely, so as not to catch the wind, and can be close planted. Conifers and evergreens, on the other hand, must be stood vertically to prevent the stems from kinking and causing irreparable damage. Large evergreens must be staked and tied and they should be well spaced out – the leaves of one must not touch those of its neighbor. Firm fine topsoil in and around the roots, then water in to settle.

When plants are delivered during a freeze and the ground is frozen, keep them in an airy cool building or shed until the weather improves. Remove any wrapping from around the foliage to allow air to circulate – but protect the roots from frost. If frosts are prolonged, give the roots an occasional soaking; they must not be allowed to dry out. Stand container-grown plants in a sheltered spot where they can be cared for until planting time. Protect the roots if frost threatens, moving plants indoors if necessary.

Planting conditions

The weather Whenever possible, set plants out during calm, mild, moist and preferably dull weather. Avoid exposing the roots to hot sun, drying or chilling winds and frost as these can be stressful to your plants. If delays are unavoidable, keep the roots covered with damp burlap or newspaper.

The ground This should be well prepared and weed free; moist but not waterlogged. Never attempt to plant on land which is baked dry and hard – water thoroughly two or three days beforehand. Frozen ground should be allowed to thaw; waterlogged land may need draining.

The plants All should be thoroughly moist at the roots before setting out or potting up. Continue to water containers until water runs out at the base, then allow them to drain for a minimum of 30 minutes before handling. If any container has dried out, stand it in a container of water with the water level up to the rim. As soon as the bubbles stop rising, take it out and allow it to drain. Soak bare-root plants for two to four hours and again allow them to drain before planting.

Tree planting

Check exact planting positions. This is vital in small spaces and near walls. Don't plant strong-growing trees closer to buildings than a distance equal to their ultimate height or you risk damage to foundations. In these situations it is much safer to pot up and grow trees in large containers. Set wall-trained trees like peach (*Prunus persica*) at least 30 cm (12 in) out from the foot of the wall.

Dig out a planting hole which is twice as wide as the rootball and half as deep again, stacking good topsoil to one side. Loosen the bottom and sides of the hole with a fork to relieve any possible compaction: roots will then grow more easily into the surrounding soil to make for quicker establishment. Fork plenty of organic matter into the bottom of the hole – well rotted garden compost or peat is excellent for the purpose – together with a sprinkling of balanced fertilizer.

Where supports are necessary, as with free-standing trees, hammer home a pointed stake. Position it off center, to one side of the hole, and preferably facing into the direction of the prevailing wind. The tree will then be blown away from the stake and won't become chafed. When calculating the length of stake needed to give stability, reckon on a quarter being buried below soil level. With the support in place, the hole is ready to receive the tree.

To get trees off to a good start, pack planting mixture around the roots. Prepare this by mixing three parts good topsoil with one part each, by bulk, of peat moss and clean coarse sand, together with balanced fertilizer at rates recommended by the manufacturer. Any other suitable soil conditioner can be used to replace the coarse sand. Where the existing topsoil is poor, it is much better to buy ready made potting mix or planting mixture rather than attempt a homemade mix. If lime-hating trees are being planted, be sure to use lime-free planting or potting mixtures.

Carefully remove the container, with the minimum of root disturbance and shorten any damaged roots back to sound tissue. Position the tree in the planting hole, close up to the stake, with its best side facing toward the main viewing point. Root wrappings from balled trees are best removed after the tree is positioned in its hole. Work planting mix in around the rootball, firming as filling proceeds. This is to eliminate possible air pockets and so ensure good soil contact with the roots. At this stage the top of the rootball should be slightly below the level of the surrounding soil.

Release any temporary bindings or ties used to hold in branches during planting and fix trees to supports with brand-name tree ties. Carry out any necessary top pruning. This will depend on the type and condition of the tree. Most ornamental trees require little pruning other than shortening weak, straggly or misplaced shoots. When planting trees in warm or mild climates, it is a common and highly recommended practice to create a dishlike depression around the tree. This is to retain irrigation water which will then seep down to the roots instead of being wasted in surface run-off. Don't make the dish any deeper than 8 cm (3 in). The base of the tree must be slightly higher than the dish, to avoid the risk of standing water remaining in contact with the trunk. In hot weather, you should shade newly planted trees from burning midday sun. Spraying spring-planted conifers and broadleaved evergreens with a suitable brand-name antiwilt preparation immediately after planting will help them to establish themselves more rapidly. Hose over regularly with clean water in the cool of the evening, following warm, dry or windy days, and keep the roots well watered.

You should leave a minimum 30–45 cm (12–18 in) collar of bare soil around the base of each tree when planting in grassed areas. This is to minimize competition for nutrients and moisture. Mulch the roots of newly planted trees in spring, once the soil has warmed up, using a generous layer of well rotted compost, peat, shredded bark or the like.

Planting shrubs and climbers

Shrubs The procedure for planting shrubs follows a fairly similar pattern to that adopted for tree planting. The one essential difference is in the staking and tying. With the exception of standards, supports for freestanding shrubs are not as a rule necessary. To calculate spacing, allow each freestanding shrub a minimum circular area about equal in diameter to its ultimate spread.

Wall shrubs and climbers Set wall shrubs and climbers at least 25 cm (10 in) out from any wall to avoid extreme dryness and make supporting easier. Borders at the foot of warm, sunny walls are notorious for dryness – the chief enemy of wall plants and climbers. In hot, dry sites the sinking of one or two drain pipes alongside vulnerable plants can help with deep watering. Set the pipes vertically, the tops level with the surrounding border, then pack round with soil. Water poured in at the top of the pipe will then reach the roots without waste.

Most climbers and many wall plants benefit from some form of support and with these plants wall-mounted trellis or wires should be installed before planting.

Formal hedging

Hedging and screening plants are set much closer together than freestanding shrubs in beds and borders. Nurseries and garden centers will usually recommend spacings appropriate to the variety and type of plant being purchased.

When setting out a row of close-planted hedging, prepare a strip of ground the length of the proposed hedge and dig out a trench at least 30 cm (12 in) deep and 45–75 cm (18–30 in) wide. Fork up the bottom, incorporating organic matter such as well rotted compost or peat, plus a sprinkling of fertilizer. If the soil is heavy, work in some coarse sand to improve the texture at the same time. Backfill with the topsoil, working in more manure, compost, peat and coarse sand and breaking down clods to a fine tilth and rake level. Peg out a taut line and insert stakes at regular intervals to mark planting positions. Take out planting holes large enough comfortably to take the roots, allowing a depth of about 30 cm (12 in) and an area 38 cm (15 in) square for smaller plants. You will find anything over 60 cm (2 ft) in height is more difficult to establish.

In warm conditions on freedraining, light sandy soil, plant the hedging in a sunken, flat-bottomed drill about 8 cm (3 in) below the surrounding soil. This way rainfall is captured, surface run-off avoided, and watering made easier. If the soil is heavy, however, and inclined to remain wet, then you should plant on a slightly mounded ridge of between 8 and 15 cm (3 and 6 in). All hedging is planted at the same depth, or slightly deeper, than the plant was before the move.

In windswept, exposed gardens it is advisable to provide some form of support to prevent windrock. If plants are blown about, a depression soon forms around the base in which water can collect and this is likely to lead to rotting. Perhaps the simplest method of support is to knock in a few stakes to take a horizontal wire. Each hedging plant is then tied individually on to the wire. Keep all hedging plants moist and mulched at least during their first, critical growing season.

Planting in beds and borders

Dig vacant beds and borders in preparation for planting perennials and bedding plants. Go down a spade deep and incorporate plenty of organic matter and sand, as for hedging. Where the soil is very acid, with a pH of 5.5 or below, apply a handful of ground limestone per sq m (yd) and just before planting, rake in a dressing of complete balanced fertilizer. If the soil is inclined to be spongy, firm by tramping, then rake level.

For maximum effect, where borders are viewed from one side, set tallest plants to the back; where long beds are viewed from two sides, set the tallest plants along the center with the shorter plants to front and rear; with circular beds set the tallest plants in the center and grade down to dwarf edging plants.

Mark out planting position by scratching the surface with a stick and set out young plants with a trowel, firming the soil around each plant with the fingers before watering in. Use a spade or fork to set out larger plants. Where perennials are set out in established borders, take out planting holes in much the same way as for trees.

Bulbs Bulbs look good interspersed in groups among other plants in beds and borders, and when naturalized in grass. Use only flowering sized, firm, undamaged bulbs. Most hardy kinds are planted in autumn. Set out half hardy varieties after the danger of frost has passed in spring and lift again before frosts return. Avoid growing bedding bulbs like narcissus and tulips more than one year in three in the same bed or you risk disease.

A good rule of thumb guide is to plant bulbs at a depth equal to three times their height. Planting depth is measured from the top of the bulb to the soil surface. It is sound practice to plant bulbs on a generous handful of sand – vital on heavy or wet soil to improve drainage and discourage rots. Fork the soil to loosen before planting at random, and only plant bulbs in straight rows for formal bedding or for cutting. When planting in grass, remove areas of sod, loosen the soil, plant and return the sods, firming back into place after adjusting soil levels as necessary.

Rock gardens, paved areas and retaining walls

Where there is any choice in the matter, you should avoid planting rocky plants under the shade of trees. The aim when planting here is to make the plants look as natural as possible, using, in the main, rock plants, dwarf shrubs and conifers, *Erica* and *Calluna*. Place upright plants at the foot of a rock face; trailers to drape over the edge; reserving cushion formers and tufty varieties for filling in. Do not plant lime haters like *Lewisia* and *Lithodora* among limestone rocks.

Using a trowel, take out small planting pockets in rock gardens and paved areas. In paved areas it is often necessary to remove the odd corner from a few of the flags, unless provision was made when the paving was laid. Bottom out the pockets with soil-based potting mix and position plants. Work more soil mix in and around the roots, again using a lime-free mix for lime haters. Finally, cover with a layer of chippings to keep the roots cool and prevent rain washing away the soil mix. Use limestone chippings for the majority of plants, but granite for the lime haters.

When planting a retaining wall, bear in mind that most plants prefer shade from mid-day sun, and that plants growing on top of a wall are particularly vulnerable to drying, by excavating extra deep pockets. In a dry stone wall – without mortar – it is relatively easy to plant in the cavities between the stones. In old stone and mortar or brick walls, poke out crumbling mortar to create planting pockets. Only attempt to plant in new brick/stone walls if planting spaces have been left specifically for the purpose.

Choose small, young, pot-grown plants – they are least likely to suffer root disturbance during planting – and line the cavity with some moist potting mix. Pack more moist peat around the rootball and ease the plant gently into the prepared cavity with a pointed stick. Firm in well.

Aquatic and bog plants

When planting a pool or pond it is particularly important to use plants which are suited to the climate and to the available water depth. Where the water depth is 30–45 cm (12–18 in) or more, plant deep water aquatics like water lily and *Aponogeton*. Floating aquatics, like *Hydrocharis* and *Stratiotes*, which grow at or near the surface without being anchored to the bottom, are suitable for almost any depth. Where fish are kept, it is important to plant a selection of oxygenating plants: aim to set out at least six or eight per sq m (yd) of surface water area. Avoid using invasive plants like some sedges (*Scirpus*) or water weeds like *Lemna* in small pools and take care not to overstock the pool initially. When plants are established, 75 percent of the water surface should be covered.

Excess light in water encourages the growth of algae – one of the main causes of the unpleasant green soup effect. Water-edge plants should be positioned in the shallow water near the pool edge or held in place on water-edge shelves by boulders, to soften the outline.

In small pools it is best to plant deep water aquatics, and oxygenators in net lined baskets filled with soil low in organic matter. After planting always put a layer of gravel or stones over the soil to prevent fish disturbing the soil and clouding the water. Balance the baskets securely on blocks so that the leaves just float on top of the water.

Planting in containers

Only use containers which are suitable for their location. For outdoor use they must be durable and frost resistant and reasonably well insulated against heat and cold. Make sure any container is well provided with drainage holes in the base and large enough to hold sufficient soil mix to sustain, water and anchor plants. For tall plants, they should be heavy enough not to blow over. Also check that containers are well designed and strongly constructed; lumber should only be treated with a suitable nontoxic preservative.

Size Use minimum 30–40 cm (12–16 in) diameter containers for trees and shrubs. Don't consider windowboxes less than 18 cm (7 in) deep and 20 cm (8 in) wide. When growing specimen plants in containers, at no time should plant width be more than three times the container width; neither should the plant height be more than four times the width of the container. When moving plants into a larger container, avoid increasing the diameter of the container by more than 5–8 cm (2–3 in) at each move.

Plunge planting It makes good sense to adopt the plunge planting technique where plants of different types and growth rates are displayed in the same container. This enables frequent changes of plants to keep up a succession of interest. Plunge planting entails setting out plants complete with pot. The pots are plunged up to their rims in soil, peat or other attractive aggregate.

Normal planting Cover drainage holes with gauze/netting and provide a good layer of pebbles or crocks for drainage. Part fill with soil-based potting mix, then plant in the way described for trees and shrubs. Alternatively, fill to within 3 cm (1 in) of the rim and set out a collection of smaller plants as discussed for beds and borders. A top covering on the soil's surface helps minimize moisture loss □

PLANT MAINTENANCE

The appearance of any beautiful garden depends as much on the health and well-being of plants, as on their original choice and setting. No matter how tasteful and expensive a selection of man-made artefacts might be in the form of statuary, containers, paving or buildings, their effect is soon nullified by plants which have become sickly, untidy or overgrown. If plants are to remain healthy after planting and give of their best, then adequate provision must be made for their routine care and maintenance.

Planned maintenance

Whenever a sizeable planting plan is envisaged, maintenance should really be considered at the planning stage – be it a complete new layout or major improvement. Landscapes linked by paving or decking with large areas of water and a blend of low maintenance trees and shrubs need little attention over the years, provided herbaceous planting is kept to a minimum. At the other extreme, fussy and elaborate planting projects are labor intensive and costly to maintain – especially those involving seasonal bedding designs which need replanting up to three times a year. Your choice of plants, as discussed earlier, should be viewed from the angle of maintenance – both workload and expense – as well as from the other important considerations of site, soil and climate.

Where hired labor or contractors are employed, and where budgeting is essential, the drawing of some form of maintenance plan and program is strongly to be recommended. Such a plan can assist in making sure that essential jobs are not forgotten and that an acceptable spread of work and expense is achieved. Obviously some flexibility is called for – minor adjustments will need to be made according to season, weather and ground conditions. During the first season a certain amount of guesswork is going to be involved, but in the second and subsequent years, more accurate judgements are possible.

An all too common approach to plant maintenance, especially in small gardens, is to react to the needs of the moment without any preconceived plan. If a plant or container is dry, it gets watered. If the grass is long, it gets cut. This approach is fine, provided it is always practical to stop other activities in order to devote time to the garden as and when plants require attention. Regardless of approach, plant care and maintenance should be careful-ly assessed in relation to work involved and resources available in the shape of money, equipment and time. It may help to know what you might be up against through the year so that you can plan your resources accordingly and on a timely basis.

Groundwork

Trees, shrubs and climbers During winter and spring, refirm the roots of newly set out plants which have been loosened by frost or wind. Take care to wait until the ground thaws and choose a time when the soil is not too wet. Then scatter topsoil over any roots which have become exposed and firm again.

It is important to keep the soil weed free after planting – for the first year or two at the very least. This is to minimize root competition for food and moisture. Once things have warmed up a bit in spring, a good routine is to surface hoe or lightly cultivate the soil, killing weed seedlings and breaking up the soil crust. Take care, however, not to loosen the plants or to damage the roots.

Then scatter dry, balanced fertilizer around all established plants, at rates recommended by the manufacturers. Water in. If the soil is dry, apply at least 10 liters per sq m (2 gals per sq yd), and repeat if it soaks in quickly. Follow this with a generous 5–8 cm (2–3 in) deep mulch of rotted garden compost, peat or bark fiber. This will help smother germinating weed seeds, keep roots cool, help to conserve soil moisture, and assist in the prevention of soil erosion. Replenish the mulch as necessary and as supplies permit, during the summer months. Where mulching materials are in short supply, simply hoe or lightly cultivate the soil between plants to create a dust mulch. Although somewhat less effective, this serves a similar purpose to conventional mulching. In later summer or autumn, when carrying out the end of season cleanup, fork in any remaining mulch. At the same time loosen up compacted soil, again taking care not to damage delicate surface roots.

In cold winter areas, protect the roots of frost sensitive plants by putting down a minimum 15 cm (6 in) layer of material such as leaves or straw, held firmly and securely in place with pinned down netting.

Border perennials Basically, follow the guidelines as set out for shrubs. One of the major differences is the need to rejuvenate many border perennials every three to five years or so – when clumps get large and overcrowded and flowering begins to suffer. Fork up large clumps of plants like *Helenium*, *Lychnis*, *Monarda* and *Rudbeckia*, then cut or tease away small, rooted outer segments. Re-plant at the same depth as before lifting, with minimum delay as the rooted segments must not be allowed to dry out. Throw away the outworn center portions. Spring-flowering plants are usually lifted in autumn; and autumn-flowering plants in spring.

Rock plants Systematically hand weed the rock garden throughout the season to keep it tidy. Otherwise weeds can quickly get a hold, become entwined and smother small, slow-growing plants. The only satisfactory way to deal with an unruly weed-ridden rockery is to rebuild it from scratch.

Invariably it is necessary to replenish soil washed away from around plants twice a year – during spring and again in autumn. Use freedraining, soil-based potting mix as a top-dressing and cover with chippings or other attractive material.

Supporting plants

Trees, shrubs and climbers Examine all stakes and ties at least once a year, similarly check supports for climbers. Make any adjustments necessary. Those which have become too slack will cause chafing; any which are too tight will restrict the flow of sap. Remove any stakes which have come to the end of their useful life and replace those where continued support is called for: trees are not fully secure from wind damage for up to several years after planting.

Border perennials By virtue of their habit of dying down at the end of each flowering season, perennials must be restaked annually. All tall, floppy plants will need supporting; one popular, easy and effective way to deal with clump-forming perennials is to push in three stakes to form an inconspicuous triangle around each plant when half grown. Soft green or brown twine can then be looped from stake to stake. Give tall plants like *Althaea*, which produce long spikes of bloom, one stake for each stem and tie it in at several points. The alternative is to use commercially made supports.

Pruning

It is important to prune many trees, shrubs and climbers for a variety of reasons. Primarily this is to ensure continuity of flowering and foliage by encouraging the production of new replacement wood; for shaping and training; and to keep plants healthy. In the average garden, pruning takes place at planting time, as part of normal routine to get the plant into a good shape and as a remedial measure with old, neglected or sickly plants.

When pruning, aim to make a clean cut, just above a good, healthy, well-placed bud –

APPENDIX

using a pair of sharp pruners. There are several basic ways to tackle pruning depending on the effect you are trying to achieve:
- Shearing – as for hedging.
- Cutting back or crown reduction – most stems and branches are shortened.
- Crown thinning – the selective removal of some shoots and branches, resulting in a more open-textured tree or shrub.

For practical purposes the method and time to prune will depend on the type of tree, shrub or climber involved.

Ornamental trees As a rule, those which are allowed to grow more or less naturally need little by way of routine pruning. This consists mainly of cutting out any dead or diseased wood back to sound tissue and shortening any misplaced, straggly, crossing or ingrowing shoots. Generally pruning of this nature is best carried out in autumn. Avoid pruning trees like *Acer*, *Betula* and *Juglans* in late winter or spring as the sap is rising, otherwise they may bleed badly and be severely weakened. Remedial pruning and surgery on old, neglected or badly diseased trees is a specialist job and you should obtain professional help.

Shrubs Spring-flowering shrubs like *Forsythia* bloom mainly on young shoots produced in the previous year. They are normally pruned as soon as flowering is over, by thinning out any worn out flowered wood, as well as weak, new growths.
- Summer- and autumn-flowering varieties like *Buddleia* and *Clematis*, bloom at the tips of new shoots formed the same year and are pruned in autumn or spring. Once a main framework of branches has been formed, flowered shoots are cut back to this framework.
- Some summer- and autumn-flowering shrubs of borderline hardiness in cool temperate zones – such as *Fuchsia*, *Ceratostigma* and *Phygelius* – are treated like herbaceous perennials and cut down almost to ground level.
- Evergreens like *Camellia*, *Pieris* and *Rhododendron*, together with dwarf conifers of naturally neat habit, need little pruning beyond shortening of straggly shoots.
- *Calluna* and *Ericas* which need regular cutting to keep them compact and busy are lightly sheared after flowering in spring or summer depending on variety. Prune winter-flowering *Ericas* in spring. Prune summer- and autumn-flowering *Ericas* and *Calluna* in autumn or early spring where winter foliage is outstanding.
- Large-leaved shrubs like *Aucuba* and *Prunus laurocerasus*, and climbers such as *Hedera colchica* are best pruned with pruners, rather than risk shearing with hedge shears or trimmers. This avoids the risk of cutting individual leaves in half, which will invariably become brown and discolored at the edges.

Bark color Trees such as *Salix* and shrubs such as *Cornus* are grown for the winter color of young bark, and are cut hard back each spring – just as the buds are beginning to burst into leaf.

Topiary Trees and shrubs, including hedging and ground cover, grown for their sheared formal effects, are lightly sheared during summer whenever necessary to keep them tidy.

Perennials Border perennials which are winter green or winter gray only need to have the odd flower stems cut down when blooming is over for the year. Use a sharp knife or pruners. Perennials which die back to soil level each winter are normally cut down almost to the ground in autumn, but, as with bulbs, not until the leaves begin to yellow.

Deep water and submerged aquatics In late summer or early autumn, it is important to remove any dead or decaying leaves and other vegetation, especially in small pools stocked with fish. If left, rotting vegetation will use up valuable oxygen in the water and give off poisonous decomposition products harmful to fish. This apart, the rotting vegetation is not a pretty sight through the winter.

Every two or three years, when aquatic plants have become matted and overcrowded, thin them out very drastically. Summer is a good time to carry out the work, when the water level has dropped and conditions are reasonably warm. This is also an appropriate time to undertake any replanting.

Deadheading Deadheading, as the word implies, is the prompt removal of faded or dead flowers. A few shrubs notably young azaleas, rhododendrons, *Syringa* and modern bush and standard roses (*Rosa*) benefit from deadheading. Never deadhead where plants are grown for their seeds or fruits.

Deadhead most border perennials, rock plants, bulbs, annuals and biennials. This is to keep plants tidy and prolong flowering. Plants may be greatly weakened if flowers are allowed to run to seed. In the case of perennials, this results in less flowers being produced the following year. Simply cut or pick off the old faded blooms or spikes. With rock plants and heaths lightly shear over with hedge shears; with bulbs it is important not to cut off any leaves.

Humidity, ventilation and watering

Humidity and ventilation During the warmest months of the year, it is vital to maintain the correct level of *humidity* – especially around indoor plants. In a greenhouse or conservatory this can be achieved by misting over foliage and by damping down floors and benches. Standing pots on moist, pebble-filled flats or saucers helps but a brand-name humidifier is less work.

Ventilation goes hand in hand with shading in an effort to keep plants cool and should ensure adequate air movement for healthy growth without damaging drafts. Ideally, aim for a ventilator to floor area of 15–20 percent. This will be able to cope with hot weather and provide the requisite number of air changes per hour. Actively growing plants need fresh air and carbon dioxide for the leaves to function properly and manufacture much needed starches and sugars. Stale, stagnant air makes for disease prone plants.

Watering Water plays a variety of roles; it is essential for absorption of fertilizer; the transportation of nutrients and food within plants; the manufacture of sugars and starches in green leaves during the hours of sunlight; and to keep plants cool. It is important to give plants pure water that is free from harmful salts. Never, for example, use water which has passed through a chemical water softener. Use only clean water, free from disease organisms. In some areas water contains a considerable amount of lime which is harmful to acid loving plants like azaleas and rhododendrons. In these situations use rainwater or select plants to suit local water conditions.

Good watering practice is to water at sowing, planting and potting – and again thereafter whenever the soil dries out. It is important to water plants before they start to wilt. Avoid wetting leaves in strong sunshine, or you risk scorching them. Always water plants thoroughly, never in dribbles which encourages surface rooting; in the case of beds, borders and lawns, aim to apply a minimum of 1 cm (½ in) of water – or 10 liters (2 gallons) per sq m (yd).

Container watering Conscientious watering is crucial here. With most container plants, the rule is water sparingly in winter and freely in summer. Newcomers to plant care may find the gauging of soil moisture content a little tricky until experience is gained. In this situation a soil moisture meter with a direct read-off dial can be very helpful. Alternatively use labellike water signals – they are pushed into the soil and change color when the moisture level varies.

Apply water to containers until it starts to trickle out at the bottom. Rewet dried out containers by immersing up to their rim in a pail/tank of clean water: take out and drain as soon as air bubbles stop rising. In warm climates, soak the roots of container plants occasionally during summer. This will flush out accumulated salts and fertilizer residues

236

and prevent a harmful build up. Never leave plants standing in water for more than 10–15 minutes before allowing to drain.

Watering methods Use a watering can with a rose, or a hose with a spray or rose attachment for watering small numbers of plants.

● Various sprinklers, ranging from small rotary to the long-throw pulse jets and oscillating sprinklers are popular for larger areas where they dispense with laborious hand watering.

● Drip or trickle systems, including soakers, are extremely useful for the deep watering of individual plants.

Protection

Frost protection Frost, and low temperatures, pose a serious hazard to many plants in cool temperate zones. Tender half hardy plants should be lifted and brought indoors to overwinter in a frost free place, if freezing conditions are likely outdoors. Similarly those growing in containers should be brought inside. Make this a regular routine with plants like *Fuchsia, Pelargonium, Lantana* and *Abutilon*, also with many bulbs, corms and tuberous plants like *Acidanthera, Begonia* and *Dahlia*.

Marginally hardy plants like some varieties of *Agapanthus, Alstromeria, Indigofera* and *Phygelius* will survive winter frost if given adequate root protection. This is also useful for a newly planted camellia or magnolia in its first winter or two. In autumn, protect the roots with a minimum 15 cm (6 in) layer of leaves or straw, held in place with pinned down netting.

Many trees and shrubs including *Acer, Camellia, Magnolia* and various *Prunus* are normally winter hardy, but suffer severely from spring frosts, when flower buds, shoots and young foliage can be blackened. The damage is worst on east-facing walls where early morning sun results in a rapid thaw after overnight frost. Shade vulnerable plants in the morning with fine mesh netting and in future choose plants known to be more tolerant to these conditions. Wall-trained fruits like peach and apricot need to be protected if blossoms are not to be frosted. Again draped netting will normally suffice.

Shading For many plants shade from strong sun is vital. Newly set out plants in open ground and containers are particularly vulnerable to strong sunlight. Fine mesh netting supported on a light frame will keep off sun effectively, as will opaque plastic sheet. Explore the possibilities of moving container plants into a shaded part of the garden.

Screening from intense sun is equally essential for most indoor plants from spring through to late summer, if overheating and excessive moisture loss are to be avoided. With houseplants, the easiest solution is to move them on to an east- or west-facing windowsill which misses midday sun. A net curtain or blind will then give additional protection where necessary. In a greenhouse or conservatory, you can use blinds, lath screens or paint-on shade to temper the sunshine.

Wind shelter Exposure to cold, freezing, or hot, drying breezes is not good for plant survival. The provision of shelter and windbreaks makes for better growth and flowering, foliage or fruit. Permeable screens of fine mesh netting or hedging are superior to solid walls and fences which cause damaging air turbulance.

Protect individual, newly set out plants from wind with netting or burlap supported on a temporary frame. A newly planted bed or border can be sheltered by erecting a screen on the windward side. A lengthy screen positioned across the direction of the oncoming wind should protect an area of up to seven times its height, given reasonably level land. When hedge planting on windy sites, it is a good idea to take out a shallow trench, using the excavated soil to make a protecting ridge.

Snow, hail and rain Heavy rain and snow have a habit of disfiguring conifers and other multistemmed trees by forcing their branches apart. At the first signs of spreading, tie in the vertical branches in autumn by encircling with inconspicuous ties. After heavy snow, shake conifers to dislodge settled falls. In areas where hail is likely to be exceptional, protect greenhouses, frames and delicate plants with hail screens; where heavy rainfall is the norm, it is sensible to use raised beds, especially on heavy soils. Container plants can be protected from deluge rains by covering the potting mix with rigid plastic collars.

Plant ailments

In hard-water areas, lime-haters like azaleas, rhododendrons and magnolias – and to a lesser extent roses – often develop yellowing leaves, owing to iron deficiency. At the first signs, apply iron sequestrene root drench, and thereafter repeat annually.

Keep a look out for pests and diseases. Many chemical companies provide helpful identification guides – ask at your local garden center. If you take the appropriate steps at the onset of trouble, you can avoid the indiscriminate use of chemicals.

Container plant care

● Keep plants well watered from spring to autumn – up to twice a day during hot weather. Water sparingly in winter.

● Feed plants with liquid balanced high potash fertilizer during the growing season.

● Every two to four years, repot long stay plants. Do this in autumn or spring using standard soil-based potting mix. In the years between, topdress by removing the top 3 cm (1 in) of mix and replacing with fresh.

● In summer, move half hardy plants outdoors. Return them indoors before autumn.

● In autumn, insulate containers which are to overwinter outdoors by encasing them in a layer of leaves or straw.

Sod care

Each spring as growth breaks away, lightly rake, stone pick and roll lawns. Then start routine mowing – once or twice weekly until growth eases off in autumn. Give an annual feed of brand-name lawn fertilizer in spring. If moss is troublesome, use a moss killer, also in spring. Apply a selective weed killer, in spring or early summer if weeds are getting out of hand □

ZONING & PLANT HARDINESS

The use of climate zone maps is an accepted and increasingly used practice for identifying plant suitability and one which is widely adopted in the USA. It helps remove some of the guesswork from garden planning and reduces plant failures.

One of the best known examples of work carried out in this field is perhaps the United States Department of Agriculture's (USDA) system of climate zone maps. Fundamentally, this is a land classification of the USA, whereby the land is subdivided into climate zones, based on minimum temperature ranges: a system which is suitable for modification and extension to suit other countries. We have chosen to adopt the same approach in this book. Selected garden plants are listed and given zone numbers/letters to correspond with the regions in which they can normally be expected to grow. To simplify things, plants are designated **C**, **M** or **W** according to their temperate needs or tolerance.

C denotes **cool** temperate plants, tolerant of average winter minimum temperatures of minus 17°C (0°F).

M denotes **mild** temperate requirements with a winter minimum temperature of minus 6°C to minus 10°C (20° to 14°F).

W indicates **warm** climate plants, including those commonly referred to as subtropical and tropical – needing frost free minimum temperatures of 2° to 5°C (35° to 40°F).

The above plant zone classifications correspond with the USDA zone ratings approximately as follows:

C = zone 7/8; **M** = zone 9; **W** = zone 10.

Plants with lower USDA zone numbers down to 5 can be grown reasonably successfully in zone 7/8; those numbered 6, 7 and 8 in zone 9; and those numbered 8 and 9 in zone 10.

Climate and plants

Climate is the sum effect of temperature, rainfall, wind, sun, snow, frost and shade on a particular area over a period of time. It is one of the major deciding factors which determines whether a plant will grow and flourish. Soil, site, care and treatment represent other important limiting criteria.

The effect climate exerts on an individual plant will depend on the type of plant. Take temperature for example. Tropical plants will flourish in high temperatures, but those originating in cool climates may suffer badly.

Conversely, frost-tender tropical plants will perish at the first touch of frost, whereas cool climate perennials, shrubs and trees will stop growing until warmer weather returns.

To sum up: plants have adapted naturally to grow and flourish in a particular climate, largely depending upon their original habitat.

Plant growth and hardiness

A plant is hardy to a particular climatic zone if it can grow successfully outdoors year-round. Trees and shrubs and other plants which are native to and hardy in, say, Australia and New Zealand are likely to suffer badly if planted outdoors in the colder climates of Britain or North America. However, under these circumstances, there is no reason why such plants should not be cultivated successfully as tender indoor plants – in a conservatory or greenhouse. So a hardy plant from one zone frequently becomes a tender plant in another.

When assessing a plant's hardiness suitability, don't ignore the variations which make up the average temperature range. For instance, a climate with an average temperature of around 10°C (50°F), which does not fluctuate more than plus or minus 5°C (10°F) will support subtropical plants. Yet in another place, with a similar average temperature, but with, say, a 12°C (25°F) variation – including winter frosts – cool temperate plants only will prove hardy.

Hardiness ratings are based on the average prevailing weather so any deviations from the norm in the form of violent fluctuations or extreme conditions can have a dramatic effect on plant hardiness, growth and survival.

The main regional zones

For the purpose of this book, we are concerned mainly with three broad climatic zones ranging from cool temperate regions to warm climate areas. Any illusion that there is a clear-cut division between one zone and the next must be dispelled at the outset. As a rule the transition is gradual and is related to latitude on a north/south axis. The temperature decreases steadily as the distance from the equator increases. As a rough guide, there is an approximate 1°C (2°F) drop in temperature for every 250 km (160 miles) traveled.

The cool temperate climate zone

Central and northern North America, the southern half of the British Isles, southern Ireland and parts of western mainland Europe enjoy a cool, temperate climate intermediate in character between hot tropical climes and cold arctic regions. Central mainland Europe generally has hotter summers and colder winters than Britain and Ireland.

Throughout temperate Europe the hours of daylight in winter are relatively short and frost can be expected anytime between September and May. The long days of summer are warm, but as a rule not unbearably hot. In average years the rainfall is normally sufficient to carry established trees and shrubs through summer without the need to water artificially. On the whole, cool temperate regions tend to suffer less from violent storms or extremes of weather than arctic or tropical areas.

There are many similarities of climate between Britain, parts of the USA and areas of southern Australia and New Zealand's South Island but one of the main differences is that summer in the USA corresponds with winter in Australia and New Zealand.

The mild temperate climate zone

The climate of nontropical parts of southern USA and much of the Mediterranean area is fairly typical of this zone. Mild winters and long hot dry summers are characteristic near sea level at least. Frosty weather is the exception and at worst expect slight touches for short spells only. Most of the Mediterranean region receives winter rain and only parts of Spain could be described as dry and arid. Some parts of South Africa also share mild climates and on occasions, along with the USA, are subject to violent hailstorms.

The differences in day length between summer and winter are less pronounced, when compared with the cooler temperate zone.

The warm climate zone

This region equates roughly with tropical and subtropical areas of parts of southern and south-east USA – plus northern Australia. Day length and night are about equal at all times and this can upset flowering response in some temperate plants, which need long days to initiate flower buds. The zone is normally frost free year-round but rainfall is somewhat variable. It ranges from arid, dry, very low rainfall areas through to wet tropical rain forests and even violent tropical storms, drought and flood are not unknown.

Geographical influences

Air Stream Belts West coast regions of the British Isles and western Europe are warmer in winter than inland areas of central Europe due to the Gulf Stream drift of warm air across the Atlantic. Similar effects are experienced in western USA, this time because of warm air coming in from across the Pacific.

Continental Climate Toward the middle of large tracts of land in central North America, central Europe and central Australia extremely high summer temperatures are the norm. But in winter the reverse is true – extremely cold, subzero conditions prevail.

Dry Climate Areas This is a problem associated mainly with warm climates and inland regions. In some coastal areas in western USA, southern and eastern Australia mountain ranges are found to collect heavy rain on the seaward side producing a lush flora. Inland, behind the hills, lie dry, arid, rain shadow areas where life is a struggle for plants. This particular set of circumstances illustrates well the extremes which can be experienced within a single climate zone.

Frost

Frost is a factor to be reckoned with in any zone. It is a commonplace problem in cool temperate zones, and to a lesser extent in the mild climate zone. Even in subtropical regions frost occasionally threatens – sometimes with devastating effects. From a zoning and plant viewpoint the critical points which determine the degree of frost and low temperature damage are: the severity and intensity of cold; the length of time frosts persist; and when or at what stage the freezing conditions strike.

Normal frost In the cool temperate zone, and to some extent in the mild climate areas, winter frost is the norm. And unless frosts are abnormally severe, plants hardy to the area will usually come through without undue harm. Dormant or resting plants can normally survive freezing conditions with less risk of injury than those which are actively growing.

It is the interval between the last spring frost and the onset of autumn frosts which largely determines the length of the growing season. This in turn not only influences sowing and planting dates, but also the period when half hardy plants can be set outdoors in safety, or indeed when they need to be moved back inside again.

Unexpected frosts These are the most damaging of all, completely cutting down lush, soft growth. Late spring frosts can be particularly devastating should they occur for example when fruit trees and other flowering plants are in full blossom. Often equally destructive as frost are temperatures which fall abnormally low for the zone.

Frost prediction Local plants, neighbors, garden centers and meteorological records will provide the gardener with invaluable information about probable frost trends.

Frost pockets These are cold sites with above average liability to frost within a neighborhood or even within a garden. For instance hollows of natural land, such as valley bottoms, surrounded by higher ground, are typical examples of potential frost pockets. Here cold air, being heavier than warm, rolls downhill and collects at the lowest point – like pools of water – and on calm, clear nights it meets heat given off from the soil resulting in a drop in temperature of soil and the air immediately above. The cold air then moves in to replace the warm and temperatures are soon lowered to freezing point. Walled gardens and any planting plan which results in completely enclosed areas are likely to trap cold air and result in artificial frost pockets. Since such frosts are due to radiation, they can occur even in subtropical regions of desert and mountain areas.

The local climate

To many, the idea of consulting zone maps before selecting plants is purely academic and will be treated as such. However, no one can afford to ignore the local climate.

Within each of the main climatic zones are pockets of ground which are noticeably warmer, or colder, than the zone average. This applies equally to fairly small areas within a garden which are at variance with the rest, so when assessing a garden site it is vital to take local factors into account.

Altitude Differences in height above sea level exert a considerable effect on temperature and for every 100 m (330 ft) rise there is an approximate corresponding drop of 0.5°C (1°F) in temperature. Wind force also increases with height.

Coast or lakeside Nearness to the sea, or to a large lake, will invariably bring about a considerable moderating influence, evening out extremes of heat and cold. In winter, temperatures will not fall so low when compared with inland areas away from water; conversely, in summer, waterside areas are cooler than inland sites.

Wind Exposure to wind has a cooling, as well as a drying effect on plants and in exposed conditions, especially near the coast, trees and shrubs frequently become lopsided owing to 'wind pruning'. Roof gardens and balconies, along with passageways between buildings, are notoriously cool, windy and drafty. Here, shelter in the form of windbreaks can improve conditions dramatically.

Aspect/exposure Planting trees and shrubs against a sunny wall, especially under a roof overhang, creates a warmer clime. This is due in part to shelter and partly to the walls absorbing heat during the day and giving off radiation heat at night. This means planting against a south- or west-facing wall in the northern hemisphere and against a north-facing wall in the southern hemisphere.

Urban effect Sheltered urban areas in towns and cities are usually a few degrees warmer in winter when compared with the surrounding countryside.

Zoning and plant lists

It is important that the plant zoning designations as outlined are viewed as a guide only, since they are subject to amendment depending on local conditions. Having checked your regional zone and then considered local peculiarities, take a closer look at the types, kinds and varieties of plants growing in the neighborhood and ask around to find out which plants grow particularly well in the area.

Container plants Bear in mind that plants are less hardy when grown in containers than in the ground. This applies in particular to plants which are overwintered outdoors. For instance, in cool temperate zones not all plants given a **C** rating can be expected to overwinter outdoors without extra protection, some are better moved indoors.

To take account of the reduced resistance to cold of container plants, sheltered and warm favored winter quarters are essential. Where winter quarters are 'only average' then use hardier plants such as cool temperate **C** plants for mild climatic zones.

Wall protection and shelter It is a well established fact that tender plants grown against a warm, sunny wall will frequently flourish, but similar plants grown only a few paces away will perish. Taking advantage of the shelter effect of warm walls it is often possible to grow plants from a warmer zone than the regional climate suggests. Plants from mild climate regions can be grown against a sunny wall in the cool temperate zone and subtropical plants can confidently be expected to grow outdoors in a mild temperate area.

East-facing walls In cool temperate areas, these are treacherous during frosty weather. Plants in bud and evergreens are vulnerable to a too rapid thaw of overnight frost in the early morning sun, resulting in irreparable damage.

Cool, less favorable conditions Whenever it is necessary to set plants in less than ideal situations, it is always advisable to use plants from a cooler zone. For example, in a mild climate area use plants from the cool temperate zone.

Indoor plants Where plants are grown indoors aim for the following minimum winter temperatures:

Zone **C**	0–4°C (32–40°F)
Zone **M**	4–10°C (40–50°F)
Zone **W**	10–16°C (50–60°F)

City Gardens

Trees for sheltered gardens in warm winter areas

Acacia M-W
Acer C-W
Albizia M-W
Aralia M-W
Arbutus C-W
Cassia M-W
Catalpa
Chamaerops W
Citrus M-W
Cornus C-W
Cotoneaster C-W
Crinodendron M-W
Cytisus M-W
Eriobotrya M-W
Eucalyptus C-W
Ficus C-W
Gleditsia C-W
Hoheria M-W
Ilex C-W
Laurus M-W
Ligustrum M-W
Magnolia M-W
Metrosideros M-W
Morus C-W
Paulownia
Piptanthus M-W
Pittsoporum M-W
Podocarpus M-W
Prunus C-W
Rhus C-W
Robinia C-W
Sophora M-W
Trachycarpus C-W

Hardy trees (All C-M)

Acer
Aesculus
Alnus
Amelanchier
Betula
Carpinus
Chamaecyparis
Cornus
Cotoneaster
Crataegus
Eucalyptus
Fagus
Ilex
Laburnum
Malus
Prunus
Pyrus
Rhus
Salix
Sorbus

Shrubs for enclosed gardens (mild areas) (All M-W unless marked otherwise)

Abelia
Abutilon
Acacia
Atriplex
Azalea C-W
Callistemon
Camellia C-W
Carissa
Carpenteria
Caryopteris
Ceanothus
Cestrum
Choisya C-W
Cistus
Clianthus
Coprosma
Cordyline
Cotoneaster C-W
Crinodendron
Cyathea
Cytisus
Desfontainea
Elaeagnus
Embothrium
Enkianthus
Eriobotrya
Escallonia
Euonymus
Fatsia C-W
Ficus
Fothergilla
Griselinia C-W
Hibiscus
Hydrangea
Jasminum
Kalmia C-W
Lantana
Leptospermum C-W
Leucothoe
Magnolia
Mahonia
Ochna
Osmanthus C-W
Photinia
Phygelius
Pieris C-W
Piptanthus
Pittosporum
Podocarpus
Prunus C-W
Punica
Pyracantha C-W
Pyrus

Rhododendron C-W
Rhus
Rosa C-W
Rosmarinus
Salvia
Sarcococca C-W
Sophora
Tecomaria
Viburnum
Xylosma
Yucca

Climbers for warm areas (All M-W unless marked otherwise)

Actinidia
Akebia
Aristolochia
Berberidopsis
Campsis
Clematis
Eccremocarpus
Fremontodendron
Humulus
Jasminum
Lapageria
Lonicera
Passiflora
Raphiolepis
Rosa C-W
Schizophragma
Senecio
Solanum
Thunbergia
Trachelospermum
Vitis
Wistaria

Perennials and ferns for warm areas

Acanthus C-W
Adiantum C-W
Agave M-W
Aloe M-W
Arundinaria M-W
Aspidistra M-W
Asplenium C-W
Carex M-W
Cyperus C-W
Dicksonia
Dryopteris C-W
Euphorbia C-W
Gazania M-W
Gerbera M-W
Hedychium M-W
Hemerocallis C-W
Kniphofia C-W
Liriope C-W
Musa W
Ophiopogon M-W

Philodendron M-W
Phormium M-W
Polystichum C-W
Sedum C-W
Yucca C-W
See Country Gardens for hardy perennials

Ground cover, rock and paving plants for warm areas (All C-W unless marked otherwise)

Acaena M-W
Acantholimon M-W
Achillea
Asarum
Calocephalus M-W
Cerastium
Ceratostigma
Chamaemelum
Convolvulus M-W
Coronilla
Cotula M-W
Crassula M-W
Cymbalaria
Cytisus
Dichondra M-W
Duchesnea M-W
Epimedium
Erodium
Festuca
Fragaria
Gazania M-W
Hakonechloa M-W
Halimium
Helianthemum
Hosta
Hypericum
Liriope
Lithodora
Lysimachia
Mazus M-W
Mentha
Mesembryanthemum M-W
Nepeta
Ophiopogon M-W
Pellaea M-W
Polygonum
Potentilla
Sagina
Santolina
Satureja
Saxifraga
Scleranthus M-W
Sedum
Sempervivum
Silene
Thymus
Vancouveria M-W
Zoysia

Bulbs, corms and tubers for warm areas (All M-W unless marked otherwise)

Achimenes *
Acidanthera *
Agapanthus C-W
Allium C-W
Alstroemeria
Amaryllis
Arisaema
Arum
Asclepias *
Begonia *
Brodiaea
Caladium *
Canna *
Chlidanthus
Colchicum C-W
Crinum *
Crocosmia C-W
Dahlia *
Dicentra C-W
Dierama
Eucomis *
Galtonia C-W
Gloriosa *
Homeria *
Hyacinthus C-W
Incarvillea
Iris C-W
Ismene *
Ixia *
Lilium C-W
Narcissus C-W
Nerine *
Polianthes *
Ranunculus *
Sandersonia *
Schizostylis
Sternbergia
Tricyrtis *
Tulipa C-W
Zantedeschia

* Will not survive frost

COUNTRY GARDENS

Trees for coastal planting

Acer C-M
Albizia M-W
Arbutus C-W
Betula C-M
Chamaecyparis C-M
Cordyline C-W
Crataegus C-M
× Cupressocyparis C-M
Cupressus C-W
Eucalyptus C-W
Ficus C-W
Ilex C-M
Juniperus C-W
Metosideros M-W
Picea C-M
Pinus C-W
Populus C-M
Prunus C-W
Quercus M-W
Sorbus C-M
Tamarix C-W
Vitex M-W

Shrubs for coastal planting

Acacia M-W
Atriplex M
Aucuba C-M
Berberis C-M
Calothamnus M-W
Carissa M-W
Choisya C-M
Cistus M
Colutea C-M
Coprosma M
Corokia M
Cotoneaster C-M
Cytisus C-W
Elaeagnus C-W
Escallonia C-M
Fuchsia C-M
Griselinia C-W
Hakea W
Halimium C-M
Hebe C-M
Hibiscus C-M
Juniperus C-W
Lavatera C-M
Leptospermum M-W
Lonicera C-M
Myrica M
Nerium M-W
Olearia C-M
Pittosporum C-M
Potentilla C-M
Prunus C-W
Pyracantha C-W

Raphiolepis M
Rhamnus M
Rhus C-W
Rosa C-M
Rosmarinus C-M
Senecio C-M
Spartium C-W
Tamarix C-W

Hedging plants for coast

Atriplex M
Berberis C-M
Buxus C-W
Caragana M
Carpinus C-M
Chamaecyparis C-M
Cotoneaster C-M
Crataegus C-M
Cupressus C-W
Dodonaea M-W
Elaeagnus C-W
Euonymus C-M
Griselinia C-W
Ilex C-M
Juniperus C-W
Kochia M
Laurus M-W
Lavandula C-M
Ligustrum C-W
Lonicera C-M
Mahonia C-M
Miscanthus M-W
Myrica C-M
Myrtus M-W
Nandina C-W
Nerium M-W
Osmanthus C-W
Photinia C-M
Pittosporum C-M
Prunus C-W
Pyracantha C-W
Rhamnus C-M
Rosa C-M
Rosmarinus C-M
Thuga C-M
Viburnum C-M

Perennials for coastal planting (All C-M unless marked otherwise)

Aloe M-W
Armeria
Arundinaria M-W
Asplenium
Aster
Aubrieta
Aurinia

Calocephalus M
Centaurea
Cerastium
Cortaderia C-W
Dictamnus
Erigeron
Eryngium
Euphorbia
Euryops
Iris
Limonium
Nepeta
Perovskia
Phlomis
Phormium
Pulmonaria
Rheum
Stachys

Ground covers for coastal planting (All C-M unless marked otherwise)

Abronia M
Arctostaphylos C-M
Atriplex M
Calluna
Ceanothus
Centranthus
Cerastium
Cistus M
Convolvulus
Coprosma
Cotoneaster
Delosperma M
Erica
Euonymus
Fragaria
Gaultheria
Gazania M-W
Hedera C-W
Helianthemum
Hypericum
Iberis
Juniperus
Lampranthus M
Mahonia
Osteospermum M
Paxistima M-W
Polygonum
Potentilla
Rosa
Ruscus
Ruta
Sedum
Sempervivum
Vaccinium
Xylosma M-W

Cottage-type garden annuals and biennials (All C-M)

Althaea
Anchusa
Aquilegia
Bartonia
Bellis
Calendula
Callistephus
Campanula
Centaurea
Cheiranthus
Clarkia
Dianthus
Digitalis
Eschscholzia
Felicia
Helianthus
Helichrysum
Humulus
Iberis
Impatiens
Lathyrus
Nigella
Primula
Reseda
Tropaeolum
Viola

Perennials for sheltered gardens (All C-M)

Acanthus
Achillea
Alchemilla
Alstroemeria
Anemone
Armeria
Artemisia
Aster
Astilbe
Astrantia
Bergenia
Brunnera
Caltha
Campanula
Catananche
Centaurea
Coreopsopsis
Delphinium
Dianthus
Doronicum
Echinops
Eremurus
Erigeron
Eryngium
Filipendula
Gaillardia
Geranium
Geum

Helenium
Helleborus
Hemerocallis
Heuchera
Hosta
Iris
Kniphofia
Liatris
Lilium
Lobelia
Lupinus
Lychnis
Macleaya
Malva
Miscanthus
Monarda
Narcissus
Nepeta
Onopordum
Paeonia
Phlomis
Phlox
Phormium
Phygelius
Physalis
Polygonatum
Portulaca
Primula
Pulmonaria
Pyrethrum
Rudbeckia
Scabiosa
Schizostylis
Sedum
Sisyrinchium
Solidago
Stachys
Trillium
Trollius
Tulipa
Verbascum
Veronica

WATER GARDENS

Deep-water aquatics and floaters (All C-M)

Azolla caroliniana
A. ficuloides
Brasenia
Hydrocharis
Nuphar advena
N. japonicum
N. microphyllum
Nymphaea alba
N. candida
N. caroliniana
N. × hybrida
N. × laydekeri
N. × marliacea
Nymphoides
Pistia
Salvinia
Stratiotes
Trapa

Submerged aquatics (oxygenators) (All C-M)

Anacharis
Callitriche
Ceratophyllum
Egeria
Eleocharis
Fontinalis
Hottonia
Lagarosiphon
Myriophyllum
Najas
Oenanthus
Potamogeton
Proserpinaca
Ranunculus
Rorippa
Tillaea
Utricularia

Aquatics needing warmth (All M-W)

Aponogeton
Colocasia
Cyperus
Eichornia
Hydrocleys
Nelumbo
Nymphaea capensis
N. coerulea
N. × hybrida
N. lotus
N. stellata
Nymphoides
Oryza
Saccharum

Thalia
Xanthosoma

Water-edge aquatics (All C-M)

Acorus calamus
A. gramineus
Alisma
Anemopsis
Butomus
Calla
Caltha
Carex morrowii
C. pendula
C. riparia
C. stricta
Cotula
Cyperus alternifolius
C. longus
C. vegetus
Damasonium
Decodon
Echinodorus ranunculoides
E. radicans
E. rostratus
Eriophorum angustifolium
E. latifolium
E. vaginatum
Glyceria
Houttuynia
Iris kaempferi
I. laevigata
I. pseudacorus
I. sibirica
Juncus bufonius
J. effusus
J. ensifolius
Jussieua grandiflora
J. repens
Ludwigia alternifolia
L. palustris
L. mulertii
Mentha
Menyanthes
Mimulus guttatus
M. cupreus
M. lewisii
M. luteus
M. maculosus
M. ringens
M. tigrinus
Miscanthus
Myosotis
Nasturtium
Orontium
Peltandra
Phalaris

Pontederia
Preslia
Ranunculus
Sagittaria japonica
S. sagittifolia
Saururus cernuus
S. chinensis
Scirpus albescens
S. cernuus
S. tabernaemontani
Sisyrinchium
Sparganium
Thalia
Typha angustifolia
T. latifolia
T. minima
Veronica
Villarsia
Zantedeschia

Submerged aquatics needing warmth (All M-W)

Aponogeton
Cabomba
Cardamine
Cryptocoryne becketti
C. ciliata
C. cordata
C. griffithii
C. wightii
Hydrotrida
Ludwigia mulertii
L. palustris
Vallisneria americana
V. spiralis

Damp loving & bog plants (All C-M)

Aconitum
Actea alba
A. rubra
A. spicata
Agapanthus africanus
A. campanulatus
A. orientalis
A. Hybrids
Anagallis
Anemone
Aruncus
Asclepias
Aster
Astilbe × arendsii
A. astilboides
A. chinensis
A. davidii
A. japonica
A. rivularis
A. Hybrids
Astrantia
Buphthalmum

Camassia
Cardamine
Chrysanthemum
Cimicifuga
Claytonia
Coptis
Dierama
Dryopteris
Eupatorium
Filipendulina hexapetala
F. palmata
F. rubra
F. ulmaria
Gentiana
Gunnera
Heloniopsis
Hemerocallis citrina
H. fulva
H. thunbergii
H. Hybrids
Hosta albo-marginata
H. fortunei
H. lancifolia
H. plantaginea
H. undulata
H. Hybrids
Inula
Iris kaempferi
I. laevigata
I. sibirica
I. Hybrids
Kirengshoma
Ligularia
Lobelia
Lysichitum
Lysimachia
Lythrum
Mimulus
Monarda
Montbretia
Myrica
Osmunda
Peltiphyllum
Petasites
Phormium cookianum
P. tenax
P. Hybrids
Phyllitis
Polygonum
Primula
Ranunculus
Rheum
Rodgersia
Schizostylis
Senecio
Tradescantia
Trollius
Zantedeschia

ORIENTAL GARDENS

Tall conifers

Abies C-M
Agathis M
Araucaria C-M
Athrotaxus M
Austrocedrus M
Calocedrus C-M
Cedrus C-M
Cephalotaxus M
Chamaecyparis C-M
Cryptomeria M
Cunninghamia M
× Cupressocyparis C-M
Cupressus C-W
Dacrydium M
Fitzroya M
Ginkgo C-M
Glyptostrobus C-M
Juniperus C-W
Larix C-M
Metasequoia C-W
Picea C-M
Pinus C-W
Podocarpus M
Pseudolarix M
Pseudotsuga C-M
Saxegothaea M
Sciadopitys C-M
Sequoia C-M
Sequoiadendron C-M
Taiwania M
Taxodium C-W
Taxus C-M
Thuja C-M
Torreya M
Tsuga C-M

Dwarf and slow-growing conifers

Abies C-M
Cedrus C-M
Cephalotaxus M
Chamaecyparis C-M
Cryptomeria M
Cupressus C-W
Juniperus C-W
Larix C-M
Microbiota C-M
Microcachrys M
Phyllocladus M
Picea C-M
Pinus C-W
Podocarpus M
Sequoia C-M
Taxus C-M
Thuja C-M
Tsuga C-M

Ferns (All C-M unless marked otherwise)

Adiantum
Asplenium
Athyrium
Blechnum
Dryopteris
Matteuccia
Onoclea
Osmunda
Pellaea M-W
Phyllitis
Polypodium
Polystichum

Grasses (All C-M unless marked otherwise)

Agrostis
Agropyron
Arundinaria M
Arundo M
Avena
Bambusa M-W
Briza
Coix
Cortaderia
Eragrostis
Eriophorum
Festuca
Glyceria
Hakonechloa M-W
Helictotrichon
Hordeum
Koeleria
Lagurus
Luzula
Melica
Milium
Miscanthus M-W
Molinia
Panicum
Pennisetum
Phalaris
Polypogon
Scirpus
Setaria
Stipa
Tricholaena
Triticum
Zea M-W

Shrubs for autumn color (All C-M unless marked otherwise)

Acer
Amelanchier
Azalea
Berberis
Callicarpa
Ceratostigma
Cercidiphyllum
Cornus
Cotinus
Cotoneaster
Enkianthus
Euonymus
Fothergilla M
Hamamelis
Nandina C-W
Parrotia
Rhamnus
Rhododendron
Rhus C-W
Spirea
Stephanandra
Viburnum

Flowering prunus – Hybrid and species (All C-M unless marked otherwise)

Prunus Hybrids
Almond M-W
Apricot M-W
Cherry
Peach M-W
Plum
Prunus armeniaca M-W
P. avium
P. cerasifera
P. cerasus
P. dulcis M-W
P. laurocerasus
P. lusitanica
P. padus
P. persica M-W
P. sargentii
P. serrula
P. serrulata
P. subhirtella
P. triloba

Evergreens for cool climates (All C-M unless marked otherwise)

Arctostaphylos
Berberis
Buxus C-W
Calluna
Camellia
Daphne
Elaeagnus C-W
Erica
Euonymus
Hedera C-W
Ilex
Kalmia C-W
Leucothoe
Mahonia
Osmanthus
Pachysandra
Pieris
Pyracantha C-W
Rhododendron
Vinca

Rock garden evergreens (All C-M unless marked otherwise)

Arctostaphylos
Berberis
Buxus C-W
Calluna
Galax
Ilex
Kalmia C-W
Leiophyllum
Lonicera
Rhododendron
Skimmia
Teucrium

Evergreens for warm climates

Arbutus M-W
Arctostaphylos C-M
Berberis C-M
Carpenteria M-W
Ceanothus C-W
Choisya C-M
Cistus M
Cotoneaster C-M
Daphne C-M
Elaeagnus C-W
Euonymus C-M
Garrya C-M
Gaultheria C-M
Hedera C-W
Ilex C-M
Kalmia C-W
Leucothoe M
Ligustrum M-W
Magnolia M-W
Mahonia M
Osmanthus C-M
Pachistima M-W
Photina M
Pieris M
Prunus C-W
Pyracantha C-W
Skimmia C-M
Stranvaesia C-M
Vaccinium C-M
Viburnum C-M

Rhododendrons for cool oriental-style gardens (All C-M)

R. arborescens
R. calendulaceum
R. canadensis
R. carolinianum
R. catawbiense
R. Gable Hybrids
R. × gandavense
R. impeditum
R. indica Hybrids
R. kaempferi
R. Knap Hill – Exbury Hybrids
R. keiskei
R. × kosterianum
R. lapponicum
R. × loderi
R. maximum
R. mucronulatum
R. nudiflorum
R. obtusum
R. schlippenbachii
R. vaseyi
R. viscosum
R. Hybrids

STONE & ROCK GARDENS

Dwarf trees (All C-M)

Abies
Acer
Betula
Cedrus
Chamaecyparis
Cryptomeria
Juniperus
Picea
Pinus
Podocarpus
Salix
Sorbus
Thuja
Tsuga

Dwarf shrubs (All C-M unless marked otherwise)

Acer
Andromeda
Arctostaphylos
Azalea (Rhododendron)
Berberis
Calluna
Calocephalus M-W
Ceanothus
Chamaecyparis
Cistus
Cornus
(Chamaepericlymenum)
Cotoneaster
Cytisus
Daphne
Erica
Euonymus
Ficus
Fuchsia
Gaultheria
Genista
Grevillea
Halimiocistus
Halimium
Hebe
Hedera
Helianthemum
Helichrysum
Hypericum
Iberis
Jasminum
Juniperus
Lavandula
Leschenaultia M-W
Margyricarpus
Microbiota
Myoporum
Penstemon
Pimelea

Polygala
Polygonum
Potentilla
Prunus
Rhododendron
Rosa
Rosmarinus
Rubus
Salvia
Santolina
Sarcococca
Spiraea
Syringa
Teucrium
Vinca

Perennials, ferns and grasses (All C-M unless marked otherwise)

Acaena M-W
Achillea
Actinotus
Adiantum
Aethionema
Ajuga
Anacyclus
Anagallis
Androsace
Anemone
Antennaria
Aquilegia
Arabis
Arenaria
Armeria
Asarina
Asperula
Asplenium
Astilbe
Aubrieta
Aurinia
Calceolaria
Campanula
Carex M-W
Carlinia
Cassiope
Cerastium
Ceratostigma
Chrysogonum
Convallaria
Convolvulus
Cotula M-W
Crassula M-W
Cymbalaria
Dianthus
Dimorphotheca M-W
Dodecatheon
Draba

Dryas
Duchesnea M-W
Echeveria
Edrianthus
Epigaea
Epimedium
Erigeron
Erinus
Eriogonum
Erodium
Erysimum
Euphorbia
Festuca
Gazania M-W
Gentiana
Geranium
Graptopetalum
Gypsophila
Helichrysum
Helleborus
Hepatica
Hernieria M-W
Heuchera
Iberis
Iris
Kalanchoe
Lamium
Leontopodium
Lewisia
Linum
Lithodora (Lithospermum)
Lotus
Mazus M-W
Mentha
Mesembryanthemum M-W
Mimulus
Minuartia
Myosotis
Nepeta
Oenothera
Omphalodes
Onosma M-W
Origanum
Oxalis
Papaver
Paphiopedilum
Pellaea
Penstemon
Phlox
Polemonium
Potentilla
Primula
Ranunculus
Raoulia
Rhodohypoxis
Sagina
Saponaria
Saxifraga
Scleranthus
Sedum

Sempervivum
Shortia
Silene
Stachys
Stokesia
Thalictrum
Thymus
Tiarella
Trillium
Tunica
Verbena
Veronica
Viola
Vittadinia
Zauschneria

Annuals and biennials (All M-W)

Adonis
Amellus
Anacyclus
Anagallis
Androsace
Asperula
Brachycome
Calandrinia
Echium
Escholzia
Felicia
Iberis
Ionopsidium
Leptosiphon
Limmanthes
Linum
Lupinus
Montzelia
Nemesia
Nemophila
Phacelia
Portulaca
Sanvitalia

Bulbs (All C-W unless marked otherwise)

Allium
Chionodoxa
Colchicum
Convallaria
Crocus
Cyclamen
Erythronium
Freesia
Fritillaria
Galanthus
Ipheion M-W
Iris
Leucocoryne
Milla
Muscari
Narcissus

Scilla
Sparaxis
Sternbergia
Tritonia
Tulipa
Zephyranthes

SHADY GARDENS

Trees (All C-M unless marked otherwise)

Acer
Aesculus
Alnus
Arbutus C-W
Betula
Chamaerops M-W
Cornus C-W
Corynocarpus M
Cotoneaster
Crataegus
Cyathea M
Dicksonia M
Ficus C-W
Grevillea M
Ilex
Laburnum
Laurus M-W
Lithocarpus M
Olmediella M
Prunus C-W
Pseudopanax M-W
Robinia
Salix
Schefflera M-W
Sorbus
Strelitzia M-W
Umbellularia M

Climbers (vines)

Aristolochia C-M
Asteranthera M
Berberidopsis M
Celastrus C-M
Cissus M
Euonymus C-M
Fatshedera M
Ficus C-W
Gelsemium M
Hedera C-W
Hydrangea C-M
Lonicera C-M
Monstera M
Parthenocissus C-M
Polygonum C-M
Rhoicissus M
Schizophragma M
Trachelospermum M

Conifers

Abies C-M
Cephalotaxus M
Chamaecyparis C-M
Cryptomeria M
Juniperus C-W
Picea C-M
Podocarpus M
Taxus C-W
Thuja C-M
Tsuga C-M

Annuals and biennials

Ageratum M
Begonia M-W
Bellis C-M
Browallia M
Coleus M
Cotula M
Digitalis C-M
Impatiens M
Lobelia M
Meconopsis C-M
Mimulus C-M
Myosotis C-M
Nicotiana M-W
Pelargonium M-W
Schizanthus M
Senecio C-M
Viola C-M

Shrubs

Abutilon M
Ardisia M
Arundinaria M-W
Aucuba C-M
Azalea (rhododendron) C-M
Azaleodendron C-M
Bambusa M-W
Berberis C-M
Brunfelsia M
Buxus C-W
Calycanthus C-M
Camellia C-M
Cantua M
Carpenteria M
Choisya C-M
Cleyera M
Cocculus M
Coffea M
Coprosma M-W
Cordyline M-W
Cornus C-W
Cotoneaster C-M
Cycas M-W
Danae M
Daphne C-M
Distylum M
Dizygotheca M
Embothrium M
Enkianthus M
Euonymus C-M
Fatsia C-M
Fuchsia C-M

Gardenia M-W
Gaultheria C-M
Griselinia C-W
Hebe C-M
Hydrangea C-M
Hypericum C-M
Ilex C-M
Itea M
Juniperus C-W
Kalmia C-W
Kalmiopsis M
Laurus M-W
Lencothoe M
Ligustrum M-W
Loropetalum M-W
Magnolia M-W
Mahonia C-M
Myrica M
Nandina C-W
Olearia C-M
Olmediella M
Osmanthus C-W
Pachysandra C-M
Pernettya C-M
Philodendron M
Pieris M
Pittosporum C-W
Prunus C-W
Pseudopanax M-W
Rhamnus C-M
Rhapis M
Rhododendron C-M
Ruscus C-W
Salix C-M
Sambucus C-M
Sarcococca C-M
Shibatea M
Skimmia M
Stachyurus M
Taxus C-W
Ternstroemia M-W
Vaccinium C-M
Viburnum C-M
Vinca C-M

Perennials, ferns, grasses and bulbs (All C-M unless marked otherwise)

Acanthus
Aconitum
Adiantum
Ajuga
Alpinia M
Anemone
Aquilegia
Arenaria
Arum
Asarum
Aspidistra M-W
Asplenium

Astilbe
Athyrium
Begonia M-W
Bergenia
Billbergia M-W
Caladium M-W
Calceolaria
Campanula
Clivia M
Colocasia M
Convallaria
Crassula
Cymbalaria
Cymbidium M
Dianella M
Dicentra
Digitalis
Doronicum
Dryopteris
Duchesnea M
Endymion
Epigaea M
Epimedium
Erythronium
Fragaria
Galax M
Galium M
Haemanthus M-W
Hakonechloa M-W
Hedychium M
Helleborus
Hepatica
Heterocentron M
Hosta
Iris
Kalanchoe M
Lamium
Ligularia
Lilium C-W
Liriope M
Lobelia
Lysimachia
Meconopsis
Mentha
Mertensia
Mimulus
Monarda
Narcissus
Ophiopogon M
Oxalis m
Pelargonium M-W
Phlox
Polemonium
Polygonatum
Polystichum
Primula
Pulmonaria
Ramonda
Ranunculus
Rehmannia

Rohdea M
Sanguinaria M
Sansevieria M
Saxifraga
Scilla
Sedum
Shortia
Sinningia M-W
Smilacina
Soleirolia
Strelitzia M-W
Streptocarpus M
Thalictrum
Tiarella
Tolmeia
Tradescantia
Trillium
Trollius
Vancouveria M
Viola
Zantedeschia M

Fruit (All C-M)

Cane fruits
Currants
Gooseberries
Strawberries

Vegetables and herbs (All C-M unless marked otherwise)

Beet
Cabbage
Carrot
Chive
Cucumber M-W
Leek
Mint
Lettuce
Salad onion
Spinach
Swiss Chard (Leaf Beet)
Tomato M-W

DRY GARDENS

Trees (inc. conifers) (All M-W unless marked otherwise)

Acacia
Aesculus C-M
Ailanthus C-W
Albizia
Arecastrum
Bauhinia
Brahea
Butia
Calocedrus C-W
Casuarina
Cedrus C-W
Celtis
Ceratonia
Cercidium
Chorisia
Citrus
Eriobotrya
Eucalyptus C-W
Fig C-W
Geijera
Gleditsia C-W
Grevillea
Juglans
Juniperus C-W
Koelreuteria
Laurus
Lyonothamnus
Lysiloma
Maclura
Magnolia
Melia
Morus C-W
Olea
Parkinsonia
Phoenix
Pinus C-W
Pistacia
Podocarpus
Populus C-W
Prunus C-W
Pyrus C-W
Quercus
Rhus C-W
Robinia C-W
Schinus
Sequoiadendron C-M
Sophora
Taxus C-W
Tristania
Ulmus
Vitex
Washingtonia
Xylosma
Zizyphus

Climbers (vines) (All M-W unless marked otherwise)

Antigonon
Bougainvillea
Cissus
Euonymus C-W
Gelsemium
Hedera C-W
Ipomoea
Jasminum C-W
Macfadyena
Parthenocissus C-W
Polygonum C-M
Rosa C-M
Senecio C-W
Tecomaria
Trachelospermum
Vitis C-W
Wisteria C-W

Shrubs

Abelia M
Arbutus C-W
Arctostaphylos C-M
Artemisia C-W
Atriplex C-W
Baccharis M
Buxus C-W
Caesalpinia M-W
Callistemon M-W
Caragana C-W
Carissa M-W
Cassia M-W
Catha M-W
Ceanothus C-W
Cercis C-W
Cercocarpus M-W
Chamaerops M-W
Chamaelaucium M
Cistus M-W
Cocculus M-W
Convolvulus C-M
Coprosma M-W
Cotinus C-W
Cotoneaster C-M
Crassula M
Cupressus C-W
Cytisus C-W
Dais M-W
Dalea M-W
Dendromecon M-W
Dodonaea M-W
Echium M
Elaeagnus C-W
Erica C-M
Escallonia C-M
Euonymus C-M

Euphorbia C-W
Fallugia M
Fig M-W
Fremontodendron M-W
Garrya C-M
Genista C-M
Grevillea M-W
Grewia M-W
Hakea W
Halimium C-W
Halimocistus C-W
Heteromele M-W
Hibiscus C-W
Hypericum C-W
Juniperus C-W
Justicia M-W
Lagerstroemia M-W
Lantana M-W
Laurus M-W
Lavandula C-W
Leucochyllum M
Ligustrum C-W
Lysiloma M
Mahonia M
Melaleuca M
Myoporum M
Myrtus C-W
Nerium M-W
Osmanthus C-W
Photinia C-M
Pinus C-W
Pittosporum M-W
Platycladus M
Plumbago M-W
Portulacaria M
Prunus C-W
Punica M-W
Pyracantha C-W
Raphiolepis M-W
Rhamnus C-W
Rhus C-W
Rosa C-M
Rosmarinus C-W
Salvia M-W
Santolina C-W
Senecio C-W
Simmondsia M-W
Solandra M-W
Sophora M-W
Spartium C-W
Symphoricarpos C-W
Tamarix C-W
Taxus C-W
Teucrium C-M
Trichostema M
Ulmus C-W
Vauquelina M-W
Vinca C-M
Xylosma M-W
Yucca C-W

Perennials, bulbs and grasses (All C-M unless marked otherwise)

Achillea
Agave M-W
Aloe M-W
Amaryllis M
Anacyclus
Arctotheca M
Aster
Baccharis M
Baptisia
Carpobrotus M
Centranthus
Cerastium
Chrysanthemum
Convolvulus
Coreopsis
Cortaderia C-W
Dianthus
Dichondra M
Dietes M
Dudleya M
Echeveria M-W
Eriogonum
Euphorbia C-W
Euryops C-W
Felicia M
Gaillardia
Gazania M-W
Gerbera M
Helianthus
Hemerocallis
Hippocrepis
Iris
Kniphofia
Leonotis M
Leucocoryne M
Liatris
Limonium
Linum
Marrubium
Narcissus
Oenothera
Pelargonium M-W
Pennisetum
Phlomis
Phlox
Phormium M
Physostegia
Polygonum
Puya M
Romneya
Sedum
Sisyrinchium
Verbena M-W
Xylosma M-W
Yucca C-W
Zauschneria
Zoysia M-W

Annuals and biennials (All M unless marked otherwise)

Calendula C-M
Callistephus
Cleome
Coreopsis
Cosmos C-M
Dahlia
Dianthus C-M
Gaillardia C-M
Gomphrena
Linum C-M
Portulaca
Tagetes
Tithonia
Verbena M-W

HOT & TROPICAL GARDENS

Flowering trees and shrubs
(All M-W unless marked otherwise)

Abelia
Abutilon
Brunfelsia *
Callistemon *
Cassia *
Ceanothus
Cistus
Desfontainea
Erythrina *
Fuchsia
Hakea *
Halimium
Helianthemum
Hibiscus
Jacaranda *
Lagerstroemia *
Lantana *
Leptospermum
Ligustrum
Magnolia
Myrtus
Nandina
Nerium
Pachystachys
Pittosporum
Sophora
Streptosolen *

Flowering climbers
(All M-W)

Actinidia
Allamanda *
Bougainvillea *
Campsis
Clematis
Clianthus *
Eccremocarpus
Ipomoea
Lapageria *
Lippia *
Lonicera
Mandevilla *
Maurandia *
Passiflora
Petrea *
Raphiolepis
Rhodochiton
Solanum
Thunbergia *
Trachelospermum
Wisteria

Flowering perennials
(All M-W unless marked otherwise)

Acanthus C-W
Adenium
Agapanthus C-W
Anigozanthus *
Asclepias
Begonia
Bletilla
Calceolaria
Canna
Chamaecereus
Clivia
Cortaderia C-W
Crocosmia C-W
Diplocyatha
Echeveria
Echinocactus
Eucomis
Euphorbia
Felicia
Gerbera
Hedychium
Helichrysum
Hemerocallis C-W
Homeria
Incarvillea
Kniphofia C-W
Lilium C-W
Lobelia
Notocactus
Oliveranthus
Pelargonium *
Phygelius
Polianthes
Ranunculus
Tigridia
Zantedeschia

Flowering annuals
(All M-W)

Ageratum
Amaranthus
Begonia
Brachycome
Capsicum
Catharanthus
Celosia
Cleome
Coleus
Dahlia
Dimorphotheca
Eschschlozia
Gazania
Gomphrena

Helianthus
Helichrysum
Heliotropium
Impatiens
Mesembryanthemum
Mirabilis
Nicotiana
Osteospermum
Petunia
Portulaca
Salpiglossis
Salvia
Sanvitalia
Senecio
Tagetes
Thunbergia
Tithonia
Venidium
Verbena
Zinnia

Foliage trees and shrubs
(All M-W)

Abutilon
Albizia *
Arundinaria
Atriplex
Beaucarnea *
Buxus
Calocedrus
Calocephalus *
Cordyline
Cyathea *
Cycas *
Dicksonia *
Dizygotheca *
Dodonaea
Dracaena
Eriobotrya
Eucalyptus
Euonymus
Fatsia
Ficus
Fuchsia
Gleditsia
Grevillea
Griselinia
Hakea *
Laurus
Leea *
Ligustrum
Lophomyrtus
Mahonia
Melianthus *
Myrtus
Nandina
Olearia
Phoenix *
Pinus
Pittosporum

Podocarpus
Pseudopanax
Salvia
Trachycarpus
Xylosma
Yucca

Foliage climbers
(All M-W)

Akebia
Aristolochia
Fatshedera
Hedera
Vitis

Foliage perennials
(All M-W)

Acanthus
Agave *
Aloe *
Alternanthera *
Arundinaria
Bambusa
Begonia *
Bergenia
Caladium *
Centaurea
Chlorophytum *
Cyperus
Echeveria *
Hakonechloa
Hosta
Iresine *
Iris
Liriope
Miscanthus
Nepeta
Ophiopogon
Pelargonium *
Phormium
Polystichum
Rheum
Sedum
Sempervivum
Syngonium *
Tradescantia *
Zebrina *
Zoysia *

Foliage annuals and biennials (All M-W)

Amaranthus
Chrysanthemum
Impatiens
Kochia
Perilla
Ricinus
Senecio
Zea
* Will not stand frost

INDOOR GARDENS

Plants for direct sun

Agave M
Aloe M
Bryophyllum M
Callistemon M
Cephalocereus M-W
Chrysanthemum M
Cineraria C-M
Clianthus M-W
Convolvulus C-M
Cordyline C-W
Crassula M-W
Dianthus M
Echeveria M-W
Eucalyptus M
Euphorbia M-W
Genista C-M
Gymnocalycium M
Lippia M
Lithops M
Mammillaria M
Nerium M
Olea M
Oliveranthus M-W
Opuntia M-W
Pelargonium M-W
Protea W
Rebutia M-W
Rhipsalis M
Rochea M-W
Rosa M

Plants for some sun (part shade) (All M-W unless marked otherwise)

Abutilon M
Acacia
Acalypha
Achimenes
Aechmea
Aeschynanthus M
Agapanthus M
Allamanda
Ampelopsis M
Ananas W
Anigozanthus
Anthurium
Aphelandra W
Araucaria C-M
Ardisia M
Arundinaria C-W
Asparagus
Azalea C-M
Bambusa
Beaucarnea
Begonia
Beloperone M

Billbergia
Bougainvillea
Bouvardia
Camellia C-M
Campanula C-M
Canna
Capsicum
Cassia
Ceropegia M
Cestrum
Chlorophytum M
Cineraria M
Citrus
Clerodendron
Clivia M
Crassula
Crossandra
Cryptanthus M
Cuphea W
Cyclamen
Cytisus
Eccremocarpus
Episcia W
Fabiana M
Faucaria M
Ficus
Fuchsia
Gardenia W
Gastera
Haemanthus
Hedechium
Hibiscus
Hippeastrum
Hoya
Hydrangea M
Hypocyrta
Hypoestes
Impatiens
Ipomoea
Iresine W
Ismene
Jasminium M
Kalanchoe
Lapageria
Lantana
Lilium M
Maranta
Musa W
Myrtus
Nepeta M
Neoregelia
Nymphaea
Pandanus W
Passiflora
Pilea
Pittosporum
Plumbago

Podocarpus
Primula C-M
Punica
Raphiolepis
Ricinus
Saintpaulia W
Sarracenia
Schlumbergera M
Sedum
Senecio
Solanum
Sprekelia
Stephanotis
Strelitzia
Streptosolen
Telopea
Tillandsia
Trachycarpus C-M
Vallota
Vriesia
Yucca
Zantedeschia
Zygocactus

Plants for bright indirect light (light shade) (All M-W unless marked otherwise)

Adiantum C-W
Alternanthera W
Anthurium
Asplenium C-W
Blechnum C-W
Brunfelsia M
Carex
Caryota M
Cattleya
Chamaerops M
Chlorophytum
Chrysalidocarpus
Cissus M
Codiaeum W
Coffea W
Columnea W
Cryptanthus
Cupressus C-W
Cyathea
Cycas
Cymbidium M
Cyperus M
Davallia M
Dendrobium
Dicksonia
Dieffenbachia
Dipladenia
Dizygotheca
Dracaena
Epiphyllum M
Fatshedera M
Fatsia M
Ficus C-W

Fittonia
Gardenia
Grevillea
Gynura W
Howea W
Nephrolepis W
Oncidium
Oplismenus
Monstera
Paphiopedilum
Pellaea
Peperomia
Phalaenopsis
Platycerium
Podocarpus
Polypodium M
Pseudopanax
Pteris
Sansevieria W
Saxifraga M
Schefflera M
Selaginella
Sinningia W
Sparmannia W
Streptocarpus
Syngonium
Tetrastigma
Tradescantia M
Vanda
Zebrina M

Plants for moderate shade (All M-W unless marked otherwise)

Adiantum
Aglaonema
Aspidistra
Calathea
Cissus
Hedera
Hernieria
Nertera
Philodendron
Rhoicissus M
Scindapsus
Soleirolia M
Spathiphyllum
Tolmeia

CONTAINER GARDENS

Trees and shrubs

Acer † C
Albizia M-W
Amelanchier † C-M
Arundinaria M-W
Aucuba C-M
Buxus C-M
Callistemon M-W
Camellia C-M
Cordyline M-W
Cotoneaster † C-M
Desfontainea M-W
Dicksonia † M-W
Erica C-M
Euonymus C-M
Fatsia M-W
Fuchsia M
Gleditsia † M
Grevillea † M-W
Hakea W
Halimium M
Hebe M
Hydrangea C-M
Hypericum C-M
Ilex C-M
Lagerstroemia M-W
Laurus M-W
Lavandula C-M
Ligustrum C-W
Magnolia † M
Mahonia C-M
Malus † C-M
Myrtus M-W
Nandina C-W
Olearia C-M
Osmanthus C-M
Pittosporum M-W
Prunus † C-M
Pseudopanax M-W
Punica M-W
Rhododendron C-M
Rosmarinus C-M
Salvia C-M
Santolina C-M
Senecio C-M
Skimmia C
Sophora † M-W
Trachycarpus † M-W
Vaccinium C-M
Viburnum C-M
Vinca C
Weigela C-M
† Tree or shrub

Climbers (vines)

Actinida M-W
Akebia M-W
Aristolochia M-W
Bougainvillea W
Clematis C-M
Cobaea M
Eccremocarpus M-W
Fatshedera M-W
Hedera C-M
Ipomoea M-W
Jasminum M-W
Lapageria W
Lonicera M-W
Mandevilla W
Parthenocissus C-W
Solanum W
Trachelospermum M-W
Vitis M-W
Wisteria M-W

Conifers

Abies C-M
Chamaecyparis C-M
Cryptomeria M
Cupressus M
Juniperus C-M
Picea C-M
Pinus C-M
Podocarpus M-W
Taxus C-M

Perennials, bulbs, ferns and grasses

Acanthus M
Achillea C-M
Agapanthus M-W
Agave M-W
Anigozanthus W
Asplenium C-M
Astilbe C-M
Athyrium C-M
Begonia M-W
Bergenia C-M
Bletilla M-W
Calceolaria M-W
Convallaria C
Cortaderia M-W
Crocosmia M-W
Cyclamen M
Dianthus C-M
Dicentra C-M
Doronicum C
Dryopteris C-M
Echeveria M-W
Euphorbia C-W
Fritillaria C-M

Galanthus C
Galtonia M
Geranium C-M
Geum C-M
Gladiolus M
Helleborus C-M
Hemerocallis C-M
Hosta M
Hyacinthus C-M
Iris C-M
Kniphofia M
Lamium C-M
Lilium C-M
Liriope M
Lupin C-M
Miscanthus M-W
Muscari C-M
Narcissus C
Nepeta C-M
Ophiopogon M-W
Pelargonium W
Phlox C-M
Phormium M-W
Polystichum M
Primula C-M
Pulmonaria C-M
Pyrethrum C-M
Rudbeckia C-M
Salvia M-W
Stachys C-M
Tulipa C-M
Veronica C
Zantedeschia M-W

Alpines and rock garden plants

Aethionema C-M
Arabis C-M
Armeria C-M
Aubrieta C-M
Aurinia C-M
Campanula C-M
Dianthus C-M
Dryas C-M
Festuca C-M
Helianthemum M-W
Iberis C-M
Morisia M
Oenothera M
Phlox C-M
Saxifraga C-M

Annuals and biennials

Ageratum M-W
Amaranthus M-W
Arctotis M-W
Begonia M-W
Bellis C-M
Browallia M-W
Calendula C-M

Callistephus C-M
Catharanthus M-W
Cheiranthus C-M
Cineraria M-W
Clarkia C-M
Coleus M-W
Dahlia M-W
Dianthus M-W
Dorotheanthus M-W
Gazania M-W
Heliotropium M-W
Impatiens M-W
Kochia M
Lavatera M-W
Limonium M-W
Lobelia C-M
Lobularia C-M
Matthiola C-M
Myosotis C-M
Osteospermum M-W
Pelargonium M-W
Petunia M-W
Phlox M-W
Portulaca W
Salpiglossis M-W
Salvia M-W
Senecio M
Tagetes C-M
Thunbergia M-W
Tropaeolum C-M
Venidium M-W
Verbena M-W
Viola C-M
Zinnia M-W

Fruit

Apple C-M
Blueberry C-M
Cane Berries C-M
Cherry M
Currants C-M
Fig M-W
Gooseberry C-M
Grape M-W
Guava W
Nectarine M-W
Peach M-W
Strawberry C-M

Vegetables and salads

Beans M-W
Beet C-M
Cantaloupe (Melon) W
Carrot C-M
Corn W
Cucumber M-W
Lettuce C-M
Onion C-M
Potato C-W
Pumpkin W

Spinach C-M
Squash W
Sweet Peppers W
Radish C-M
Tomato M-W
Zucchini (Squash) M-W

Herbs

Basil M-W
Chives C-M
Coriander M
Garlic C-W
Marjoram M-W
Parsley C-M
Rosemary M-W
Sage M-W
Tarragon M-W
Thyme M-W

Y

yarrow, 103
Yucca, 44
   Y. elephantipes, 109
   Y. recurvifolia, 102

Z

Zantedeschia aethiopica, 80
Zauschneria californica, 103
zebra rush, 90, 188

The following people have given valuable help and assistance with this book, and to those who have allowed their garden to be photographed we wish to thank them all and acknowledge their kindness.

England and Europe
David Brooks, London
Chris and Judy Burnett, Surrey
Robert and Christine Evans, London
Hans and Bertie de Graaf, Holland
The Rob Herwig Garden, Holland
Cameron Mackintosh, London
Tom Monroe, Surrey
Wolfgang Mueller, Germany
Hannah Peschar, Sculpture Gallery, Ockley, Surrey
Michael Paul, London
Pieter Plomin, Germany
Gary Rogers, Germany
Ivan Ruperti, Switzerland
Mien Ruys, Holland
Ulrich Timm, Germany

U.S.A.
Derek Fell
Hiroshi Makita
George Waters

Australia and New Zealand
Anchor Pools, Sydney
The Armstrong Family, Melbourne
Sally and Tony Arnold, Melbourne
Paul Bangay, Melbourne
Chris and Karen Collins, Auckland
David Coombes, Auckland
Rick Eckersley, Melbourne
The Fearman Family, Sydney
Paul and Julie Fleming, Melbourne
Michael Hayman, Sydney
Tony Holdenson, Melbourne
Christine Hubay, Melbourne
Brian Huxham, Melbourne
Arno King, Auckland
Margaret Knight, Melbourne
Maggie Lockwood, Melbourne
Nookie Monahan, Melbourne
Barbara and Michael Perkin, Auckland
Stuart Pittendrigh, Sydney
Marcia Resch, Melbourne
Michelle Shennen, Sydney
Paul Sheppard, Melbourne
Ray Turner, Sydney
Annie Wilkes, Sydney
Peter Wydburd, Sydney

Special thanks is offered to the following:
John Duane, for his sketches, text and designs
David Palliser, for his help with text
Desmond Whitwell – plant consultant
David Carr – plant consultant
Arno King – plant consultant
Joanna Chisholm – consultant
Richard Bird – index
Fred Ford & Mike Pilley of Radius – paste-up

Gardens and garden designers are credited where information is available:
Anchor Pools 138B, 169 (Main pic.)
The Balmain Garden Centre 72, 122IB, 125I
Michael Balston 33, 34, 35, 124BR, 163B
Paul Bangay 152
David Brook 76, 129, 139T
Graham Burgess 102
Roberto Burle Marx 22, 23, 24, 25
Beth Chatto 45, 46, 47, 83I
Chelsea Flower Show 35, 70B, 85T, 178TL, 181TL, 190R
Gilles Clement 18, 19, 20, 21
Jane Coleman 172T
Trevor Crump 110L, 132L, 157
Rick Eckersley & Lisa Stafford (Eco Landscape Design) 36, 37
Paul Fleming (Black Bamboo) 1, 93, 140L, 146BL
Arthur Degeyter (architect) 101T
Arthur Degeyter (architect)/Paul Deroose 160
Richard Haigh & Annie Wilkes (Parterre) 14, 15, 16, 17, 151
The Rob Herwig Garden 77B, 89BL, 101BL, 116L, 119T, 124TR, 133BL, 134BL, 143B, 182, 185
Brian Huxham (Prestige Pools) 146BR, 170 (Main pic.), 171, 172BL
Hiroshi Makita 58, 59, 60, 94, 115B, 144L
Wolfgang Muller 140R, 161T
Natural Swimming Pools 170BR
Oehme, van Sweden 42, 43
Walda Pairon 74, 150R, 153
Anthony Paul 8, 9, 11 13, 68, 69, 87B, 108L, 109, 123, 146T, 172BR, 189L
Anthony Paul/John Duane 10, 12, 64, 65, 66, 79T, 98, 122L
Stuart Pittendrigh 67T, 103BR, 124L, 150L
Pieter Plommin 118T, 147
Angus Prentice 75B, 125 (Main pic.)
Ivan Ruperti 31, 90T
Mien Ruys 50, 51, 52, 53, 54, 55, 70T, 85BR, 86, 110R, 111T, 111B, 112, 119B, 120, 128, 131T, 134T, 141, 142T, 174, 183TL, 183TR, 190L, 202, 203
Takashi Sawano 48, 49, 96T, 118B, 121T
Gunther Schulze 95L
Horst Schummelfeder 89BR
Paul Sheppard (Lotus Landscapes) 96B, 97, 99R
Brian Taylor 149T
Ton ter Linden 207B
Ulrich Timm 56, 57
Ray Turner 73, 122IB, 125I
Piet van Veen 143T
André van Wassehoven 90B
Henk Weijers 38, 39, 40, 41, 87T, 92, 122IC
Betsie Wijnhoven-Fleuren 117 (Main pic.)
Jacques Wirtz 27, 28, 29, 130

All photographs by Ron Sutherland with the exception of the following which were taken by:
Valerie Brown 42T
Karl-Dietrich Bühler/EWA 84, 127L
Camera Press 31T, 89T
Gilles Clement 18B, 21
Henk Dijkman 8B, 38, 39, 40, 41, 87T, 92, 122IC
Derek Fell 58BL, 58BR, 59, 60, 94, 115B, 144L
Marijke Heuff, Amsterdam 27, 74, 78, 79B, 82, 90/IC, 101T, 117B, 130, 133TL, 143T, 145T, 150R, 153, 160, 175, 176R, 177T, 178R, 179T, 183BR, 191L, 195, 198, 207B
Jerry Harpur 43I
Georges Leveque 18T, 19, 20, 28, 29, 81, 180
Guiseppe Molteni 137
Anthony Paul 58T, 98I, 142B, 154BL, 164, 181BL, 196BL
Ivan Ruperti 31I, 90T, 161B, 192R
Caroline M. Segur 43 (Main pic.)
Wolfram Stehling 95L, 99L, 121BR, 144R
James van Sweden 42B
Frank Taegar 89BR
Ulrich Timm 56B, 5T
W. George Waters 22, 23, 24, 25, 103BL
Steven Wooster 64, 131B, 176L, 181TL, 183BL, 184BR, 190R
Brian Yale 163C

T = top   B = bottom
L = left   R = right
C = centre   I = inset